Sunset Travel Guide to
OREGON

By the Editors of Sunset Books and Sunset Magazine

Lane Publishing Co. · Menlo Park, California

Acknowledgments

Many Oregonians have generously shared their information and suggestions during the preparation of this book. We hope it will assist Oregonians in discovering new facets of their state and aid visitors as they travel in Oregon.

We especially wish to acknowledge the assistance of the Oregon State Highway Division, Travel Information Section, especially Frank Howard; the Oregon Historical Society, especially Millard McClung; Mimi Bell; Phil Brogan; and Gordon Clark.

Other individuals who have contributed to or reviewed portions of the manuscript include Suzanne Abram, Floyd Acarregui, Christine Barnes, Mike Hanley, Wayne Moncur, Cay Kershner, and Donald Smith.

We appreciate the invaluable cooperation of dozens of officials from the U.S. Forest Service, the National Park Service, the Bureau of Land Management, the U.S. Army Corps of Engineers, various state and county agencies, city and regional chambers of commerce, and a number of private organizations and companies throughout the state.

Edited by Cornelia Fogle

Design: Cynthia Hanson

Cartography: Vernon Koski

Cover: Surrounded by greenery, Goodpasture Bridge spans the McKenzie River just off State Highway 126 east of Springfield. This local landmark is one of some 60 covered bridges still standing in western Oregon. Photographed by Roger Flanagan.

Executive Editor, Sunset Books: David E. Clark

First Printing June 1976

Library of Congress No. 74-20020. ISBN Title No. 0-376-06613-X. Lithographed in the United States.

Contents

Special Features

Oregon

Preserving its past and shaping its future

Wheat harvest begins on the rolling lands of the Columbia plateau north of Enterprise.

Skiers enjoy Mount Bachelor's powder snow and spectacular scenery from November through June. Cross-country skiers find many forested routes.

Dense green forests, snow-capped mountains, unspoiled ocean beaches, wheat-covered prairies, wilderness lakes and rivers, awesome desertlike plateaus—few states can match Oregon's natural splendor or the exceptional variety of recreational pursuits it offers.

Renowned for its forests and fertile farm lands, Oregon's Willamette Valley was the destination of pioneers who journeyed westward in creaking Conestoga wagons in the mid-19th century, following the well-worn ruts of the Oregon Trail. These early settlers—who became farmers and merchants and loggers—were home seekers rather than adventurers; fortune seekers turned south to the gold fields of California.

The westward trek continues even now, but today's immigrants are urban refugees, searching for open space and traditional values and bringing new vigor to their adopted state.

What makes Oregon special?

What makes Oregon a special place? What attractions draw visitors in ever-increasing numbers? What qualities in the land and its people contribute to the Oregon mystique? Why do its residents—newcomers as well as old-timers—regard the state so protectively?

Pastoral wayside parks *along the Umpqua (above) and other western Oregon rivers invite travelers to pause for a picnic, fishing, and other waterside fun.*

Fun at the beach *absorbs this young fellow at Sunset Bay State Park.*

A land of scenic splendor

Nature passed out scenery with a lavish hand in the Pacific Northwest. Bordered on the west by the Pacific Ocean, Oregon has a dramatic 400-mile coastline varying from waveswept headlands to broad sandy beaches backed by lushly forested mountains.

The Columbia River, the region's great artery, flows for some 300 miles along the state's northern border with Washington. To the east lies Idaho, partially separated from Oregon by mile-deep Hells Canyon, carved over eons by the waters of the Snake River. California and Nevada butt the state's southern border.

Oregon's backbone is a majestic string of snow-capped dormant volcanoes—the Cascade Range—dividing the state into two distinct regions. Most of the state's population lives on the moist, heavily forested western side of the Cascades; east of the mountains, a broad high plateau stretches eastward to the Blue Mountains and the lonely land of the Great Basin.

Fed by numerous tributary streams draining the coastal and Cascade mountains, the Willamette River meanders through the broad Willamette Valley. Major southern Oregon streams are the Rogue and Umpqua, both emptying into the Pacific. East of the Cascades, the Deschutes and John Day rivers drain vast areas of the state, carving deep canyons on their northward route to join the mighty Columbia.

Variety in climates and seasons

In Oregon you can have it wet and green or high and dry. The folklore about the rain isn't *all* true.

West of the Cascades, you're engulfed by a sea of green trees and lush farm lands; this land is watered by rain clouds that drop their moisture as they nudge against the coastal and Cascade mountain ranges. Most of the rain falls during the mild winter, between November and mid-April. Gentle "Oregon mist" soaks the Willamette Valley, but on the western slopes of the coastal mountains, drenching downpours can exceed 100 inches of rainfall annually. Little rain falls during the warm, pleasant summer, but coastal towns often are wreathed in morning and evening fogs.

The lush Rogue and Umpqua valleys of southern Oregon enjoy the mild moist weather of western Oregon, but temperatures are slightly warmer and the climate a little drier.

East of the Cascades you experience greater extremes in temperature. Air masses moving across the mountains have lost most of their moisture, so central and eastern Oregon have less rain, more snow, and abundant sunshine. Temperatures are colder in winter and warmer in summer.

Oregon's 11,000-foot variation in elevation and its northern latitude influence a delightful progression of changing seasons. When spring or autumn arrives in Oregon, you know it.

Sightseeing highlights

Oregon's varied attractions allow the resident or visitor to choose from a broad array of intriguing destinations.

Along the coast, travelers enjoy dozens of state parks and recreation areas; among favorite stops are the Fort Clatsop National Memorial, the OSU Marine Science Center, the Cape Perpetua Visitor Center, and the Oregon Dunes National Recreation Area and its coastal lakes.

Focus of the Willamette Valley is Portland, center of urban activity. Other busy towns are Salem, the state capital, and the university towns of Eugene and Corvallis. Along the Columbia, visitors thrill to the many waterfalls of the Columbia Gorge and the massive dams at Bonneville and upriver.

Nearly every Oregon outdoorsman has his favorite lake or trail in the Cascades, but most visitors head for Mount Hood's Timberline Lodge, the Bend country, or Crater Lake National Park. The McKenzie Pass Highway is a memorable cross-Cascade route. In southern Oregon, you'll want to see the Oregon Caves, Ashland's Shakespearean Festival, and Jacksonville, and perhaps take a boat trip on the Rogue.

East of the Cascades, you can enjoy the grandeur of the wide-open spaces. You'll see various facets of this spacious country along the Cascade Lakes Highway, at Lava Lands Visitors Center and touring the lava country, at Cove Palisades State Park, and at John Day Fossil Beds National Monument.

Near the state's eastern border, look for remnants of the Oregon Trail, the alpine wilderness of the Wallowa Mountains, ghost towns, the surprising beauty of Steens Mountain, and the impressive canyons of the Snake and Owyhee rivers.

Oregon—a state of mind

Oregonians exhibit a protective pride in their state, a consciousness of its unusual appeals and potential, and a desire to keep their land unspoiled. To them—and to many visitors—Oregon is a special place. But why?

Love of the outdoors. The pioneer spirit surfaces in a need to feel close to and comfortable with the land. Oregon's forests and farm lands, its seashore, mountains, and desert are never far away. They are a part of an Oregonian's daily life, enriching the spirit and offering a sense of roots and oneness with the land.

Concern for the quality of life. Many Oregonians have consciously chosen to live in Oregon's slower-paced, less urban society. They prefer its informal life style, enjoy its city greenery and clean roadsides, exult in its unspoiled places, and rely on its

Spectacular 178-foot South Falls is just one of 14 waterfalls in lushly wooded Silver Creek State Park east of Salem. A hiking trail goes behind the misty falls.

extensive recreational resources to soften the scrapes of daily life. Many are actively involved in preserving and enhancing the livability of their environment.

A pride in its past. One cannot separate Oregon from its history, for a knowledge of the past explains much about the present.

You'll see vestiges in every part of the state—markers along the routes traveled by early explorers and pioneer wagon trains, century-old houses and churches still in use, covered bridges and ghost towns, sites of conflict between Indians and settlers or cattlemen and sheepmen.

Community groups have preserved and restored many historic buildings, and you'll find museums depicting Oregon's colorful past scattered throughout the state.

A willingness to try new ideas. Oregon has traditionally been a receptive ground for new ideas, and this trend has accelerated in recent years.

State and local governments and Northwest industries have spent vast sums improving air and water quality in Oregon. Roadside and campsite litter has been drastically reduced. Forestry and agricultural industries are developing new uses for former waste products. Statewide land use planning—with plenty of local input—is underway. A system of bikeways is being developed with state funding to encourage this enjoyable and nonpolluting form of transportation.

Self-reliant and friendly people. Oregonians are doers, not talkers. An independent lot, they work hard and take satisfaction in a job well done.

Cities and towns thrive on a "do-it-yourself" spirit; residents enthusiastically support their community music and art groups, theaters, museums, garden clubs, and other local activities. Persons following different life styles work together toward a common goal.

Towns of manageable size. Oregon's cities and towns are manageable in size. The state's only large city is Portland, with a population of 375,000, followed by Eugene (95,000) and Salem (76,000). Only three additional towns—Corvallis, Springfield, and Medford—top 30,000 population. Approximately 2.3 million people now live in Oregon, two-thirds of them in the Willamette Valley.

Universities and community colleges add cultural stimulation to larger towns throughout the state. Even in the urban centers, life has a human scale—you'll discover downtown parks and greenery, fountains of tumbling water, and delightful shopping complexes.

A concern for the future. Some new residents want to be the last immigrants across the Oregon border. Many have experienced elsewhere the problems of unchecked growth, and they see a chance for Oregon to avoid the mistakes of other, more urban states. Oregonians know they have a good life and—understandably—they don't want to see it spoiled.

Carving its way *through central Oregon's broad plateau, the John Day River exposed ancient fossil beds now highlighted in John Day Fossil Beds National Monument.*

The state's population has doubled in the last 30 years; native Oregonians are now outnumbered by residents born elsewhere. But this new blood has stimulated Oregon's arts, education, industry, politics, and social activity. The state still has its forest refuges and backwoods towns, but today its urban centers hum with contemporary life.

Oregon's opportunity lies in shaping its future to retain its basic values, yet adapting to the needs and expectations of its people.

Enjoying yourself in Oregon

Few states can equal Oregon for scenic attractions, and you'll find recreation opportunities to match. You can enjoy urban activities or head for the mountains, the coast, or the desert. If you prefer, explore back roads, relax at a resort or guest ranch, or attend a rodeo or local celebration.

You can pursue your favorite sport or hobby—rockhounding for agates or thundereggs, playing golf or tennis, bird watching, cycling—or learn more about Indian culture, local history, ghost towns, wildflowers, marine biology, covered bridges, Oregon wines, fossils and geology, or Northwest artists.

Discover the pleasure of off-season travel with its uncrowded facilities and invigorating weather. Seek out autumn foliage or spring wildflowers, watch storm-tossed waves crash against coastal headlands, go ski touring through untracked forest, or fish through the ice of a frozen lake.

Parks and campgrounds

Oregon has an unparalleled system of state parks, roadside rest areas, and scenic waysides to serve

Fishermen gather in this pleasant pine-shaded Forest Service campground along the Deschutes River south of Sunriver.

Informative signs identify Oregon's state parks and other travel facilities.

the traveling public in all parts of the state. Campgrounds dot the national forests and other public lands, and county and local parks supplement the recreational opportunities.

For a listing of Oregon's many parks and information on their facilities and recreation activities, write to the state Travel Information office (address on page 11).

State parks are generally open for day use throughout the year, weather permitting; the camping season extends from mid-April through October. Six coastal parks (see page 45) and Valley of the Rogue State Park remain open for camping in winter. Some state parks accept campsite reservations. Dogs and other pets are allowed in state parks but must be kept on a leash or otherwise confined.

In state parks, a fee is charged for overnight camping, but not for day-use activities. Some county parks charge a use fee.

Hundreds of additional campgrounds have been developed in the national forests and on other public lands. Fees are charged at many Forest Service and BLM campgrounds. For detailed information, contact the U.S. Forest Service or Bureau of Land Management (addresses on page 11).

For current detailed information on parks and campgrounds, including local and private parks, see *Sunset Western Campsites* (revised annually).

National forests and wilderness areas

Oregon's 13 national forests and 11 wilderness areas offer almost unlimited chances to enjoy the great outdoors. Forest roads wind through the trees to wooded campgrounds, fishing streams, tree-rimmed lakes, lava flows, and other attractions. Trails lead to remote lakes and waterfalls.

Oregon's magnificent mountain wilderness areas offer outdoorsmen the chance to leave the world of motorized vehicles and take to the trail on foot or horseback. A free wilderness permit is needed for a trip into eight of the areas; the Gearhart, Kalmiopsis, and Hells Canyon areas do not require a permit. Further information can be obtained from the appropriate national forest where your trip originates. Permit applications may be requested by mail or phone.

Forest Service offices can also provide information on road and trail conditions, packers and outfitters operating in the national forests, and marked cross-country ski trails and snowmobile routes for winter sports enthusiasts.

Other national areas include Crater Lake National Park, Fort Clatsop National Memorial, Oregon Caves National Monument, and John Day Fossil Beds National Monument, all administered by the National Park Service; and Oregon Dunes National Recreation Area and Hells Canyon National

Recreation Area, both administered by the U.S. Forest Service.

Fishing and hunting

The opening of trout season each spring triggers a migration of anglers to favorite sites along Oregon's rivers, creeks, lakes, and reservoirs. Trout fishing and seasonal runs of salmon and steelhead attract the most attention, but the dedicated fisherman can cast his line at any time of year somewhere in Oregon waters. Coastal harbors draw deep-sea fishermen in search of salmon.

Resident and nonresident anglers need to purchase fishing licenses; season, 10-day nonresident, or 1-day licenses are available. Salmon and steelhead fishermen need tags.

Hunters in Oregon try for blacktail deer and Roosevelt elk west of the Cascades, mule deer and Rocky Mountain elk east of the mountains. There are also limited hunting seasons for other big game as well. Upland game birds include ringnecked pheasant, chukar and Hungarian partridge, quail, blue and ruffed grouse, and sage grouse. Many hunters await autumn flights of migratory waterfowl. Hunting licenses are required for nongame as well as game animals and birds. Tags are necessary for big game.

Current information on fishing and hunting regulations, licenses, and tag fees is available at local sporting goods stores or from the Oregon Department of Fish and Wildlife (see page 11).

Boating on Oregon's waterways

If you're attracted to the water, Oregon offers plenty of lures. You can cruise along the Willamette, challenge white-water rivers in a rubber raft or drift boat, sail or water-ski on broad lakes and reservoirs, or paddle your canoe or kayak down a placid stream or across a wilderness lake.

Portions of eight Oregon rivers—the Rogue, Illinois, Sandy, Clackamas, Deschutes, John Day, Minam, and Owyhee—are state-designated scenic waterways.

Small boats can safely navigate many Oregon rivers; commercial operators and Oregon river guides conduct white-water river excursions through several challenging river canyons. River runoff information is available from the River Forecast Center in Portland (phone 221-3811).

To obtain information on the state's boating facilities, see page 11.

Life at the beach

The coast exerts a magnetic pull on many travelers. Some relax in the stimulating marine climate; others pursue activity-filled days that leave an observer weak. State parks and waysides line this scenic shore, offering dozens of sheltered picnicking and camping areas. No other area of the state has such an array of tourist accommodations available.

Beachcombers prowl the sands looking for agates and unusual shells, contorted pieces of driftwood, or prized glass fishing floats. At low tide, clammers dig along coastal bays and estuaries and tidepool explorers take a look at marine life uncovered by receding waters.

Anglers are everywhere—fishing from shore or boat on coastal rivers and bays, heading out to sea in search of salmon, casting into the surf from beaches, jetties, and rocky promontories.

Children wade and splash in the surf, build sand castles, or fly kites, while their elders may try surfing or hang gliding. You can hike coastal trails, watch the waves, go crabbing, take a boat trip or a dune buggy ride, buy salt-water taffy, watch shore birds and sea lions, or explore coastal towns for unexpected delights. Coastal restaurants offer such local specialties as clam chowder, freshly caught seafood, and homemade huckleberry pie.

Driving Oregon's highways and byways

Two broad interstate freeways cross the state. The primary north-south route is Interstate 5, cutting like a ribbon from the Columbia River south through the Willamette, Umpqua, and Rogue valleys to the California border. Interstate 80N follows the Columbia east from Portland, paralleling the route of the Oregon Trail to Ontario and the Idaho border.

U.S. 101 closely follows Oregon's scenic coast. East of the Cascades, the north-south highways are U.S. 197-97 (The Dalles-California Highway) and U.S. 395, which cuts from Hermiston across central Oregon to Lakeview and California.

Three additional east-west highways cross the state. U.S. 26 begins in Astoria and cuts eastward via Portland, Mount Hood, Madras, Prineville, and John Day to Vale. Crossing the center of the state is U.S. 20—from Newport to Corvallis, Albany, Bend, and Burns to join U.S. 26 at Vale. The Winnemucca to the Sea Highway (see page 129) connects the main southern Oregon towns.

Most Oregon secondary roads are paved routes. In national forests, all-weather roads are generally graded gravel, suitable for passenger cars; logging truck traffic may be heavy during the week, so keep to your side of the road and stay alert.

If you plan to venture off the main routes into deep forest or the desert, inquire locally about road conditions before starting out. Be sure that your car is in good working order and carry drinking water. Some mountain routes are not suitable for cars pulling trailers.

Main traffic regulations are noted on the official state highway map, available free from the state Travel Information office (see page 11).

For more information

Tourism is one of Oregon's major industries, and travelers will find a network of visitor information centers throughout the state. Large blue and white signs direct you to sources of local information. If

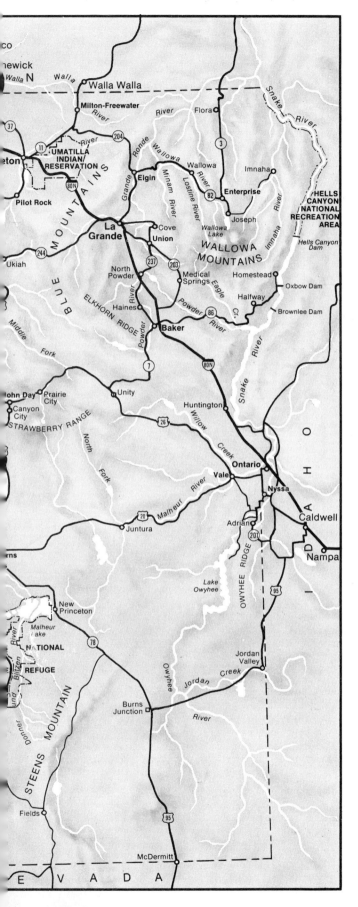

you write ahead, address your inquiry to the local chamber of commerce.

State information centers are located along main routes leading into the state—at Portland and Ashland on Interstate 5, at Astoria and Brookings on U.S. 101, at Klamath Falls on U.S. 97, and at Ontario on Interstate 80N (open May to October).

In state rest areas along major highways, Travel InfoCentre gazebos display information about nearby points of interest, local accommodations, and travel facilities. A coinless telephone enables you to call ahead for reservations or other travel services.

Telephoning to Oregon from out of state is simplified by the fact that *the area code for the entire state of Oregon is 503.*

State agencies. You can obtain a free highway map and general information about Oregon from the Travel Information Section, Oregon State Highway Division, State Highway Building, Salem, OR 97310 (phone 378-6309).

Persons with special interests or hobbies can obtain folders on Oregon parks, golf, skiing, boating, salmon fishing, rockhounding, bikeways, climate, fall vacations, and festivals and events. Also available are publications on the Mount Hood-Columbia Gorge Loop, the Oregon Trail, Lewis and Clark Trail, and other subjects. If you are interested, request a list of industrial tours.

For information on state parks, contact the State Parks and Recreation Branch, Oregon State Highway Division, Trade and High streets, Salem, OR 97310 (phone 378-6305). From Memorial Day to Labor Day, you can call toll free within Oregon for camping information (phone 1-800-542-0294).

Questions on fishing, hunting, clamming, and crabbing should be directed to the Oregon Department of Fish and Wildlife, 1634 S.W. Alder Street (P.O. Box 3503), Portland, OR 97208 (phone 229-5403).

Information on boating facilities, laws, and safety requirements is available from the Oregon State Marine Board, 3000 Market Street N.E., Salem, OR 97310 (phone 378-8587).

Federal areas. For a list of offices of Oregon's 13 national forests, write to the U.S. Forest Service, Pacific Northwest Region, P.O. Box 3623, Portland, OR 97208 (phone 221-2877). Maps of each national forest and certain topographical maps may be purchased (50 cents each) by mail or at Forest Service offices and district ranger stations.

For recreation information on BLM lands, write to the Bureau of Land Management, P.O. Box 2965, Portland, OR 97232 (phone 234-3361).

To learn more about recreation on reservoirs in western Oregon and along the Columbia River, write to the U.S. Army Corps of Engineers, Public Affairs Office, Box 2946, Portland, OR 97208 (phone 221-3768).

For information on guides and packers, consult Forest Service officials, local chambers of commerce, and Oregon Guides and Packers (P.O. Box 722, Lake Oswego, OR 97034).

Portland, the river city

Parks and flowers brighten this busy port

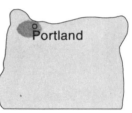

Portland

Wading children *enjoy cool waters of Forecourt Fountain on a warm summer day.*

Splendid rhododendron displays *are at their peak during April and May in the American Rhododendron Society test gardens in Crystal Springs Lake Park.*

One of the West's most attractive cities, Portland lies at the confluence of Oregon's two major rivers —the Columbia and the Willamette. Known as the City of Roses, it glows with flowers in spring and summer as rhododendrons, azaleas, and roses burst into bloom. Dozens of parks stud the city with greenery.

The fertile Willamette Valley was the goal of most pioneers who wended their way westward on the Oregon Trail. In the winter of 1844-45, two New England emigrants—A. J. Lovejoy of Boston and Francis Pettygrove of Portland, Maine—laid out a 16-block town site on the west bank of the Willamette and tossed a coin to see which one would name the new town. Commerce flourished in the young city, spurred by the discovery of gold in California —and later in Oregon—and the development of steamboat transportation on the rivers.

Today Portland is one of the busiest ports on the Pacific Coast and gateway to the vast Columbia River Basin. Spectacular towers are changing the city's skyline; yet many splendid 19th century structures are being preserved and restored.

First impressions

Described by one writer as "the biggest small town in the West," Portland is a medium-size metropolis

The placid Willamette separates downtown Portland from residential areas east of the river. Wooded foothills are backed by the snowy peak of Mount Hood.

Gaslight era landmarks are Skidmore Fountain and New Market Theater.

of nearly 375,000 people, hub of a metropolitan area of more than 1,070,000 population. Manageable in size, it is a friendly, forward-looking city. Highways radiate from Portland to all parts of the state.

Dominating the city are its rivers and its greenery. Visitors find themselves constantly crossing the Willamette on various highway bridges, 10 of which span the busy river.

The pioneers who carved Portland out of the wilderness so loved the forest that they preserved great chunks of it. A greenbelt of parks covers the city's western hills. Mature trees and landscaping add a gracious note to downtown park blocks. Home gardens thrive, and neighborhood parks are sprinkled through residential areas.

Portland's site at the mouth of the Willamette Valley, sheltered on west and east by the Coast and Cascade mountain ranges, enjoys a mild climate seldom disturbed by extreme temperatures. Though Portland lies at the same northern latitude as Minneapolis, its climate is warmed by the Japanese Current flowing south off the Oregon coast.

Sliced by its river

Though you can often see snow-capped mountains from the city's high view points, Portland is oriented to the Willamette River, a watery lifeline dividing the city into two distinct halves.

The west bank (Portlanders say "west side") is

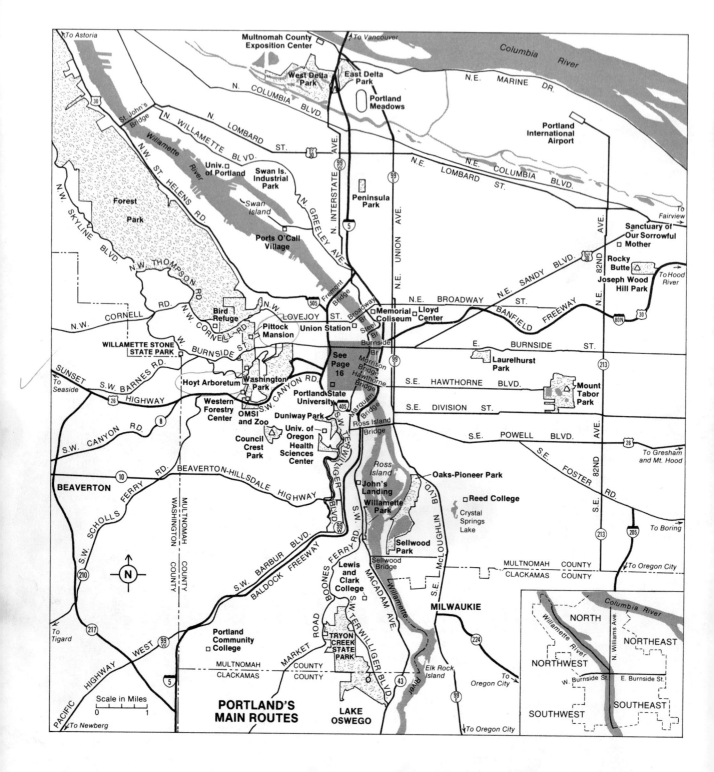

PORTLAND'S MAIN ROUTES

old Portland, containing the downtown business district, the principal parks, and perhaps a fifth of Portland's residential area. Its hilly terrain offers marvelous views of river and mountains.

Most Portlanders sleep east of the river. Generally the east bank area is level, but it does include several lofty parks (Rocky Butte and Mount Tabor) as well as Portland's airport, Memorial Coliseum, and Lloyd Center, a vast shopping complex.

A broad river cutting through the heart of a city presents some problems. Until relatively recent years, periodic floods caused extensive property damage, and industries poured impure waste products into the Willamette. Now upriver dams check potential flood waters, and an ambitious river cleanup program and improved access (see page 66) have brought a new boom in river-oriented recreation.

A city of parks and gardens

Portland is liberally sprinkled with greenery; some 160 parks and civic gardens provide welcome open space for city dwellers. Landscaped downtown blocks open up the business district, and many newer buildings include gardens and plazas. Numerous riverside parks line the banks of the Willamette. In the neighborhoods, grassy areas provide walkways and benches for adults and playgrounds for children. Massive plantings of roses and rhododendrons brighten parks and home gardens.

Along the west side hills, a string of contiguous parks provide a forested band extending for 9 miles. Much of it remains undeveloped—a thick virgin forest only a few minutes from the city center. At one end is wild Forest Park, laced with hiking trails; at the other, busy Washington Park, hub of the city's outdoor activities.

An event-filled summer park program features outdoor concerts, nature studies, sports events, art and craft classes, and such special events as open-air theater and traveling zoo exhibits of "touchable" animals.

A network of highways

Major highways encircle Portland's central district and fan out in all directions.

Interstate Highway 5—Oregon's main north-south highway—links the city with the Willamette Valley and southern Oregon.

The city's primary east-west highway is Interstate Highway 80N (U.S. Highway 30); it cuts eastward through the Columbia River Gorge and across northeastern Oregon, paralleling the overland route of the Oregon Trail. Westward, U.S. 30 follows the Columbia downstream to Astoria.

Interstate Highway 405 curves around the west side of the business district. It provides a link between Interstate 5 and westbound U.S. 30 and U.S. Highway 26. Eastbound, U.S. 26 becomes the Mount Hood Highway.

State highways 99W and 99E lead south from Portland to link a number of Willamette valley towns. State Highway 43 follows the river's west bank south to Lake Oswego and West Linn. Interstate Highway 205 cuts across the northwest corner of Clackamas County to join Interstate 5 with State Highway 213 and eastbound highways.

Finding your way around

Portland is divided into five districts, cut by three arteries—the Willamette River, Burnside Street, and N. Williams Avenue (see map insert).

Early in your visit, stop at the Visitor Information Center, 824 S.W. 5th Avenue, for sightseeing suggestions.

If you're visiting the city but have no car, you can travel around by rented car, taxi, or Tri-Met bus. The Gray Line Sightseeing Company offers a bus tour covering Portland's best-known sights.

Scenic drives

From the wooded west side hills, you can see the city laid out below—the sparkling river and its bridges, downtown skyscrapers, and the residential districts sprawling to east and south.

Take S.W. Vista Avenue south of Canyon Road (U.S. 26) through the city's older, close-in, elegant residential districts, where you'll see gracious houses and well-tended gardens ablaze with flowers; the city's highest point—1,074-foot Council Crest—offers fine views. Or drive up Burnside Street into the western hills, through forest rarely found so near the heart of a busy city.

Ask at the Visitor Information Center for a map detailing three scenic drives of the city's west side, east side, and northwest district. The routes pass most of Portland's main points of interest, wind through attractive residential areas, and skirt busy industrial districts. Signs mark the routes.

Exploring by Tri-Met bus

Most city destinations and nearby suburban communities can be reached by public transit. Tri-County Metropolitan Transportation District (locally known as Tri-Met) operates approximately 75 bus lines serving Multnomah, Clackamas, and Washington counties. You'll find a map of bus routes in the Yellow Pages of the telephone directory; for route and schedule information, call 233-3511. A customer assistance office is located at 522 S.W. Yamhill. Effective July 1, 1976, single bus rides are 40 cents; a monthly pass is $14. Exact fare is required; tickets are also available.

Passengers can ride free if they board and disembark within a 288-square-block downtown area called "Fareless Square." It is bordered by N.W. Hoyt Street, the Willamette River, S.W. Market Street, and the Stadium Freeway (Interstate 405).

Portland's new downtown transit mall, on S.W. 5th and 6th avenues between West Burnside and Madison streets, is under construction and is scheduled for completion by December, 1977. Through auto traffic and on-street parking will be banned from these streets.

Local sightseeing tours

Bus tours of Portland and vicinity are offered by the Gray Line Sightseeing Company, 921 S.W. 6th Avenue (phone 226-6755). A daily 3-hour bus tour covers Portland's major attractions. Other bus tours feature the Columbia River Scenic Highway, the Mount Hood Loop, and the Oregon Coast.

From mid-June to mid-September the *Columbia Sightseer* makes leisurely all-day boat trips upriver through the Columbia Gorge to Bonneville Dam, and excursions downstream from Portland, amid riverport traffic, to the Trojan Nuclear Plant site and Astoria.

Portland Walking Tours conducts 2-hour guided walks of downtown Portland and the Old Town district on a flexible schedule. Individuals interested in learning about Portland's history, architecture, and public art can join one of the "open walks" conducted on the first Saturday of each month and several times monthly in summer. For information on scheduled walks and fees, contact Portland Walking Tours, P.O. Box 4322, Portland, OR 97208, or phone 223-1017.

Downtown Portland

Like most cities, Portland is constantly changing. In recent years, many exciting new developments have been taking place downtown and along the waterfront.

Distinctive office buildings are going up. New landscaped plazas add more open space to the business district. A concerted effort is being made to preserve historic buildings, many of which have been renovated for use as shops or offices.

Two relatively new bridges—the Marquam and Fremont—span the Willamette. A new downtown riverfront park and other imaginative developments are transforming Portland's waterfront, providing added opportunities to enjoy the Willamette River.

Stroll around downtown Portland and take a look at some of these innovations for yourself.

Downtown greenery and open space

Early city fathers foresightedly set aside complete downtown blocks as landscaped open space. Today these unique park blocks offer greenery in the heart of the city's business district.

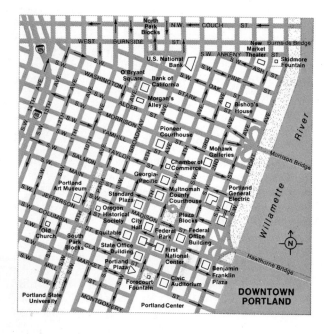

Plaza Blocks. Two downtown blocks bounded by S.W. 3rd and 4th avenues and Salmon and Madison streets were donated to the city in 1852. Lownsdale and Chapman squares, often referred to as the men's and women's blocks, are separated by stately old Elk Fountain.

Park Blocks. Two other large park areas were also set aside more than a century ago. Originally they were planned to form a park belt, a bit of serenity girdling the city's downtown district.

The South Park Blocks extend 13 blocks along Park Avenue south from S.W. Salmon Street through the Portland State University campus. Stately elms and maples and gracious gardens give this area an old-fashioned air.

North Park covers six blocks, bounded by N.W. Glisan and S.W. Ankeny streets. It borders Portland's "skid road" district.

O'Bryant Square. This busy brick plaza between S.W. Stark and Washington streets is the first block in a new city effort to link up the North and South Park blocks in a continuous greenbelt.

The square has rapidly become a favorite gathering place, with lunch time "brown baggers" coming here on pleasant days. A three-tiered fountain shaped like a rose dominates the square; nearly 250 rose bushes surround it.

Federal Park. Newest of the downtown parks, this square block of greenery (bordered by Madison and Jefferson streets and S.W. 3rd and 4th avenues) faces City Hall and the new Federal building. It lies directly south of the Plaza Blocks parks.

Landmarks old and new

Classical old public buildings intermingle with dramatic new office towers in Portland's downtown district. Here are a few sites worth noting:

Pioneer Courthouse. Recently restored, the century-old Pioneer Courthouse (often called the Pioneer Post Office) occupies a full block in the center of downtown Portland. It faces S.W. 5th Avenue between Morrison and Yamhill.

Built in the early 1870's, the historic Italianate structure now houses the U.S. Ninth Circuit Court of Appeals and a downtown branch post office.

Mohawk Galleries. A former dry goods store at S.W. 2nd and Yamhill was converted into a complex of professional offices in 1963. Designed to harmonize with the old buildings in the area, the offices surround a landscaped interior courtyard.

Morgan's Alley. This lively little shopping arcade, between S.W. Park and Broadway at Washington, was created during the remodeling of the Morgan Building. Restaurants and shops, offering a wide selection of food and goods, open onto the gallery —especially pleasant to visit on a rainy day.

Multnomah County Courthouse. Occupying an entire block at S.W. Salmon between 4th and 5th avenues, this colonnaded granite building was built between 1909 and 1914; it houses county offices.

City Hall. A stately, four-story Italian Renaissance structure built in 1895, City Hall dominates S.W. 5th between Madison and Jefferson. Polished granite columns support its circular portico.

Old Church. The city's oldest existing church stands a few blocks west of the business district at the corner of S.W. 11th Avenue and Clay. Now maintained by a secular preservation society, it began service in 1883 as the Calvary Presbyterian Church; in 1948 it became the Metropolitan Baptist Church. A fine example of "carpenter's Gothic" architecture, the church is open to visitors from 11 A.M. to 3 P.M. Tuesday through Saturday. Organ concerts are presented every Wednesday at noon, played on the old organ brought around Cape Horn.

Civic Auditorium. This handsome structure, newly built in 1968, is located at S.W. 3rd Avenue between Clay and Market streets. The auditorium is noted for its outstanding acoustics, and it has a seating capacity of 3,000 persons. The Portland Opera, Oregon Symphony, and Portland Junior Symphony perform here, along with touring musical attractions, stage plays, and dance troupes.

Wood paneling and Italian marble are used throughout the interior of the auditorium. Modern paintings and sculpture decorate three glass-fronted foyers overlooking the Forecourt Fountain.

Forecourt Fountain. One of the focal points of the downtown district is the people-pleasing Forecourt Fountain, located across from the Civic Auditorium at S.W. 3rd and Clay. Bordered by green lawns and trees, the fountain has tumbling waterfalls and frothy pools that delight strollers, shoppers, and children—who go wading on warm days.

The water is on daily except Wednesday from 9 A.M. to 11 P.M., recirculating 13,000 gallons of water each minute.

Behind the fountain, the 25-story Portland Plaza is a cloverleaf-shaped condominium.

Portland Center

Landscaped walkways connect the handsome office buildings, high-rise apartments, and shopping arcades of Portland Center, an 80-acre urban renewal project south of Civic Auditorium. Bounded by S.W. Front Street and 4th Avenue, it extends south from Market Street to the Stadium Freeway (Interstate 405). The project, begun in 1958, has brought new vigor to the downtown area.

Five tall apartment buildings overlooking the river are linked to modern office buildings by pedestrian malls and small Pettygrove Park—a delight of grassy mounds and tree-lined paths.

Farther south, the cascading waters of Lovejoy Fountain create a pleasant setting amid the apartment buildings surrounding Lovejoy Park.

New silhouettes on the Portland skyline

In recent years, a number of new office buildings have added gracious touches to the business district, and more striking office centers are in the

Schoolchildren learn about old-time forestry methods and equipment in the Georgia-Pacific Logging Museum, one of several fine exhibits devoted to the timber industry.

final planning or construction stages. Landscaped plazas, the use of art and sculpture, and modern design details add new downtown interest. Among the distinctive new structures are these:

U.S. National Bank Plaza. Accenting the north end of downtown Portland at 555 S.W. Oak is this bold, granite and glass seven-story building. Constructed in the shape of a trapezoid, it features a landscaped plaza and a long, high, enclosed arcade of specialty shops and restaurants. An adjacent 37-story tower is on the drawing boards.

Georgia-Pacific Building. Art and sculpture transform this 30-story structure at 900 S.W. Fifth into a vast gallery, where more than 450 works of art—purchased from Oregon artists—are on display throughout the building. If you look closely at the building, you'll note unusual architectural design details—all horizontal lines are slightly curved, the floor rises slightly toward the center, and the building's Doric columns taper toward the top of the tower. Don't miss the logging museum (see page 23) on the concourse level.

First National Center. This pair of buildings is linked by a bridge over S.W. 4th Avenue. The striking 40-story building at 1300 S.W. 5th Avenue is Oregon's tallest structure; an outstanding collection of works by Oregon artists is displayed here.

Benjamin Franklin Plaza. Rising on S.W. Front Avenue, this distinctive 18-story tower overlooks the river between Jefferson and Columbia streets. Faced in handsome red brick, it is a striking addition to the skyline.

Federal Office Building. Facing the City Hall across a landscaped park, the new 17-story General Services Administration Building houses most of the

Saturday Market shoppers find pottery, macramé, jewelry, and other handmade merchandise in the open-air bazaar. Street musicians add to the festive atmosphere.

Elegantly restored Bishop's House on S.W. Stark Street formerly housed church offices and a Chinese speakeasy.

city's Federal agencies and the offices for Oregon's congressmen. Its underground garage is topped by Federal Park.

Portland General Electric Company. A three-block headquarters is now under construction facing S.W. Front Avenue between Taylor and Main streets. When completed late in 1976, the complex will include shops, restaurants, auditorium, conference center, and an outdoor skating rink.

Old Town is getting spruced up

Portland's Old Town is making a comeback. In the 19th century, the downtown waterfront—roughly bounded by Front and 3rd avenues, N.W. Everett and S.W. Stark streets—was the center of commercial activity, and the area displaying the city's finest architecture. But as the city expanded, its business center shifted, and the classic buildings grew dilapidated. The West Burnside area became Portland's "skid road."

Now the district is getting a new lease on life. Entrepreneurs are refurbishing store fronts, cleaning up old brick, polishing wrought iron embellishments, and restoring historic buildings. Two downtown historic districts have been designated—the Skidmore-Old Town area and the Yamhill district. Shops and restaurants are moving into renovated buildings, and Old Town is becoming one of the city's liveliest shopping areas.

You may be able to join a walking tour (see page 16) through Portland's historic district, now a mix of social and economic elements. If you explore on your own, here are a few highlights:

Shops and restaurants. Many lively new shops mingle with vintage businesses that have been in the area for generations. The adventurous shopper will find specialty shops—arts and crafts, furniture, mod clothing, imports, housewares, antiques, old books—as well as restaurants and coffee houses amid the old hotels, grocery stores, and empty store fronts. The shops are concentrated on streets north and south of W. Burnside Street at the west end of the Burnside Bridge.

Saturday Market. On Saturdays from May until Christmas—rain or shine—the parking lot of the Import Plaza store at N.W. 2nd and Davis is transformed into an open-air market as craftspersons set up their stalls around the smokestacks of the old battleship U.S.S. Oregon. From 10 A.M. to 5 P.M. you can browse and socialize to the sounds of street music. Expect to find fresh flowers and plants, foreign foods, and quite a variety of handmade merchandise.

Skidmore Fountain. Focus of the area is a restored classic fountain at S.W. Ankeny and 1st—a sentimental link with Portland's gaslight era. Stephen Skidmore, who arrived in the wilderness village in 1850 as a lad and prospered in Horatio Alger style, bequeathed funds to the city for a fountain "where horses, men, and dogs might drink."

Unveiled in 1888 to public acclaim, the handsome

fountain was rated the loveliest piece of statuary west of Chicago—though eastern art critics patronizingly implied its beauty would be wasted on Portland. The fountain's plaza became the favorite meeting place in turn-of-the-century Portland.

After some years of neglect, water again splashes into the old fountain's octagonal pool, flowing out of decorative lions' mouths into four horse troughs.

New Market Theater. Not far from the fountain you'll see the facade of the New Market Theater, opened in 1875 at 49 S.W. 1st Avenue, between Ankeny and Ash. The city's leading theater during the gaslight era, today only its ornate facade and vaulted carriage entrance remain.

Bishop's House. One of the most elegantly restored old buildings is this handsome structure at 219 S.W. Stark Street. Built in 1879, it housed administrative church offices until 1900, then was tenanted by several diverse establishments—including a Chinese speakeasy.

Union Station. Located on N.W. 6th, the rambling, red brick train station, with its handsome tile-roofed clock tower, welcomed its first passengers in the 1890s. Today, Amtrak trains stop here daily.

Police Historical Museum. Police artifacts from the 19th and early 20th centuries have been assembled in the Portland Police Historical Museum at 115 N.W. 1st Avenue. The museum is housed in a renovated 70-year-old building—the working precinct station for policemen in the north Burnside area. You enter the museum from the alley.

Among the items displayed are arrest logs written in flowery penmanship, early fingerprint cards, old murder weapons, and turn-of-the-century police uniforms and equipment. Police officers working in this historic area wear uniforms of the 1890s.

Oregon Historical Society

Persons interested in the colorful history of the Northwest will find the Oregon Historical Society an enjoyable place to visit. Housed in a spacious new building at 1230 S.W. Park Avenue, the century-old Oregon Historical Society is open daily except Sunday from 10 A.M. to 5 P.M.

Exhibits highlight such features as historic ship models of the Northwest coast, Indian heritage of the Oregon country, pioneer crafts and trades, and 19th century printing. An original 1845 covered wagon is displayed along with pioneer artifacts, and a collection of miniature historic wagons offers a delightful record of early-day transportation.

Numerous books and other items relating to Oregon history may be purchased in the book shop.

The society maintains an active publishing program, and scholars make extensive use of the society's vast library collection of historical manuscripts and nearly a million photographs.

Portland Art Museum

Housed in a classically simple red brick building designed by architect Pietro Belluschi, the Port-

Tall trees and green lawns of the South Park Blocks form a landscaped mall through Portland State's campus. Sculpture pool is located near S.W. Montgomery Street.

land Art Museum faces the landscaped greenery of the South Park Blocks. Its calm facade belies the vigorous program inside; it is recognized as one of the outstanding small museums in the U.S.

In addition to collections of paintings and sculpture, the museum has an excellent exhibit of Northwest Coast Indian Art and permanent collections of pre-Columbian artifacts and Asian, West African, and classical Greek art. Oregon artists are presented in one-man and group shows. Traveling exhibitions change every 4 to 6 weeks. An outdoor sculpture court on the museum's north side displays the work of a number of sculptors.

The museum is open Tuesday through Sunday afternoons from noon to 5 and Friday evenings until 10. For a schedule of public events, write to the museum at 1219 S.W. Park. The museum sponsors special shows, films, lectures, concerts, and art classes for young people and adults. A rental and sales gallery offers the work of many Oregon artists. On the lower level, a museum shop has excellent reproductions of museum sculpture and jewelry, art books, and prints.

Portland State University

Young and vigorous, Portland State is Oregon's fastest growing university with an enrollment of more than 15,000 students. Just a short walk from the city center, the peaceful campus extends south from S.W. Market Street to Jackson. Stroll along the wide promenades of S.W. Park Avenue, past broad lawns shaded by ancient elms (part of the early South Park Block plantings).

The park blocks are a favorite campus gathering spot—chess and checker players compete across

Guided tours of the Port of Portland offer summer visitors a look at waterfront facilities and operations.

tile-topped game tables, and students relax on the lawns and benches. Flower-filled containers add a bright touch. On sunny days, entertainers often perform at noontime on an outdoor stage.

Rediscovering the waterfront

For decades Portlanders caught only glimpses of their river. Buildings, docks, and warehouses cut the Willamette off from public access and view.

Nowhere is Portland's vitality more in evidence than in the ambitious projects now underway along the Willamette waterfront. Long-range planning, public funds, and private investment are being combined in a number of dramatic ventures.

The busy Port of Portland encompasses modern cargo-loading facilities, specialized vessels, a ship repair yard, and industrial parks.

Bridges span the Willamette

In Portland you can expect to cross the Willamette again and again. Ten traffic bridges span the river, linking the city's west side business districts with east side residential areas. Built and rebuilt over the past century, Portland's bridges vary considerably in style and character.

Pedestrian walkways on the bridges (on all except the Marquam and Fremont freeway spans) give you a splendid view of the river and its traffic. Sturdy tugboats push loaded barges, maneuver freighters, or tow log rafts along the busy water-

way. Pleasure craft of all types and sizes share the river with ocean-going vessels and river craft. Perhaps you'll see drawbridges in action; they are opened on signal from approaching river traffic.

A look at Portland's busy port

Downstream from Fremont Bridge is the bustling Port of Portland. It transforms Portland from a medium-size inland city into an international port. The Port of Portland operates five marine terminals that handle general and bulk cargoes in a variety of specialized shipping methods—including containerized vans, cold storage, and roll-on roll-off traffic. Other specialized cargoes handled here include imported cars, logs, and bulk grain and ore shipments. The publicly owned port also operates a pair of industrial parks, ship building and repair facilities, a dredge and stern-wheel tug, and a commercial complex on Swan Island.

Port tours. In summer, free guided tours of the port are conducted each Wednesday and Thursday afternoon. You need to register in advance by calling the Port's Community Development Department (233-8331, ext. 268).

From central points, buses transport tourists to the harbor area to see various waterfront industries and port facilities—cargo handling equipment, container docks, grain elevators, floating dry docks, and automobile unloading docks.

Container loading. At John M. Fulton Terminal 6 on the Columbia River, the port provides a large public observation area on the third floor of its administration building where you can watch containerized cargoes being loaded. The terminal operates only when ships are in port, so telephone (286-9671) before visiting.

To reach Terminal 6, take N. Marine Drive west from Interstate 5 to North Portland Road and then turn onto the terminal access road.

Ports O'Call Village. This three-level international bazaar of restaurants, specialty shops, and landscaped plazas is part of Port Center, a port-owned riverfront "office-park" being developed on the southern side of Swan Island. From a four-story observation tower, you have an unobstructed view of river traffic and the activities at the port's Terminal 2, directly across the river.

Stern-wheeler on the Willamette. If you see a steamboat churning through Willamette waters, a sparkling curtain of spray spinning off her paddle wheel, you needn't rub your eyes in disbelief. It's the *Portland,* believed to be the last commercially operated steam-driven stern-wheeler in the world. River pilots consider her a vital harbor tool, but to sentimentalists she's a romantic symbol of the past.

A downtown riverfront park

One of the most exciting prospects for downtown Portland is the riverfront esplanade, a narrow strip of land stretching 22 blocks along the Willamette's west bank, from the Steel Bridge south to S.W. Columbia Street.

Conceived as a long-term project, the esplanade will be developed over the next 10 to 20 years. Harbor Drive was closed to traffic in mid-1974, the concrete was ripped up, and lawns and trees are being planted between Front Avenue and the river. A promenade will stretch along the Willamette.

Plans—which include citizen suggestions—call for a relatively undeveloped park with broad urban vistas. Areas will be set aside for shops and restaurants, a large lagoon, pleasure craft marina, and large open spaces for Rose Festival events. Walkways and bicycle paths will link the esplanade to the downtown area.

East Bank Esplanade

Across the river, a mile-long riverside promenade extends between the Burnside and Hawthorne bridges. Separating the river and Interstate 5, this landscaped city park strip offers a spectacular but noisy place to stroll, fish, cycle, or just sit admiring the city skyline or watching river traffic. Flowering trees, evergreens, and shrubbery soften freeway sounds and create a more parklike atmosphere.

To reach the promenade, walk up the ramp that begins near S.E. Belmont and Water streets at the east end of the Morrison Bridge.

Johns Landing, a riverfront village

In conjunction with Portland's downtown revival, one of the city's oldest industrial areas, on the Willamette's west bank south of Ross Island Bridge, is being privately restored to active use. Stretching for nearly a mile along the waterfront, between S.W. Flower and Carolina streets, the 70-acre Johns Landing project is designed to be a self-contained riverfront village.

A former furniture factory at 5331 S.W. Macadam has been remodeled into the Water Tower, a nostalgic shopping arcade containing more than 50 specialty shops and restaurants and a floor of offices. The sturdy, rambling charm of the old factory has been retained. A three-story etched glass mural decorates the shaft of the outside elevator.

Parks along the Willamette

As the Willamette River has been revitalized, Portlanders have gained new enjoyment from recreation on and along the water. You'll find picnic areas, boat ramps, a garden of rare plants, an amusement park, and view points where you can watch the ever-changing parade of river traffic.

Kelley Point Park. Northern gateway to the Willamette Greenway, this large park has been created on marshlands at Portland's northwestern tip, where the Willamette joins the Columbia.

Picnickers can spread their lunches in a grassy meadow or broil meals on barbecue grills; beach fires are also permitted. You can watch river boats from the shore.

To get to the park, leave Interstate 5 at the N. Marine Drive exit (near the Multnomah County Fairgrounds) and drive west on that road about a mile. Signs direct you to the park entrance.

Willamette Park. On the west bank of the river north of Sellwood Bridge, this park offers a public boat ramp and a fine spot to picnic and watch boats.

Oaks Amusement Park. First opened in 1905 to coincide with the Lewis and Clark World's Fair, the Oaks Amusement Park has provided fun for several generations of Portland families. Located on the east bank of the Willamette just north of Sellwood Bridge, the private park has an old-fashioned charm. Families enjoy its numerous rides and midway attractions, the city's largest roller-skating rink, and shaded picnic areas overlooking the river. For information on park hours, phone 233-5777.

Elk Rock Island. This Portland-owned island, just off shore from the city of Milwaukie, is a 16-acre wooded park in the middle of the Willamette River. The island is accessible by boat and—in summer— by wading from Milwaukie. You can watch boaters and water-skiers or follow winding footpaths amid the park's rare and unusual plants and trees.

The western hills

The forested hills west of the Willamette contain some of Portland's most inviting residential districts and an outstanding string of city parks.

Here you can hike through wilderness, enjoy flower gardens, study Northwest native trees and shrubs, tour an elegant mansion, visit an excellent science museum, stroll through a wildlife sanctuary, and drive through forest corridors.

Spiral ramp *leads to a mile-long landscaped city promenade along the east bank of the Willamette River.*

Rose fanciers head for Washington Park's rose test gardens, where more than 10,000 bushes bloom throughout the summer.

Students learn about electricity at the Oregon Museum of Science and Industry.

Washington Park and its gardens

Largest and busiest of Portland's city parks, Washington Park offers varied diversions for all ages. Summer evening concerts are a Portland tradition. Forests and broad grassy lawns give way to two outstanding gardens in the park's northeast corner. Athletes will find tennis courts and a municipal pitch-and-putt course.

In the southern part of the park are the popular Oregon Museum of Science and Industry (OMSI), the Western Forestry Center (see page 23), and the Zoological Gardens.

International Rose Test Gardens. Most outstanding of the city's rose gardens, this site is a Northwest showplace in June; roses continue to bloom until early fall. More than 10,000 bushes—including hundreds of rose varieties—are planted on a terraced slope overlooking a splendid city panorama. On summer weekends you may see a wedding party grouped in a secluded part of the garden.

Japanese Garden. You stroll through a roofed gate into a quiet oriental world of weeping willows, stone lanterns, and gently falling water, all captured in five classic gardens. Developed entirely from private donations, the garden meanders over 5½ acres of woodland, opening onto views of the Portland skyline. Cherry trees blossom in April.

A free shuttle bus transports visitors from the parking lot to the main gate. The garden is open from April through October, weather permitting. For information on hours and fees, phone 223-1321.

Portland Zoological Gardens

One of the oldest zoos in the country (since 1887), the Portland Zoo covers 40 acres of land at 4001 S.W. Canyon Road, just north of U.S. 26. The zoo is open daily from 10 A.M. to dusk. For information on fees, zoo railway schedules, and special events, phone 226-1561.

Special attractions include African animals and birds in the African Grasslands section, Siberian tigers, and chimpanzees who paint and perform in sign language. Children can pet and mingle with small animals in the Children's Zoo, and baby animals can be seen in the nursery.

Miniature trains of the Portland Zoo Railway take zoo visitors along a winding 4-mile route through Washington Park's woodlands. You can ride on a streamlined, diesel-powered "Zooliner" or in cars pulled by a wood-burning steam locomotive. Weather permitting, the trains operate daily in spring and summer, weekends only in winter.

Oregon Museum of Science and Industry

Science is fun for both children and adults at this fascinating museum, a unique local institution whose influence extends far beyond Portland. Popularly known as OMSI, it is located north of U.S. 26 at 4015 S.W. Canyon Road. The museum is open daily from 9 A.M. to 5 P.M., with extended hours on weekends and in summer.

Often the visitor is a participant in the engrossing natural and physical science exhibits. Viewer-operated electricity demonstrations, planetarium shows, and a transparent lady dramatizing parts of the human body are just a sample. You can tour the aerospace hall, command the pilot wheel of a ship's bridge, study Oregon fossils, see how the heart works from a walk-in model, and learn about modern agriculture from an indoor greenhouse, an operating beehive, and hatching chicks.

OMSI exists solely on its wide popular support; is was built and is supported entirely by donations of money, time, materials, and services. School and family programs offer science enrichment classes, summer camps, field trips, and opportunities for laboratory research in the OMSI Community Research Center. The "science shop" has a fine selection of popular scientific field guides, science equipment, and kits for young researchers.

Hoyt Arboretum, a gardener's treasure

If gardening is your pleasure, you won't want to miss outstanding Hoyt Arboretum. Native Northwest trees, shrubs, ferns, and wildflowers have been collected in a rambling, hilly woodland adjacent to Washington Park.

Seven miles of cool shady trails and numerous identification markers make the arboretum a delight to the casual visitor as well as the botanist. Outstanding tree species from around the world grow side by side with the natives.

S.W. Fairview Boulevard divides Hoyt Arboretum into two sections; conifers are planted west of the road, and most deciduous trees grow in the east section. Most trails begin near the administration building, where you can pick up a map of the arboretum and its paths. Behind the parking area are picnic tables and a picnic shelter in a meadow.

Forest Park—city wilderness

A vast city wilderness park offers hikers and equestrians more than 30 miles of trails just a few minutes northwest of downtown Portland. The 5,000-acre park follows the shoulder of the Tualatin Mountains for 6½ miles above the Willamette. A trail map is available from the city's Bureau of Parks (phone 248-4315).

Winding through the natural forest corridor of Portland's western hills is the Wildwood Trail, a 14-mile scenic path recently designated a National Recreation Trail. Beginning at the Western Forestry Center in Washington Park, it winds through Hoyt Arboretum, passes near the Pittock Mansion, and continues through the woodlands of Forest Park. Hikers occasionally see deer wandering through the woods, and in October, brilliant autumn foliage mingles with the evergreens.

When road and fire conditions permit, motorists can make a leisurely drive through the luxuriant woods along Leif Erikson Drive—a primitive, graded dirt road winding through the park. To enter the drive, follow N.W. Thurman Street to its junction with the forest road. Turnouts allow you to picnic or enjoy sweeping views.

The splendid Pittock Mansion

In a parklike setting nearly 1,000 feet above the city, a mansion built in French Renaissance style reflects the highest standards of early 20th century craftsmanship.

Arriving in Portland in 1853 as an English lad of 16, Henry Pittock rose from newspaper printer to owner in 8 years. Between 1909 and 1914 he built

Oregon's fascinating timber industry on display

For more than a century, Oregon's history and economy have been closely linked to its forests. Logging and the processing of wood and wood products remain the state's foremost industry.

Two excellent Portland museums highlight different aspects of the timber industry. Throughout the state, sawmills, plywood plants, and pulp and paper mills offer tours to visitors.

Georgia-Pacific Logging Museum. Old-time logging comes to life in this museum in downtown Portland. Located on the concourse level of the Georgia-Pacific building at 900 S.W. Fifth Avenue, the free exhibit is open Tuesday through Friday from 10 A.M. to 3 P.M.

A turn-of-the-century logging cart with 10-foot-high wheels first catches your eye. You move on to enjoy a movie about early railroad logging, historical photo displays of life in logging camps, and large dioramas depicting early-day and modern logging practices. Occasionally, an old-time logger stops in, and he'll reminisce of the days before power saws and mechanical log-hauling equipment took over the industry.

Western Forestry Center. Across the parking area

from OMSI, two rustically majestic wooden buildings offer intriguing exhibits on forestry and the multifaceted wood products industry. You can visit the center at 4033 S.W. Canyon Road daily from 10 A.M. to 5 P.M.

Its best-known attraction is a 70-foot "talking tree," a lifelike Douglas fir soaring to the roof of the main structure. With the push of a button, colored lights point out various parts of the tree as a taped presentation explains how trees feed and grow.

Two floors of displays—dioramas, motion pictures, and automated exhibits—illustrate the forest's life cycle, multiple uses, and harvesting and manufacturing operations, plus the wide array of products derived from wood. One exhibit displays woods from 505 different trees—every species native to North America.

Plant tours. Many lumber mills and wood products plants welcome visitors. You can tour sawmills and plywood plants and see wood pulp made into various kinds of paper, particleboard, and other useful products. Some plants have regularly scheduled tours; others request advance notice. □

Antiques shoppers head for the old Sellwood district, where refurbished buildings along S.E. 13th Avenue contain nostalgic items of the "good old days."

an elegant home on the brow of a hill overlooking the city. Purchased by the city in 1964, the mansion has been restored and is now open to the public.

Outside, the building is distinguished by graceful terraces and stone balustrades. Dominating the interior is a magnificent central staircase finished with a polished hardwood handrail and bronze supports. Ornamental plaster work, marble and hardwood floors, and hand-carved mantelpieces contribute to the elegance. The mansion has a central vacuum cleaning system, an elevator to all floors, and room-to-room telephones.

A modest fee is charged to tour the house, but the Pittock Acres Park grounds are open without charge. Hours vary by season; phone 248-4469 for information.

To get to the Pittock mansion, go west on Burnside; a mile beyond N.W. 23rd Avenue, turn right on N.W. Barnes Road; then make another right turn on N.W. Irving Avenue and follow signs into the park.

A bird refuge and wildlife exhibits

Bird watchers will enjoy a visit to the Audubon House and Pittock Wildlife Sanctuary, just a few minutes' drive from the city center at 5151 N.W. Cornell Road. About 1½ miles of trails wind through the grounds, which are kept in a natural state. You'll probably see small mammals and hear song birds. Waterfowl settle on the half-acre pond.

Inside Audubon House you can examine natural history exhibits ranging from butterfly collections to paintings of western birds. The sanctuary is open to the public daily. Audubon House is closed on Wednesdays and Sundays.

Other west side parks

Among several dozen parks in the hills, here are a few of special interest:

Macleay Park. This forested park, between Pittock Acres and Forest parks, is a good place to bring a picnic. N.W. Cornell Road cuts through the park, and you'll find many turnouts and trails.

Willamette Stone State Park. This tiny wooded preserve atop the Tualatin Mountains—near N.W. Skyline Boulevard at N.W. Royal Road—surrounds a surveyor's monument. Placed in 1851, the stone marked the point from which all lands in Oregon were surveyed; now all boundaries from Puget Sound to California are measured from this point. You look westward from the site over the Tualatin Valley.

Council Crest Park. Highest point in the city, this hilltop park in the southwest district offers fine views in all directions. The statue *Mother and Child* by Frederic Littman is a favorite of many Portlanders.

Duniway Park. If you're a lilac fancier, you'll enjoy the fine collection in Duniway Park, located at S.W. 6th Avenue and S.W. Sheridan Street just south of Interstate 405. In May you'll find several hundred mature shrubs blooming in a natural 4-acre saucer of land. Joggers run on the park's ¼-mile track.

Terwilliger Boulevard Park. This forest corridor follows the mountain ridge between Interstate 405 and State Highway 10. Turnouts along the east side of the roadway afford views of the Willamette and southeast Portland. Cyclists will find a bicycle trail along the route, and joggers can exercise at fitness stations beside the trail.

Tryon Creek State Park

Oregon's first metropolitan state park, this 600-acre wilderness preserve borders a wooded canyon between Portland and Lake Oswego, offering a glimpse of what the Portland area probably looked like 150 years ago.

Threatened with sale to a private developer, the land was preserved through citizen effort and the unique cooperation of two cities, two counties, and state and Federal governments. Dedicated volunteers constructed the park's trails under the supervision of park and forestry officials and raised $130,000 to build a nature center.

Along its 7-mile course to the Willamette, Tryon Creek cuts a ribbon through lushly forested foothills. Accessible only by trail, the park is a haven for urban hikers, cyclists, and horseback riders. Along the path you enjoy such serendipitous forest pleasures as wildflowers, occasional beaver dams, and the sight of small animals and birds.

Blending into the forest setting is the Nature

Center, open daily from 9 A.M. to 5 P.M., containing exhibits of the park's plant and animal life. A naturalist is on duty Wednesday through Sunday. Trained volunteer guides conduct nature walks through the park at 1 and 3 P.M. on weekends and on weekdays by request. The park has 7½ miles of narrow, hand-built foot trails and 3½ miles of separate horse trails. Part of the Terwilliger Boulevard bike path runs through the park.

East side destinations

In contrast to the forested hills west of the Willamette, Portland's east side stretches across a flat valley toward the Cascades. Dozens of neighborhood parks are sprinkled throughout the residential area.

Memorial Coliseum

Located on the northeast side of the Willamette between the Broadway and Steel bridges, versatile Memorial Coliseum is the site for conventions, ice shows, rock band concerts, circuses, fairs, and indoor athletic events. Basketball draws good crowds —the Portland Trail Blazers play NBA league games here, and each December top college teams compete in the Far West Classic tournament.

Busy Lloyd Center

One of the Northwest's first and finest shopping complexes, Lloyd Center offers a massive retail center just east of the Willamette River. It is reached from N.E. Broadway or Interstate 80N.

Landscaped pedestrian malls are lined with more than 100 businesses, ranging from major department stores to local specialty shops. A favorite gathering place is the covered open-air ice-skating rink where you can watch students practice or take to the ice yourself. Special mall exhibits highlight arts and crafts, flower displays, and youth activities. Restaurants, banks, and professional offices round out Lloyd Center's facilities.

Mount Tabor, an extinct volcano

This large park in southeast Portland has its own extinct volcano, now used in summer as an outdoor theater. Geologists say the volcanic activity occurred about 10 million years ago.

The road circling Mount Tabor's grassy summit affords some fine views of the distant downtown area, the rivers, and the lower Willamette Valley, with Mount Hood looming on the eastern skyline.

Sanctuary of Our Sorrowful Mother

The tranquility of an outdoor cathedral impresses visitors to this religious shrine, located at N.E. 85th Avenue and Sandy Boulevard. Outdoor Mass is held in the grotto at noon on Sundays from May through September. An elevator transports visitors to the cliff top to see more landscaped gardens and a panoramic view of the Columbia.

Rhododendron test gardens

More than 2,500 rhododendrons are planted in the Portland test gardens of the American Rhododendron Society in Crystal Springs Lake Park. Located near S.E. 28th Avenue and Woodstock Boulevard just southwest of Reed College, the gardens cover a wooded island in the lake as well as part of the mainland park. A footbridge links the two areas, and pathways wind through the gardens. Blossoms are at their peak in April and May.

Sellwood's Antique Row

A thriving group of antique and specialty shops has brought new life to Portland's old Sellwood district. Capitalizing on the growing interest in antiques, an enterprising colony of entrepreneurs has revitalized the old area.

Some 15 antique stores and a handful of compatible shops—some housed in old gingerbread-decorated buildings—stretch along a 12-block area of S.E. 13th Avenue southeast of Sellwood Park. Saturday is the busiest day of the week as window-shoppers crowd the stores and sidewalks in search of a nostalgic treasure.

A modernized international airport

In early 1977, Portland unveils an expanded and modernized Portland International Airport on its site beside the Columbia in northeast Portland.

Ice-skaters practice their jumps and spins on Lloyd Center's open-air ice rink. Watch students practice—or glide onto the ice yourself.

Festival queen and princesses wave to spectators from a flower-bedecked float as the Rose Festival's colorful parade winds through the city.

Modernization brings spacious new ticket counters, an expanded and more efficient baggage claim area, colorful lounge areas, a nursery and children's lounge, and a meditation room. Wall coverings depict familiar Oregon scenes and spotlight the state's major industries.

North Portland

Interstate 5 and other main thoroughfares cut through Portland's northernmost district. North of the business area, state 99W and 99E merge into Interstate 5 just south of the Columbia River.

Peninsula Park. A short detour east of Interstate 5 on N. Portland Boulevard takes you to Peninsula Park, where more than 700 varieties of roses bloom in the Sunken Rose Garden from late May into autumn. The rose garden is located in the southern part of the park, near the corner of N. Ainsworth and N. Albina.

Multnomah County Fair and Exposition Center. This sizable arena on the Columbia's south bank hosts the city's largest shows and expositions—among them the spring Home and Garden Show, the Multnomah County Fair, and the annual Pacific International Livestock Exposition held each November. Portland Meadows Race Track and West Delta Park and Golf Course are located nearby.

Marine Drive. This riverside road parallels the south shore of the Columbia. During the sailing season, you can watch sailboats and yachts maneuvering in the mile-wide river.

Activities and events

Metropolitan Portland has activities going on the year around—opera and symphony performances, dramatic and musical plays, arts and crafts exhibits, professional and amateur sports events, tours of local industries, and seasonal festivities.

Opera, symphony, and theater

Portland's major musical events—including touring attractions—take place in the Civic Auditorium at S.W. 4th and Clay. Local newspapers list the current offerings. For information on program schedules and ticket availability, consult the opera and symphony associations.

The Oregon Symphony Orchestra plays to full houses during its winter season. In addition to a regular series with guest artists, it presents youth and pops concerts and performances around the state. The Portland Opera is young in years (it was organized in the late 1960s), but it has drawn rave reviews for its presentations.

A number of theatrical groups, led by the 50-year-old Portland Civic Theatre, schedule dramatic and musical plays throughout the year.

A resurgence in arts and crafts

The reviving interest in handicrafts, coupled with a growing appreciation of art, has caused dozens of Portland galleries to flourish. Art and sculpture—much of it by Northwest craftsmen—adorns new office buildings and parks.

The Portland Art Museum (see page 19) sponsors a continuing schedule of exhibits and events. A number of local galleries feature paintings, weaving, basketry, ceramics, jewelry, and sculpture by Northwest artists and craftsmen. Local newspapers report current exhibitions.

The sporting life

In recent years Portland has assumed a more active role in professional sports, with league entries in soccer (the Portland Timbers), basketball (Trail Blazers), and baseball (Mavericks). Soccer, football, and baseball games are played in Portland Civic Stadium, S.W. 18th and S.W. Morrison; basketball contests take place in Memorial Coliseum; the Portland Buckaroos independent hockey team meets opponents at the Jantzen Beach Ice Sports Arena.

In season, you'll find horse racing at Portland Meadows, greyhound racing at Fairview Park, and motorcross and sports car races at the Portland International Raceway near West Delta Park.

A half-dozen public golf courses are located within the city, and numerous others only a short drive beyond; the Portland Chamber of Commerce can provide a listing of facilities and addresses. Tennis courts, swimming pools, and children's playgrounds are located in various city parks; for information on park facilities, consult the Bureau of Parks (1107 S.W. 4th, phone 248-3580).

Check Portland newspapers for current information on sailboat racing, ice-skating competitions, hiking trips, bicycle excursions, and other sports activities.

Portland's colleges

Portland is a college town, yet no single school dominates the city. Many campus activities are open to the public.

Largest, lustiest, and youngest of the major 4-year schools is Portland State University (see page 19). University of Oregon students enrolled in the schools of medicine, dentistry, and nursing take their professional work in Portland at the university's Health Sciences Center.

Other 4-year colleges and universities are Lewis and Clark College, University of Portland, Reed College, and small Columbia Christian and Warner Pacific colleges.

Portland Community College provides a wide variety of educational offerings to the entire community. Marylhurst Education Center, formerly a Catholic girls' college, offers many innovative community education programs; its wooded campus is located on State 43 south of Lake Oswego.

A museum for children

Scaled to a child's size and keyed to his interests, the Portland Children's Museum offers an interesting change of pace for young museum-goers.

Located at 3037 S.W. 2nd Avenue, the museum features a doll collection, various exhibits in low glass cases, and live animals—some of which may be gently handled. Maintained by the city's Bureau of Parks, the museum also has summer classes. For additional information, phone 227-1505.

Tours through industrial plants

If you plan ahead, you can visit any of several dozen Portland business and industrial firms that offer tours through their plants. Some schedule tours on a regular basis, but most request advance notice.

For a list of companies offering tours, write to the state Travel Information office (address on page 11) or contact the Portland Chamber of Commerce.

June is Rose Festival time

In early June Portland assumes its role as the City of Roses, when it honors the flower in a 10-day civic celebration climaxed by a tremendous floral parade. The International Rose Test Gardens in Washington Park and other city rose gardens are groomed to be at peak bloom during the annual Rose Festival.

The fast-moving series of events includes coronation of a royal court, boat races and a water carnival, sports events, bicycle races, a rose show, and a ski race at Timberline on Mount Hood. U.S. and Canadian naval ships hold open house along the sea wall near downtown Portland. Indian performers from many western tribes gather for a 3-day encampment in East Delta Park during the

Historic Sauvie Island—a rural retreat

Only 20 minutes from downtown Portland lies Sauvie Island, an unspoiled wedge of greenery at the confluence of the Columbia and Willamette rivers. Separated from the city's busy industrial fringe, the island is a pastoral retreat.

Here you'll find thriving farms, oak and cottonwood groves, sandy river beaches, and lakes and marshes teeming with birds and other wildlife. You can watch oceangoing freighters on the Columbia, hike the island's beaches, canoe its waterways, bicycle along level roads, picnic in sunny meadows, and visit a historic house. Many fishermen simply set up a chair on the beach, throw a line in the river, and relax.

Long before white men arrived, Indian tribes from the Columbia and Willamette valleys gathered here. In 1792 the island was noted in the journal of Lt. William Broughton, an English naval officer under Captain George Vancouver. Lewis and Clark landed here in 1805; they called it Wappato Island. The island was the site of a Hudson's Bay Company fur trading post (Fort William) and a pioneer dairy worked by Laurent Sauvé, for whom the island is named.

Island roads. A loop road covers the southern part of the island, with side roads branching north-

ward along Multnomah Channel, to Sturgeon Lake, and along the Columbia. Most of the dry land is farmed, and you're likely to see signs advertising home-grown produce for sale. The island's northern half is a waterfowl management area; duck hunters come here in late autumn.

Territorial farm museum. The restored two-story Bybee-Howell house near the southern end of the island reflects life in the Oregon country on the eve of statehood. Territorial settlers lived an isolated, self-contained life here, and to some extent that feeling remains.

Built by James F. Bybee in 1856 on a Donation Land Claim, the house was sold 2 years later to a neighbor, Benjamin Howell. The house remained in the Howell family until 1961, when it was sold to Multnomah County for a historical park.

Following several years of research and restoration, the house was opened to the public in 1967 and is now a National Historic Landmark. Furnishings in the house reflect the pre-Civil War era. Behind the house, apple trees dominate the pioneer orchard, planted with more than 160 different varieties of fruit trees found in early Oregon orchards. Native plants have been collected in a pioneer garden. ☐

festival; they erect a tepee village, perform traditional dances, and sell Indian food and crafts.

Other annual Portland highlights include the Multnomah County Fair in midsummer and the Pacific International Livestock Exposition in November.

Other nearby attractions

When a Portlander thinks of a day excursion, his first idea is often a drive through the Columbia Gorge, an outing in Mount Hood National Forest, or a quick trip to the beach—all less than 2 hours from Portland.

But you can also find a pleasing change of pace nearer the city. Some suggestions are listed below; you'll find additional ones in the Willamette Valley chapter.

Alpenrose Dairyland

Children can get acquainted with farm animals and enjoy other activities at Alpenrose Dairyland, a sprawling, 60-acre working dairy just west of Portland. Weekends are the best time to visit. Bring along a picnic lunch.

Well-known children's tales are made real with live animals in Storybook Lane. In the Baby Animal Barn, youngsters can pet the calves, lambs, colts, and kids. On Sunday afternoons small visitors can ride the dairy's Shetland ponies while their older brothers and sisters enjoy quarter midget action and watch amateur bicycle races in the park's Olympic-style velodrome. Many permanent exhibits —old music makers, antique wagons and motor vehicles, a doll collection—add to the fun.

Annual festivities include an Easter Egg Hunt and the Americana Pageant that spans several days around July 4. Other special events are announced in advance.

To reach Alpenrose Dairyland, take State 10 to Shattuck Road, turn south, and continue about ¾ mile to 6149 Shattuck Road.

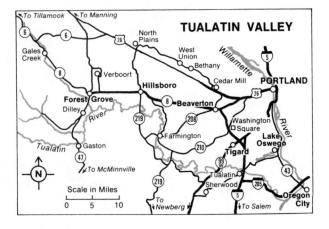

The Tualatin Valley

Now one of the state's fastest developing areas, the fertile Tualatin Valley was once alive with beaver and was a favorite hunting ground of Hudson's Bay Company trappers. Lured by the rich valley soil, the first settlers arrived about 1840.

Broad, busy State Highway 8 is Washington County's "main street," linking the towns of Beaverton, Hillsboro, Forest Grove, and many smaller communities. The Tualatin River meanders through the valley; its name comes from the Indian word *twality*, meaning lazy river.

Despite its rapid growth, the valley is still prime agricultural land. Pleasant secondary roads follow the earth's gentle contours through the farming country. Small communities with 19th century churches are a pleasant surprise.

Local celebrations. Forest Grove turns into a tintype of the 1890s on the first weekend of March when the town holds its annual Barbershop Ballad Contest and Gay '90s Festival. Many townspeople dress in period costumes, merchants grow beards, and surreys and horseless carriages reappear. Highlighting the event-filled weekend are the evening barbershop quartet competitions, attracting groups from all over the Northwest.

Hillsboro hosts its Happy Days Celebration in July and the Washington County Fair and Rodeo in August. Sherwood has a Robin Hood Festival in July, and Tualatin sponsors an August Crawfish Festival.

Beaverton. Nine miles west of Portland, Beaverton is the center of a rapidly growing research and electronics industry.

The Northwest's largest enclosed shopping center—Washington Square—is located south of Beaverton off State Highway 217. Opened in 1973, it houses more than 100 retail stores and specialty shops (including six department stores). Skylights and vaulted ceilings accent the climate-controlled mall, and landscaped garden courts offer benches for shoppers.

Pioneer churches. During the years of the westward migration, settlers of varying religious and national backgrounds settled in the valley. Each group built its own church, some of which still stand. Several are located near the West Union Road, north of U.S. 26.

The Tualatin Plains Church, locally known as the Old Scotch Church, was built in 1878 about 4 miles north of Hillsboro; almost surrounded by trees, the little white structure stands among the gravestones of its pioneer cemetery.

Giant sequoias. More than a century ago, an unsuccessful gold seeker named John Porter returned home from California carrying a gunny sack of redwood cones from the giant sequoia. From this simple beginning, trees he propagated have grown tall and thick. You'll see them scattered about Forest Grove and flanking the south entrance of the Washington County Courthouse in Hillsboro.

On Porter Road between State 8 and Verboort, two long rows of giant sequoias flank the lane leading to the farmhouse where Porter once lived.

In the community of Verboort, the Catholic Church has giant sequoias grouped at each corner of its grounds. Here you can experience the "cathedral feeling" that a grove of these tall trees exudes. On the first Saturday in November, the community holds its annual Verboort Sausage and Kraut Dinner, serving thousands of persons who come from miles around.

Pacific University. Founded as Tualatin Academy in 1849, this Forest Grove school is one of the oldest colleges in the West. On the campus you can visit the Old College Hall; built in 1850, it was the first frame building on the Tualatin plains. Constructed of hand-hewn timbers and topped with a graceful bell tower, the building housed classes until 1948, when it was converted into a museum.

Water recreation. A new reservoir dams the waters of Scoggin Creek near Gaston in the foothills of the Coast Range. Though built primarily for flood control and irrigation, it also offers a new water recreation area for metropolitan families. Located at the mouth of a timbered valley, the lake is stocked with bass and trout and bordered by bridle paths and bike trails.

Lake Oswego

Waterside living keynotes the friendly community of Lake Oswego, built around the shores of the 3½-mile-long private lake. Boaters and water-skiers enjoy skimming through the lake waters, and apartment dwellers can lean over their balcony railings to feed the ducks.

At the mouth of Oswego Creek, George Rogers City Park offers a tree-shaded picnic area, a small beach, and a public boat landing on the Willamette. The massive stone chimney is a remnant of the Oswego Iron Works, a foundry occupying this site from 1867 to 1908.

A pleasant town for strolling, Lake Oswego has an interesting selection of restaurants and boutiques. Each June the town holds a community arts festival featuring exhibitions, an outdoor bazaar of arts and crafts, and performing arts.

A paved bicycle trail parallels State 43 between Lake Oswego and West Linn; it intersects Old River Drive, where you can cycle leisurely near the Willamette. Mary S. Young State Park lies along State 43 between the two towns; you can enjoy picnicking, fishing, and hiking in the park.

Clackamas County byways

On county back roads you'll make your own pleasing discoveries—colorful lily fields near Gresham, blooming in summer; produce stands offering fresh-from-the-farm vegetables; simple roadside signs advertising home businesses or pets for sale.

Many historic or scenic attractions in the Willamette Valley are within an easy drive of Portland.

Looking for a handout, ducks swim below the balconies of waterside apartments at Lake Oswego. Residents enjoy boating and water-skiing on the lake .

Blue Lake Park

Families and groups enjoy this popular Multnomah County park, 15 miles east of Portland off Interstate 80N near Fairview. The park's 900 picnic sites get heavy use, and visitors can swim, fish, or go boating as well. The children's play area features imaginative playground equipment.

The scenic Sandy River

A favorite destination for family outings, the Sandy River flows from Mount Hood's glaciers through the foothills east of Portland; it joins the Columbia near Troutdale. In 1805, Lewis and Clark named it the Quicksand River; their explorations are commemorated at a state park near the mouth of the river (see page 36).

Upstream parks. Two popular parks provide pleasant spots to fish or picnic with a view of the river. Dabney State Park, 19 miles east of Portland on the Columbia River Scenic Route, has a swimming area. Oxbow County Park borders the river near U.S. 26; scenic campsites and hiking and bridle trails lure visitors.

Pristine gorge. A 6-mile stretch of the river, from Dodge Park to Oxbow County Park, is wild and isolated, accessible only by boat. Steep 400-foot cliffs have protected this stretch of wilderness where deer and elk browse and water birds dive for fish along the rocky shore. Quiet pools alternate with a series of white-water rapids. Federal and state agencies and the Nature Conservancy, a private organization, have joined forces to preserve the gorge as a semiwilderness recreation area.

Along the Columbia River

Follow the Northwest's highway of history

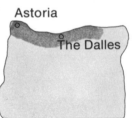

Astoria

The Dalles

Surf fishermen prepare for a day of fishing near the mouth of the Columbia.

Sun glistens on the plunging waters of Wahkeena Falls. A short trail leads from the parking area through luxuriant forest to the waterfall.

No single physical feature has influenced the development of the Pacific Northwest more than the Columbia River and its tributaries. Rising in the Canadian Rockies, the river meanders through British Columbia and eastern Washington, collecting the waters of many other rivers along its route. It then veers westward, carving an awesome channel through the Cascade Mountains on its 1,243-mile journey to the sea.

Long before the first white men sailed up the Columbia, prehistoric tribes recorded their own presence by carving petroglyphs on the cliffs above the river.

Indian tribes settled near the Columbia, fishing for salmon, trapping animals, and trading among themselves.

The entrance to the great river of the West was not discovered until 1792, when a Yankee sea captain and trader, Robert Gray of Boston, sailed several miles upstream on his ship *Columbia*. He traded with the Indians, noted the appearance of the country, and named the river after his ship. Five months later Lieutenant William Broughton, an English naval officer serving under Captain George Vancouver, explored the river nearly 100 miles inland.

Early exploration and settlement of the Oregon Territory depended in large part on the Columbia

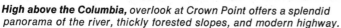
High above the Columbia, *overlook at Crown Point offers a splendid panorama of the river, thickly forested slopes, and modern highway.*

Log rafts *and other river traffic use navigation locks to by-pass dams.*

—the only water-level route from the country's interior to the sea. Explorers and fur trappers paddled their canoes along the river highway. Tired pioneers completed their grueling overland journey by rafting their wagons and livestock through the Columbia's hazardous gorge.

The discovery of gold brought a great influx of immigrants, and boats steamed up the rivers, providing transportation and communication between the scattered settlements, farming areas, and mining districts.

As you drive along Oregon's great river, you'll see a cross section of the state—sandy beaches, quiet farm lands, industrial ports, forested mountains, sparkling waterfalls, valleys of fruit orchards, vast wheat fields, livestock ranges, and arid plateau.

The hand of man is visible, too, shaping the river to his needs. Commercial ships and pleasure craft can now navigate 465 miles inland to Lewiston, Idaho, on the Snake River.

Huge freighters load lumber and wheat for foreign ports, and tugboats maneuver barges and log rafts along the waterway. Massive dams barricade the river for power and irrigation. Roads curve around hillsides and through promontories, and numerous roadside parks invite you to enjoy the river's many moods.

Tall-masted fishing boats of Astoria's commercial fleet moor just west of the interstate bridge. Sportsmen depart on deep-sea fishing trips from nearby Warrenton.

Spiral frieze on Astoria Column depicts events in town's history. You climb a spiral stair to the viewing platform.

The Lower Columbia

In the years following Lewis and Clark's epic overland journey, fur traders arrived and established outposts. In 1811 members of John Jacob Astor's Pacific Fur Company sailed up the Columbia, selecting a site on the south shore for their fort.

Astoria became the first permanent settlement and trading center in the Oregon country. Its major growth and the settlement of other lower Columbia river towns occurred in the 1840s and '50s as overland immigrants arrived and ships entered the harbor in growing numbers. Many of the settlers were New Englanders, and logging became the principal industry. By its 100th birthday, Astoria was the second largest city in Oregon.

From Astoria U.S. Highway 30 parallels the twisting river upstream to Portland. Small towns are scattered along the route, but it's a quiet drive through wooded countryside and farm lands until you near Portland.

Astoria's maritime flavor

At the turn of the century, Astoria rivaled San Francisco in size and splendor, and a hint of those glory days remains. Wealthy merchants and sea captains built elegant houses on the terraced hillsides overlooking the river. Much of the old town was destroyed by fire in 1922, but at least a dozen fine old Victorian houses still remain.

To see some of these houses (not open to the public), drive along Duane, Exchange, Franklin, and Grand streets between 8th and 17th streets. Precise locations of historic buildings are marked on a city map, available from the Chamber of Commerce office in the Port of Astoria Building.

On the city's northern slopes, two and three-story wooden frame houses face the busy river traffic. A sizable fishing fleet anchors in the shadow of the massive 4-mile-long toll bridge linking Oregon and Washington.

Many Astoria residents are of Scandinavian ancestry. Annually in mid-June the city hosts a Scandinavian Midsummer Festival with a parade, folk dancing, Scandinavian foods, arts and crafts demonstrations, and booths displaying Scandinavian articles.

The view from the Astoria Column

One of the best vantage points from which to orient yourself is the Astoria Column, crowning 700-foot Coxcomb Hill. Signs point the way from the city center.

If you are willing to climb the enclosed spiral staircase to the top of the monument—166 steps in all—a magnificent view awaits. You can see the city encircled on south and east by wooded hills, the Columbia River with its waterfront docks and wharves, the great span of the interstate bridge, the Pacific Ocean, and Young's Bay.

During a squall you can watch thunderheads pile high on the foothills. At sunset, the waters turn to silver as colors spread across the sky. An evening visit offers a different sight—the river's navigation pattern outlined in lights, bisected by the glittering bridge, with the lights of communities and highways beyond.

Constructed in 1926, the 125-foot column was patterned after one built by the Roman emperor Trajan in 114 A.D. A multicolored pictorial frieze spirals 535 feet around the outside of the column. It depicts major events in Astoria's history—the exploration of the Columbia River, the founding of Astoria, and the settlement of the territory.

Museums depict a colorful past

In a city steeped in the history of the Columbia River and the settlement of the Northwest, two splendid museums and additional exhibits provide a nostalgic look at Astoria's eventful past.

Maritime heritage. The history of the Columbia River and its ports dominates the Columbia River Maritime Museum at 16th and Exchange streets, just a block south of U.S. 30. Soon the museum will be housed in a spacious new building now under construction on the Astoria waterfront.

All the exhibits relate to things nautical; you see sailing-ship models, early sea charts, whaling and fishing equipment, plus figureheads and ship hardware from vessels of historical note and ships wrecked at the mouth of the Columbia. The museum is open daily (closed Mondays from October through April).

An outstanding feature of the maritime museum is an actual seagoing vessel, the lightship *Columbia*, moored at the foot of 17th Street next to the new museum site. It marked the mouth of the Columbia River for more than a half-century before being retired in 1961. The Coast Guard ship *Yocona* is moored alongside.

History in a Victorian mansion. The Clatsop County Historical Museum, 8th and Duane streets, is housed in the former home of Captain George Flavel. Constructed in 1883 of lumber freighted around Cape Horn, the two-story frame building is a striking example of pioneer architecture set amid spacious landscaped grounds. You can identify it by a three-story tower at one corner and by its frosting of fancy wood trim.

Inside you'll see paintings, shipwreck photos, and other lore of the Pacific Northwest. The mansion's six elaborate fireplaces, all different, were built of rare imported wood panels shipped around the Horn. Fireplace tiles came from various European and Asian countries. The museum is open daily from 10 A.M. to 5 P.M. from June to mid-September, closed on Mondays the rest of the year.

Fort Astoria. At 15th and Exchange streets, a historical marker and partial reconstruction of the fort indicate the site of the first American outpost west of the Mississippi River.

Fishing—sport and livelihood

Along the wharf, the Chinook salmon still reigns. Tall-masted fishing boats sail out to sea in search of tuna and salmon, and on weekends, smaller vessels ply the channel or head westward toward the rougher waters near the Columbia Bar. Sport fishermen compete for the biggest catch during the Astoria Regatta each summer; other events during the 4-day celebration include water sports events, dances, and a salmon barbecue.

Most of Astoria's commercial fleet ties up at the West Mooring Basin, just west of the interstate bridge; often you'll see fishermen working on their boats or repairing nets. If you are interested in watching the catch processed and packed, inquire about guided tours of the Bumble Bee Sea Foods plant a few blocks to the east.

The thriving community of Warrenton, west of Astoria, is the charter boat center for salmon fishing. From June to September, ocean trawlers take sports fishermen out for the day in search of Chinook or silver salmon. Private boats can be launched and moored in Hammond, north of Warrenton.

Side trips from Astoria

Astoria's prime location offers a choice of excursions—traveling inland to wooded hills, roaming nearby beaches, or tracing the footsteps of Lewis and Clark.

Young's River Falls. One favorite picnic spot is Young's River Falls County Park, located about 15 miles south of Astoria on the Young's River Loop Road. You drive through rich green dairy country along the river. Daisies and buttercups dot lush pastures in spring. From the parking area, a path drops down to the base of the falls. The loop road intersects State Highway 202 at Olney.

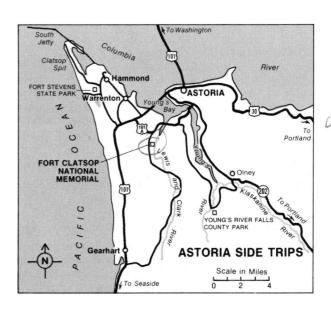

Built of logs, Fort Clatsop replica shows layout of Lewis and Clark post. Trails lead to river landing and a spring.

Into the Coast Range. From Astoria, State 202 meanders southeast along the North Fork of the Klaskanine River, climbing through coastal rain forests of spruce and hemlock to Fishhawk Falls. On the eastern slope of the range, you enter the pastoral Nehalem Valley at Jewell.

Clatsop Spit. Hardy souls willing to gamble on the weather will find the beaches near the mouth of the Columbia a quiet world of sand dunes and beach grass, where the only sounds are the clang of ocean buoys and the trill of meadowlarks. Paved roads cut across the salt flats between river and ocean. The oceanside road leads to a lookout where you can climb to a viewing platform. Below, waves crash against the enormous boulders of the South Jetty, which curves like a long arm eastward. You can watch the ocean-to-river traffic moving cautiously; the treacherous sandbars at the mouth of the Columbia have claimed hundreds of vessels.

Fort Clatsop National Memorial

Six miles southwest of Astoria, on the western bank of the Lewis and Clark River, you can visit the site of Fort Clatsop, headquarters of the Lewis and Clark expedition during the winter of 1805-06.

A full-scale replica of the original fort has been constructed, based on the floor plan and dimensions drawn by Captain Clark. It is open daily from 8 A.M. to 5 P.M. in winter, to 8 P.M. in summer. Admission is free. Picnic tables are located on the grounds.

Overland to the Pacific. Meriwether Lewis and William Clark led the first official United States exploring expedition—an arduous 2½-year journey across the vast North American continent. Their explorations provided the first detailed knowledge of the Northwest, awakening an inter-

est that lured trappers and settlers into the region and helped make Oregon an American—rather than a British—territory. For a brochure on the Lewis and Clark Trail in Oregon, write to the state Travel Information office (address on page 11).

The journals kept by Captains Clark and Lewis provide a valuable historical record of their cold, rainy winter in the Oregon country. The men chronicled not only their explorations and struggle to live off the land but also details of their surroundings. They observed and carefully described the trees, birds, animals, and fish they found, often accompanying their writings with drawings. Their maps were the first accurate and useful records of the topography of the regions through which they journeyed. Indians were frequent visitors to the fort, and the journals record the dress, appearance, customs, and way of life of the local Clatsop, Chinook, and Tillamook tribes.

Visiting the site. Equipment used during the expedition and maps tracing its route are displayed at the visitor center; you can also watch a slide program, "The Voyage of Discovery." Books and pamphlets about the expedition and frontier exploration can be purchased here.

A replica of the original fort, built of the "streightest and most butifullest logs," was constructed on the site in 1955 to mark the expedition's 150th anniversary. In its sheltered clearing, the reconstructed fort appears surprisingly small. Only 50 feet square, it housed 33 men through the winter. A 15-star flag flies atop the flagpole.

In summer costumed personnel describe the dress and life of the expedition, demonstrate the loading and firing of a flintlock rifle of the Lewis and Clark era, and hollow out a log canoe.

Short trails, corresponding to those used by members of the expedition, lead to the camp's fresh-water spring and the canoe landing. A 32-foot dugout canoe, similar to those used for river travel, can be seen near the river below the fort.

The river route

As you head up the Columbia from Astoria, you catch occasional glimpses of the water. From Clatsop Crest, savor a final panoramic view before U.S. 30 winds up into the forested hills of the Coast Range. Picnickers enjoy the woodsy setting of Bradley Wayside State Park.

At Westport a toll ferry transports cars around wooded Puget Island and across the river to Cathlamet, Washington. Local Tom Sawyers bicycle down to the wharf and dive off into the water.

Trees shield river views as you drive east through dairying and farm lands toward Clatskanie. Located in a wooded valley on the Clatskanie River, the town was named for a small tribe of Indians that once lived nearby. Boating and fishing are popular on both the Columbia and Clatskanie.

A bridge—the only one between Astoria and Portland—spans the Columbia at Rainier, providing access to Longview's mills and other industries on the Washington shore. From the hill west of Rainier you have a fine view of the river and the cities several hundred feet below.

Nuclear power comes to Oregon

In recent years interesting new structures have been built along the Columbia between Rainier and Goble. Put into operation in late 1975, the uranium-fueled Trojan nuclear power plant provides a major new source of electrical energy for the region. Its curved cooling tower has become a new landmark along the river.

For information about the plant, stop at the Visitor Information Center just off U.S. 30 at the entrance to the plant. Public areas—including picnic grounds, a recreation lake, and a wildlife viewing shelter—are being developed. A large natural lake, wintering grounds of wild whistling swans and other birds, has been preserved in its natural state.

Old river towns

Pioneer loggers from New England first settled in Columbia City and St. Helens in the 1840s. As the towns grew, businesses clustered along the waterfront. From U.S. 30, side streets lead several blocks north to the river, where the towns' older sections retain the informal charm of a slower-paced era.

Columbia City. One of the most attractive 19th century houses along the river, the Caples House overlooks a scenic stretch of the Columbia from its site at First and I streets. Built in 1870, the house (originally the home of a pioneer doctor) and several outbuildings have been restored and furnished as a museum. The buildings are open daily except Monday.

St. Helens. Named for the snowy peak often visible to the northeast, St. Helens is not only a river port and market center but also the county seat. The Columbia County Courthouse, built in 1906 of locally quarried stone, has been a lower Columbia landmark for decades. A historical museum on the upper floor is open Wednesday, Thursday, and Friday afternoons. The courtroom resembles a setting from a western movie.

The town's oldest structure is the Knighton House, built by the town's founder in 1847. Spared in the 1904 fire that burned many of the town's wooden buildings, the house has been moved to 155 S. 4th Street from its original site near the courthouse.

Pastoral retreat. Historic Sauvie Island (see page 27) lies just northeast of U.S. 30 on the western outskirts of Portland where the Willamette River enters the Columbia.

The Columbia River Gorge

The most spectacular stretch of the Columbia River Highway lies upriver from Portland. East of Troutdale, the river cuts its path through the Cascade Range. Clear streams tumble down the wooded hillsides, plunging over the steep basaltic cliffs in jubilant waterfalls.

Two highways follow the river's route—Interstate Highway 80N, the water-level freeway; and the Columbia River Scenic Highway, a section of the old road that winds high above the river through forests and past waterfalls.

Numerous state parks in the gorge offer picnicking and rest areas. Campsites are available in Lewis and Clark and Ainsworth state parks. Parks

Trojan visitor center offers exhibits on nuclear energy and view of 499-foot cooling tower and other buildings.

Steamboats linked the scattered river settlements

The river boats that plied the Columbia and her tributaries are now only memories, but in their day the hard-working stern-wheelers added an important chapter to transportation in the Pacific Northwest.

Introduced during the 1850s, the steamboats operated wherever business was available and water was deep enough. Tired pioneers and their covered wagons were transported downstream from The Dalles to Portland on the final portion of their 6-month overland trek. Each new gold discovery brought crowds of miners, who were ferried upstream with their machinery and supplies toward the gold fields. Settlers relied on the river boats not only to ferry passengers and cargo, but also to bring mail and news.

By the end of the 1860s, the steamboats were a vital transportation link in the shipping of wheat flour to European markets. Portland became the state's major sea and river port, while Oregon City gained importance as the center of navigation and portage on the Willamette.

Stern-wheelers pushed up the Willamette Valley as far as Eugene, up the Tualatin to Forest Grove, up the Yamhill to McMinnville, and up major coastal rivers as well. On the Columbia, boats left regularly for Astoria and downriver ports and traveled upriver to The Dalles—with service continuing all the way to Lewiston, Idaho. Passengers and freight were portaged around dangerous waterfalls and rapids; a connecting steamboat waited to continue the trip.

Legends grew around the sturdy boats, and their personable captains often acquired a heroic aura. Children heard tales of the little *Mary* that rescued settlers during the Indian uprising in 1856, of the elegant *Daisy Ainsworth* with her Belgian carpets and glittering chandeliers, of the sturdy *Olympian* that forged all the way upriver to Bonneville through solid ice during the winter of 1886 to rescue passengers of a snowbound train, of Sunday excursions through the Columbia Gorge on the opulent *Bailey Gatzert*.

The shrill whistle of an arriving steamboat was the signal for townspeople to gather at the wharf, and the occasion took on the appearance of a social gathering. But a trip on one of the excursion boats was a real thrill.

Portland families journeyed by steamboat down the Columbia for their summer outings at the ocean. Trips upriver to The Dalles through the Gorge left a lasting impression. The hospitable crew often permitted passengers to visit the pilot house, and sometimes a child was allowed to pull the whistle as the boat neared a landing. In a holiday atmosphere, passengers often gathered in groups to sing.

As railroads were built and roads improved, river travel diminished, though some stern-wheelers still plied Oregon rivers during the early decades of the 20th century. □

---

along the scenic route have forest trails to waterfalls and view points. Two parks near the riverside freeway—Rooster Rock and Benson—provide facilities for boat launching, swimming, and fishing.

Recreation on the lower Sandy River

Lewis and Clark State Park near the mouth of the Sandy River is a favorite day trip for Portlanders. Broughton Bluff, a target of rock climbers, towers several hundred feet above the river.

During the annual spring smelt run—usually in late March—eager fishermen wade into the river, long-handled dip nets in hand, to scoop up the small silvery fish. Shad fishing is excellent in the lower Sandy in late May and June. Fishermen and boaters use the boat ramp and families find plenty of sites for camping, picnicking, and swimming.

Larch Mountain

Another favorite destination of Portland residents is Larch Mountain, approximately 38 miles east of the city. Larch Mountain Road branches off the Scenic Highway east of Corbett, passing through hilly farm land and tree-lined corridors on its way to the summit. In late summer you'll see huckleberry pickers gathering berries along the road.

A steep ¼-mile trail leads from the picnic grounds to Sherrard Point; from this view point, you can see five major peaks, the Columbia River, and Portland. A 7-mile trail descends from the picnic area along Multnomah Creek to the Scenic Highway.

Waterfalls in abundance

The old Columbia River Highway was an engineering classic—the first paved road across Oregon's Cascades and one of the most ambitious and most scenic roads ever built in the Pacific Northwest. Following its construction in 1915, it remained for 37 years the only route along the steep Oregon cliffs of the Columbia Gorge. It is still one of the region's loveliest drives.

You can poke along at a leisurely rate, enjoy views of the river from high overlooks, catch the spray of wispy waterfalls, and if you wish, park your car and explore some of the inviting trails on foot. Moss-covered sections of the highway's original walls and railings add a charming note.

The old road—now called the Scenic Highway—starts beside the Sandy River at Troutdale, 16 miles east of Portland via Interstate 80N. It winds through rural country, then climbs to the Crown Point view point, passes through several wooded state parks, and rejoins the freeway about 5 miles west of Bonneville Dam.

The 24-mile scenic route is enjoyable in itself, but the best rewards are found at the stops. Waterfalls, formed by tributary streams, cascade over the cliffs toward the river. Short trails lead to the falls and view points; walks of just a few hundred feet take you into the forest, beyond the sight and sound of automobiles.

One of the finest falls is Latourell, which drops straight and narrow into a shadowy pool. The names of Bridal Veil Falls, Mist Falls, Wahkeena (Indian for "most beautiful"), and Horsetail Falls offer hints of their appearances. One of the best, the falls of the Oneonta Gorge, cannot be seen from the road; the 800-foot trail to Oneonta Falls lies up the stream bed, between nearly vertical canyon walls green with moss and ferns.

Biggest and best known of the falls are the two drops of Multnomah Creek; at 620 feet, the waterfall is the highest in Oregon. An interpretive center explains the geology, history, and Indian legends of the gorge. A trail curves up to the often-photographed footbridge across the chasm.

A hiker's paradise

For the hiker, the forest trails of the Columbia Gorge offer a feast of choices—you can walk a few hundred feet to a waterfall view point, put a picnic in your knapsack and head up a woodsy creek trail on a day hike, or strike off on a weekend back packing trip. The Oregon portion of the Pacific Crest Trail begins near the Forest Service work center east of Cascade Locks.

Horses are permitted on the Pacific Crest and Herman Creek trails, but all other routes are reserved exclusively for hikers. Large sign-maps at trailheads indicate the routes, and trails are well marked. Many are suitable for family trips, though some trails edge along cliffs.

Framed by greenery, Multnomah Falls drops 620 feet in a pair of lovely waterfalls. Hikers can follow a trail across the bridge and up Multnomah Creek.

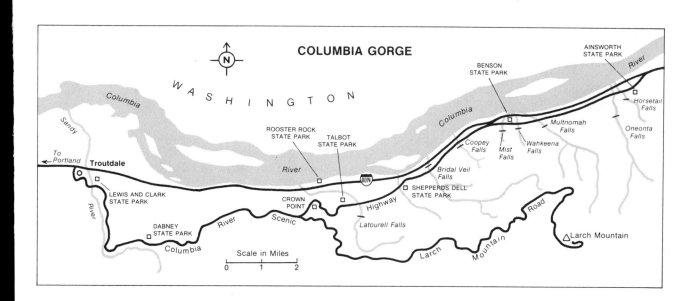

At Bonneville Dam you learn how the dam operates and watch migrating fish. Bradford Island separates spillway and navigation lock from the powerhouse.

In the Hood River valley, fruit trees frame Mount Hood views. Roadside stalls offer apples and cider in autumn.

Among numerous short family excursions are the trails up Wahkeena, Multnomah, and Horsetail creeks. On the delightful trail through Oneonta Gorge, you make your way from rock to rock through the narrow canyon. Water is shallow, so a misstep isn't serious.

Longer trails follow the rim of the gorge or wind down from Larch Mountain. Back packers enjoy beautiful Eagle Creek Trail with its numerous waterfalls, Herman Creek, or other trails connecting with mountain lakes on the eastern ridges of the Cascades.

For a map of hiking trails in the Columbia Gorge area and information on current trail conditions, stop at the Columbia Gorge Ranger Station in Troutdale.

Bonneville, granddaddy of Columbia dams

First of the massive Federal dams to harness the power of the mighty Columbia was Bonneville, built in the late 1930s about 40 miles east of Portland. It was named for Captain Benjamin de Bonneville, who had explored the Northwest a century earlier.

Constructed in two sections, the dam barricades separate river channels on either side of Bradford Island, an ancient Indian burial ground. The powerhouse lies between the Oregon shore and the island, while the spillway dam stretches from the island north to Washington. Behind the dam, Lake Bonneville stretches 48 miles upriver.

Inside the new, glass-walled visitor center on Bradford Island, exhibits explain the operation of the dam and how fish migrate upstream. Guided tours leave at regular intervals. Families picnic overlooking the river.

You can walk alongside the fish ladders or watch the fish through underwater viewing windows at the center. From a canalside walkway, visitors can watch large boats, barges, and pleasure craft pass through the 500-foot-long navigation lock.

Immediately downstream, a state fish hatchery raises thousands of salmon and steelhead. A self-guided tour shows you how the hatchery works, and you learn about fish found in the Columbia. On weekdays you can visit the Corps of Engineers Hydraulic Laboratory, where scale models of various dam projects are built and tested. A shady picnic area is located near the hatchery.

The upper gorge

Angling for salmon and steelhead is popular just below the dam and on Lake Bonneville. Waterside parks provide boat launching ramps and facilities for camping, picnicking, fishing, and water sports.

Bridge of the Gods. Indian legends tell of an ancient natural bridge that once arched across the Columbia near Cascade Locks. Today a manmade toll bridge spans the river, but massive boulders beneath the waters could be remnants of the legendary Bridge of the Gods.

Cascade Locks. Numerous rapids or cascades blocking the gorge of the Columbia proved a serious hazard to pioneer wagon trains and river traffic. Until navigation locks were completed in 1896, travelers were forced to portage around this rocky hazard. The community commemorates its "reason for being" annually in mid-September with a Portage Days celebration featuring an Indian-style salmon bake, arts and crafts booths, and a flea market.

Cascade Locks Park, with camping facilities and a small boat harbor, is operated at the site of the old Government Locks. The former canal lock is popular with fishermen; Indians still fish here with long-handled dip nets as their ancestors did. In the lock tender's residence, built in 1905, a museum contains mementos of local Indians and early settlers, the old portage road, and 19th century steamboats and railroads. The Pony Engine, the first steam locomotive used in the Northwest, is also on display.

A new museum, featuring the history of sternwheelers on the Columbia, will open during 1976 in the Cascade Locks Park Visitor Center.

The fertile Hood River valley

The town of Hood River lies at the foot of an extremely scenic and fertile valley. South of town, the snowy cone of Mount Hood rises dramatically. Thick forests and dozens of sparkling streams descend its flanks. Vast fruit orchards spread across the valley floor. Hood River is a major town on the Mount Hood Loop (see page 98), one of the state's most scenic drives.

Soon after pioneers settled here in the mid-19th century, they realized fruit grown in the rich valley was of superior quality, but it was not until 1900 that the first apples were shipped to east coast markets. The 20-mile-long Hood River valley is Oregon's largest apple growing region; additional thousands of acres are planted in pear and cherry trees.

Port Marina Park, beside the Columbia, offers tourist information, a picnic area, swimming beach, and small boat marina. You'll often see sailboats on the river, their sails filled by the brisk winds blowing up the gorge.

A number of local industries offer tours of their operations. During harvest time (August to December) you can watch fresh fruit being processed for canning and packing.

Blossom Day, celebrated on the first Sunday after April 20, is a favorite time for touring the orchard country. An old-fashioned Fourth of July and the Hood River County Fair in late July mark the summer season. On Labor Day you can watch hardy participants set out on the Columbia Cross Channel Swim.

Touring the fruit country

A 50-mile scenic tour, well marked by signs, guides you through the best of the valley. Beginning in the town of Hood River, your route introduces local points of interest, travels through peaceful farm lands and orchards, offers spectacular views of Mount Hood, and passes appealing picnic spots on the banks of the Hood River.

Though the valley is best known for its apples, acreage planted with Bartlett and Anjou pear trees now exceeds land in apple orchards. Local fruit, both fresh and canned, is shipped throughout the United States and abroad.

In spring the valley is a frothy sea of fragrant blooms. Though all the fruit varieties don't blossom at once, by mid-April the orchards take on a festive look. Wildflowers bloom along the roadside in summer.

Autumn brings a nip to the air and fall color to the forested hills around the valley. Views of white-capped Mount Hood are framed by the branches of fruiting trees, and orchards bustle with harvest activity. Most of the fruit is sold on contract, but a few farms have roadside stands and sell cider and boxes of freshly picked fruit to passers-by.

Loop trip. The scenic loop goes south along State Highway 35, detouring to Panorama Point overlook for a sweeping vista of orchards stretching to the base of Mount Hood. You return through Parkdale and Dee along the Hood River.

South of Parkdale, unimproved roads lead to lava beds along the northeastern slope of the mountain. A children's play area and good fishing are attractions at Zibe Dimmick State Park on State 35 east of Parkdale. Camping is permitted at Tucker County Park, 5 miles southwest of Hood River.

Lost Lake. A favorite subject of photographers is Lost Lake, about 30 miles southwest of Hood River in Mount Hood National Forest. The peak rises in glacial majesty behind the lake. In summer the woods are full of pink rhododendrons; autumn brings ripening huckleberries. The road to the lake is closed by snow in winter.

A Forest Service campground is located on the lake shore, and a resort (open May to September)

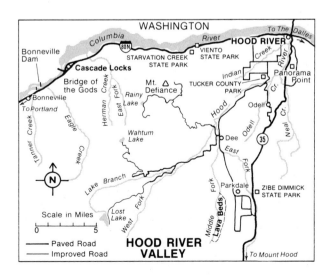

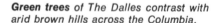

Green trees of The Dalles contrast with arid brown hills across the Columbia.

Passenger train transports summer visitors from Seufert Park, near The Dalles Bridge, upriver to the dam.

offers accommodations and supplies. Boats and canoes may be rented in season, but no motorboats are permitted on the lake. Fishing is good in nearby streams. Hikers can enjoy views of Mount Hood on the 3-mile trail encircling the lake.

East of the Cascades

Beyond Hood River the forest thins, and you become increasingly aware of a change in climate. As you enter the semiarid plateau region east of the Cascades, the great banded cliffs stand out more sharply above the river, and the hills take on the warm yellows and delicate greens of wheat and grass.

On its winding journey through the desert areas of eastern Oregon and Washington, the Columbia follows the rugged channel that it has cut during many centuries.

Fifteen miles west of The Dalles, signs lead motorists off Interstate 80N for a 7-mile climb through ponderosa pine, scrub oak, and well-groomed orchards to Rowena Crest, a plateau nearly 750 feet above the river. The road curves up Rowena Loops, part of the old Columbia River Scenic Highway. The view point is part of Mayer State Park, which also offers picnic facilities down

by the river, as well as fishing, swimming, and a bathhouse.

Memaloose State Park, 11 miles west of The Dalles along Interstate 80N, has camping and picnic sites. It overlooks Memaloose Island, once an important Indian burial ground but now almost submerged by the waters of Lake Bonneville.

The Dalles, end of the Oregon Trail

Bordering a great crescent bend of the river, The Dalles lies approximately 189 miles from the river's mouth and 82 miles east of Portland. The historic town is the trading hub of north-central Oregon's thriving agricultural economy. Fruit orchards, primarily sweet cherries, begin at the city's outskirts. Inland, great wheat and livestock ranches provide major income.

The Dalles gained its chief fame as the town at the end of the Oregon Trail. Yet thousands of years before the trappers and pioneer wagon trains arrived, primitive groups migrated down from the Bering Straits and scratched strange picture writings on the rocks overlooking the Columbia. Later, Indian tribes gathered for generations near Celilo Falls to trade and fish for migrating salmon.

In 1805 Lewis and Clark stopped here overnight after taking their large canoes through the frightening rapids. But it was the French fur trappers of

Hudson's Bay Company who gave the site its name; they noted a similarity between the Columbia's basalt walls and the flagstones *(les dalles)* paving the streets of their native villages.

Two missions had been established by the time the first pioneer wagon train arrived in 1843—the vanguard of a vast overland migration that streamed across the plains for several decades. Most of the pioneers went on toward the rich lands of the Willamette Valley.

After gold was discovered in Idaho and eastern Oregon in the early 1860s, miners surged into The Dalles, and the town boomed as an outfitting center. Wagons piled high with freight lumbered through on their way to the mines and livestock ranges. Steamboat service on the Columbia increased. Stages rumbled in from Canyon City, Umatilla, and interior settlements.

During the third week in July, the town recalls those bygone days with Fort Dalles Days—a week-long festival featuring fiddlers' contests, street dances, cowboy breakfasts, a 4-day rodeo, and a huge western parade.

A look at The Dalles

The Dalles today combines its pioneer heritage with the demands of a modern agricultural center. Barges loaded with wheat and other cargo maneuver along the river, and small boats are launched or moored in the town's boat basin.

You'll see these sights on a circuit of the town.

Old courthouse. The original Wasco County Courthouse, built in the late 1850s, has been moved from its old location to a new downtown site on West 2nd where it is being restored. It will become an addition to the city's information center.

At the time the courthouse was built, Wasco County encompassed a vast area of 130,000 square miles—from the Cascades to the Rockies and from the Columbia River to the California border, the largest county ever formed in the United States. In Oregon alone, 17 counties have been formed from the original Wasco County.

Historic churches. Two 19th century churches have been preserved. St. Paul's Church, built in 1875, is a former Episcopal church at 5th and Union streets; it contains geological exhibits and local fossils.

St. Peter's Catholic Church, at Lincoln and West 3rd, is a red brick Gothic structure built in 1897. Recently restored, it is open for tours, lectures, and other local functions. Each of its 36 stained-glass windows was given in memory of a pioneer family. The pipe organ was constructed of rare tigerwood, the railing and altars of Italian marble, and the ceilings of embossed tin; those ceilings rise to a height of 75 feet. Gargoyles glare from downspouts on the steeple, and a chanticleer weather vane tops the spire.

Oregon Trail marker. In the city park at 6th and Union streets, a basalt marker indicates the end of the Oregon Trail.

Pulpit Rock. Pioneer missionaries preached to local Indians from the basalt rock near 12th and Court streets; now it is used for Easter sunrise services.

Fort Dalles Museum. The old post surgeon's quarters—built in 1858 (during the Yakima Indian wars) and the last remaining building of Fort Dalles—house this museum of pioneer memorabilia. The building helped transform the fort from a hardship post to a comparatively comfortable one.

Located at 15th and Garrison streets, the board-and-batten structure is distinguished by pointed shingles lapped to create a six-sided design, a gabled room extending over a side veranda, and square-topped windows of leaded glass hooded with decorative cornices. Inside are five handsome manteled fireplaces. On the grounds, sheds house early-day wagons, autos, and tools.

The museum is open daily except Tuesday from May through September; it is closed on Mondays and Tuesdays the remainder of the year.

Bigfoot Museum. The Dalles has become the research center for study of the mysterious primate variously called Bigfoot or Sasquatch (believed to be a relative of the Abominable Snowman or Yeti of the Himalaya Mountains). For more than a century, sightings have reported the shy, hair-covered, manlike creatures roaming the Cascade forests.

Peter Byrne, who has spent many years studying the phenomena, has assembled exhibits relating to the search for Bigfoot in a museum at 6th and Hostetler. It is generally open during the summer season, but visiting hours change frequently. Inquire locally for more information.

Scenic drive. This pleasant road loops high above town to a view point overlooking the city, where you can gaze upriver to The Dalles Dam. Sorosis Park is a green oasis under the pines, with picnic tables, a children's play area, rose garden, and horseshoe pits. The road winds down the eastern slope past the entrance to the oak-shaded pioneer cemetery, burial place of many of the city's early settlers.

Rail trip to the dam. The state's newest railroad operates on the old portage railroad right-of-way, providing free shuttle service for visitors to The Dalles Dam. Painted red, white, and blue, the engine and passenger car leave from Seufert Park every half-hour from 10 A.M. to 6 P.M.—daily from June through August, Thursday through Monday during September. At the dam, you can get off for a 45-minute tour.

Access to Seufert Park is from N.E. Frontage Road, east of U.S. Highway 197 just south of The Dalles Bridge.

The Dalles Dam—an old fishing site

Three miles east of The Dalles stands another link in the Columbia's chain of multipurpose dams. Completed in 1960, The Dalles Dam is primarily a hydroelectric project; yet its contributions to river navigation are more interesting.

Until the present century, the turbulent waters —climaxing in the rocky gash of Celilo Falls— formed a major obstacle to river traffic on the Columbia. Passengers and cargo had to by-pass the falls—first along Indian trails, then on a portage wagon road, and after 1863 by a 13-mile rail trip from The Dalles to Celilo. Finally in 1915 an 8½-mile canal replaced the railroad. Now a navigation lock aids river traffic around the dam.

You can visit the powerhouse, see the fish ladders and fish counting station, and walk out over the spillway to watch small pleasure boats and huge grain barges pass through the 650-foot navigation lock. The visitor center—where you board the train for the return trip—has scale models to explain how the dam works, as well as exhibits on the Lewis and Clark Expedition and local history. A grassy picnic area nearby overlooks the spillway.

Celilo Falls, and the old canal as well, were submerged by waters backed up by the dam. Celilo Park marks the site of the old Indian fishing grounds, where generations of tribal fishermen speared or netted salmon from the river while perched precariously on flimsy wooden scaffolds jutting over the frenzied white water.

At Biggs another bridge crosses the Columbia to Maryhill on the Washington shore. Maryhill Museum of Fine Arts, housed in a replica of a chateau overlooking the river, displays one of the most diversified art collections in the Pacific Northwest.

Harnessing water power at John Day Dam

Upon its completion in 1968, the John Day Dam marked the final step in harnessing the waters of the lower Columbia. It crosses the river near Rufus, about 30 miles upstream from The Dalles, just below the mouth of the John Day River. The dam has an awesome power-generating capacity—reputedly the largest of any single hydroelectric dam in the free world; at peak efficiency, it produces 59 million kilowatt hours daily, about one-fifth of all the Northwest's hydroelectric power.

Interstate 80N skirts the dam and the south shore of Lake Umatilla. From highway parking areas, a pedestrian tunnel leads to the dam. Uniformed guides point out its interesting features, and visitors can take a self-guided tour along a marked route through the powerhouse and into the fish viewing room. The dam's navigation lock (near the Washington shore) can lift ships 113 feet in about 15 minutes.

Numerous recreation areas dot the shores of Lake Umatilla, stretching some 76 miles upriver. Part of the reservoir is managed as a waterfowl refuge, where ducks, geese, and other migratory waterfowl stop on their flight along the Pacific Flyway. Philippi Park, on the John Day River, is a camping and picnicking area solely for boaters.

During the building of the dam, several towns had to be relocated. The entire town of Boardman

Visitor attractions at Columbia dams

The four dams along Oregon's Columbia— Bonneville, The Dalles, John Day, and McNary— are part of the vast Columbia Basin project harnessing the river and its far-flung tributaries for electric power, river navigation, irrigation, flood control, and recreation. Dams are operated by the U. S. Army Corps of Engineers. Each dam has its special features, but all share common attractions. Public areas are open daily during daylight hours.

Information centers. You can inquire on arrival about visitor facilities, tours, recreation areas, and suggested activities. Explanatory displays and literature provide information about the dam, the river, and its fish. Brochures are available detailing recreation facilities and nearby points of interest. Bonneville has a new visitor center, completed in 1975; its upper deck provides a fine view of the dam and Columbia Gorge.

Viewing fish. From March to November salmon, steelhead, and shad migrate from the ocean up the Columbia, heading for their upstream sprawning grounds. The major salmon migration occurs in the fall.

At each dam, a stairlike series of pools—called fish ladders—permit the fish to reach the reservoir waters above the dam. Fish seldom jump up the ladders, but instead swim through submerged openings from one pool to the next until they reach the top of the dam. They pass through fish counting stations where each fish is identified

and its passage recorded. Walkways extend along the outdoor fish ladders, and underwater viewing windows allow a close look.

Tens of thousands of salmon and steelhead are raised and released annually by the Bonneville fish hatchery; exhibits explain the life cycle.

Navigation locks. At each dam you can watch river traffic pass through a navigation lock, going upstream or downstream around the dam. Lock passage is free to all vessels. Tugboats push barges and log rafts through the locks, and small pleasure boats travel from one reservoir to another. Loaded barges transport petroleum products and agricultural chemicals inland and move grain downstream for shipping to world markets.

Changing the water level in the lock at Bonneville dam—first of the projects and farthest downriver—can lift or lower an 8,000-ton ship 70 feet in about 15 minutes. The lock at John Day Dam, with a maximum lift of 113 feet, is the highest single-lift lock in the world.

Recreation areas. Each reservoir has numerous riverside parks along both the Oregon and Washington shores. You'll find picnicking and camping facilities, boat launching ramps, and opportunities for water sports. Fishermen pull in salmon (primarily Chinook, blueback, and silver), steelhead, whitefish, rainbow trout, shad, and bass. Migratory waterfowl stop along the shores of Lake Umatilla. □

Barge leaves a pattern of ripples in its wake as it passes Twin Captains Rock on the shore of Lake Wallula.

Counting stations identify and record the fish as they swim upstream. Fish ladders allow them to by-pass dams.

was moved, as well as the business districts of Arlington and Umatilla. Highways and railroads were rerouted, and buildings were transferred from the area now filled by reservoir waters.

Up the lonely river

In the vast wheat lands and livestock ranges of eastern Oregon, settlements are smaller and farther apart.

State rest areas are located along Interstate 80N near Boardman. For years this town was a sleepy settlement best known as a highway gas stop in the midst of sagebrush and tumbleweeds. Relocated during the building of John Day Dam, Boardman teems today with new agri-business development—large-scale cattle raising and farming, new potato processing plants, and a modern industrial park. A new riverside park offers camping and picnicking facilities, a swimming area, boat ramp, and protected small craft harbor.

East of Boardman, U.S. Highway 730 forks northeast toward Umatilla and Washington's tri-cities area. Umatilla, named for a local Indian tribe, is a popular water sports center. There are boat ramps and picnic areas in a city park on the east shore of the Umatilla River just south of the bridge. Umatilla Park and Marina, on the Columbia, just west of the interstate bridge, is one of the most modern on the river; the complete marina includes over-

night camping facilities and trailer hookups, boat ramps and docks, a picnic area, and a gravel swimming beach. A wildlife park near the bridge provides good bird watching.

McNary Dam

Easternmost of the four dams along Oregon's northern border is McNary Dam, located just east of Umatilla. Access to the dam is from U.S. 730. Completed in 1953, the dam is named for the late Charles McNary, former U.S. Senator from Oregon.

Picnic areas, boat ramps, and swimming areas are available near the dam along the Oregon shore. Recorded messages at stopping points explain the dam's features. You can watch the fish through viewing windows in the fish ladders on both sides of the dam. From a gallery in the powerhouse you see its 14 generator units.

To reach the navigation lock and its observation deck, you'll need to cross the Umatilla Bridge to the Washington side of the river and take a spur road from State Highway 14.

Hat Rock State Park, situated on the shore of Lake Wallula 9 miles east of Umatilla, is reached by a spur road off U.S. 730. Water sports enthusiasts enjoy the reservoir's numerous picnic sites, sheltered swimming beach, and boat launching ramps. Lawns and trees add a refreshing spot of greenery.

Down the Oregon coast

Explore or just relax along this inviting shore

Poised above the waves, fisherman awaits his chance, dip-net in hand.

At trail's end, hikers enjoy a splendid view of surf crashing in Hart's Cove and the unspoiled sweep of coastline in the Cascade Head Scenic Area.

Oregon's ever-changing shoreline is a land of contrasts—broad sandy beaches and rugged promontories, dense forests and rolling dunes, sheltered coves and grassy headlands, towering mountains and hidden lakes. Seldom do you find such a varied coastline and rich array of diversions in close proximity as along the Oregon coast. The entire 400-mile shoreline belongs to the people of Oregon, dedicated and developed for public use.

U.S. Highway 101 extends the full length of the coast—winding beside the sea, cutting through forests, curving around headlands. With the aid of a few side roads, it provides an intimate look at the shore. Dozens of state parks and waysides provide access to the ocean.

Many Oregonians have their favorite spots to which they return again and again. Travelers with limited time often sample a single section of the coast; others leisurely explore its entire length or settle in a favored location for an extended stay.

In the bracing sea air, vacationing families spend long days roaming quiet beaches, clambering over rocky promontories, hunting for agates, probing piles of driftwood, and gazing into hidden tidepools. They can frolic in the surf, build sand castles, fly kites, hike coastal trails, dig for clams, or cast fishing lines in the nearest surf or stream.

For a change of pace, they can visit art galleries and cheese factories, drive or bicycle inland roads, play a round of golf, or take a boat trip.

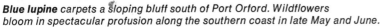

Blue lupine carpets a sloping bluff south of Port Orford. Wildflowers bloom in spectacular profusion along the southern coast in late May and June.

Hunting for agates, beachcomber scans the wet sands north of Newport.

Coastal communities bustle with vacationers from mid-June through Labor Day, but generally the best coastal weather comes in autumn, after the crowds have left. In summer, winds can be chilly on even the sunniest days, and low-hanging fog often blankets the coastal belt in mornings and evenings. Winter storms lure hardy beachcombers and storm watchers.

Coastal accommodations run the gamut from elegant resorts and modern motels to simple housekeeping cabins. The northern half of the coast has been developed more extensively, but you will find ample lodging along the entire coast.

State parks normally remain open for day-use activities throughout the year, but most camp-grounds are closed from November to mid-April. Six of the coastal state parks remain open for year-round camping—Fort Stevens, Cape Lookout, Beverly Beach, Jessie M. Honeyman, Bullards Beach, and Harris Beach. Many private parks are open the year around.

The historic north coast

Less than 2 hours from Portland, the busy northern Oregon coast attracts numerous vacationing families. Here you'll find long sandy beaches, forested headlands, offshore rocks, dairy pastures, and secluded coves. Busy beach resorts offer a multitude of activities. Coastal sites recall the historic Lewis and Clark Expedition, Indian legends, and tales of marine adventure.

Migrating salmon attract fishermen to north coast streams from late spring into fall. Good steelhead rivers include the Nehalem, Trask, Necanicum, Kilchis, and Nestucca.

Charter boats and guides are available in many coastal ports for fishing on the rivers or at sea.

Many art galleries have sprung up in north coast towns—especially around Cannon Beach and Lincoln City—and a number of craftsmen make their headquarters here. You can inquire at local visitor information centers about galleries displaying the work of Oregon artists.

Main routes from Portland across the Coast Range are the Sunset Highway (U.S. Highway 26), the Wilson River Road (State Highway 6), and the Salmon River Road (State Highway 18). Slower routes, often less crowded on weekends, are the Columbia River Highway (U.S. Highway 30), the winding forest roads through Mist and Jewell (State Highways 47 and 202), and State Highway 22 heading northwest from Salem.

Astoria—where river and ocean meet

Located just inside the mouth of the Columbia, Astoria has come a long way since its days as a fur trading post. Business center of Clatsop County, Astoria is also a fishing center, shipping port, and departure point for cross-Columbia bridge traffic.

A few miles southwest, you can visit Fort Clat-

sop, the 1805-06 winter headquarters of the Lewis and Clark Expedition. (See page 32 for more information about Astoria and interesting side trips.)

The Oregon coast hiking trail

Hikers are getting a spectacular new coastal trail that, when completed in the early 1980s, will stretch nearly 350 miles from the Columbia River south to the California border. It will provide a marvelous chance for close-up glimpses of this varied coast. The northernmost portion of the Oregon Coast Trail—from the Columbia's South Jetty 62 miles south to Tillamook Bay at Barview—was dedicated in 1975. Signs have been placed along the route, and a map brochure is available.

Many parts of the trail are not new. Before the Coast Highway (U.S. 101) was completed in the 1930s, travelers made their way along the packed sand beaches on foot and by car, ferrying across estuaries and heading inland only when stopped by rocky headlands. Early-day hikers and pack animals followed Indian trails across coastal capes.

New sections of trail are under construction to link existing segments. When possible, the route follows the beach; other portions wind over headlands, through parks, and along coastal roads.

The trail can be enjoyed on a day trip or on longer outings. If you don't mind wet weather, you can use it at any time of year. Experienced hikers prefer to walk with the prevailing winds—from north to south in summer, the reverse in winter.

Hikers are cautioned to carry a canteen of water (especially on long beach stretches), to be prepared for wind and rain, and *never* to turn their backs on the ocean. ("Sneak" waves or "high rollers" sweep several people out to sea every year.) Binoculars, a map and tide table, and a pair of dry socks and shoes may add to your enjoyment.

Fort Stevens State Park

One of Oregon's largest and most modern campgrounds, this park lies about 12 miles west of Astoria, stretching 4 miles along the beach. You can go beachcombing, clam digging, and surf casting. On the beach is the battered hulk of the *Peter Iredale*, a British schooner that went aground in 1906.

Inland, several long, shallow lakes attract swimmers, boaters, and fishermen. A 2½-mile trail follows the wooded shore of Coffenbury Lake, and a ½-mile nature trail is posted with identification signs. Seven miles of paved bicycle trails wind through the park. Campsite reservations are recommended for busy summer weekends.

The park now includes most of the old Fort Stevens Military Reservation that guarded the mouth of the Columbia from the Civil War until 1947. Battery Russell, at the fort's northern end, was fired on by a Japanese submarine in 1942— the only recorded attack on a mainland U.S. fortification since the War of 1812.

The big guns are gone now, but you can still see

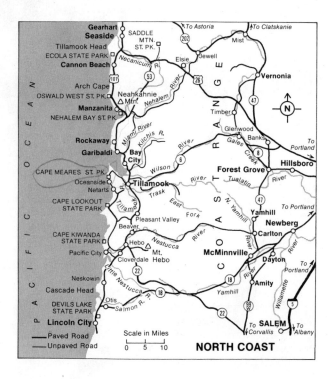

NORTH COAST

the elaborate concrete emplacements and deserted officers' quarters. The state is currently restoring the fort, and a new interpretive center recounts its history. Battery Russell is open to the public, but the rest of the fort can be visited only with a guide. You can arrange for a tour at the registration booth at the entrance to the park's camping area.

Beach resorts and splendid parks

South of Fort Stevens, you can walk in solitude for miles along the wide, windswept beach, regaining the company of man only as you near Gearhart.

Wherever the surf beats in unhampered, razor clams are abundant. Or you can look for crabs, cut off from the sea as the morning tide ebbs across troughs between sandbars. Surf fishing is often productive. For a change of pace, play a round of golf or go horseback riding.

Seaside. One of Oregon's favorite beach resorts and a major convention center, Seaside combines a lively entertainment district with ample accommodations and a broad, sandy beach. An aquarium exhibits trained seals and marine life found off the Oregon coast. Fronting the Pacific for nearly 2 miles are Seaside's famed promenade and impressive beach houses—some of them passed down through several generations of Oregon families.

A few blocks south of Seaside's main street is the site where members of the Lewis and Clark Expedition boiled sea water to provide salt for the group's return trip. Their salt cairn has been reconstructed on Lewis and Clark Way.

For close-at-hand fishing, try the Necanicum River, which flows through the center of town; it's a good stream for sea-run cutthroat, salmon, and steelhead. If you'd like to go riding, you can arrange for saddle horses.

Activity-minded Seaside offers events the year around—among them marathon beach runs in August and February, the Miss Oregon Pageant in July, arts and crafts shows in March and August, and a Beachcombers Festival in February.

Ecola State Park. North of Cannon Beach, a paved but narrow road climbs up the southern bluff of Tillamook Head to a craggy perch above the ocean. Open for day use only, Ecola has developed picnic areas overlooking magnificent panoramas and trails leading to dramatic view points.

Extending along the coast for 6½ miles, Ecola has two sandy beaches along its southern edge. Rock fishing is excellent in a steep-walled cove on the north side of Ecola Point (the main picnic area). Farther north, you'll find interesting tidepools along Indian Beach and Indian Point; often you'll see surfers at Indian Beach.

The park road continues north to Tillamook Head, most northerly of the picnic areas, and view point for the old Tillamook Lighthouse, perched atop a wave-swept rock a mile offshore.

Cannon Beach. Named for a cannon washed ashore in 1846, Cannon Beach extends along a scenic 7-

Surfers in wet suits ride the Pacific breakers into shore. Often you will see surfers in action at Ecola's Indian Beach.

mile strand. Pocketed between Tillamook Head and Arch Cape, this long, curving beach is enjoyed for surf fishing, swimming, and clamming.

Offshore stands Haystack Rock, a massive monolith rising 235 feet above the sea. Gulls and other sea birds nest in its rocky crags, and the tidepools around its base are alive with starfish, sea anemones, and other intriguing examples of marine life.

In recent years a number of artists and craftsmen have settled in the area, and Cannon Beach has become a major art center of the Oregon coast.

In summer the popular university-sponsored Haystack program combines family recreation with learning. Nationally known instructors lead 1 and 2-week seminars and workshops in music, writing, and visual arts. A separate children's program emphasizes art and outdoor activities. For more information, write to Haystack, Box 1491, Portland, OR 97207.

Portland State University students present summer stock theater in July and August. And each summer there is an annual Sand Castle Building Contest where competitors create fanciful architectural masterpieces and sculptured figures from wet sand; date depends on minus tides.

The climb up Saddle Mountain

Four miles south of Seaside, U.S. 26 sweeps inland along the Necanicum River through the coastal forests to Portland. Just east of Necanicum junction, a paved road climbs 7 miles north to Saddle Mountain State Park.

You have two good reasons to hike to the top of

Saddle Mountain—a splendid view and rare alpine wildflowers in spring. Allow 2 to 3 hours for the 3-mile climb, and wear hiking boots if you have them. Fill your canteen at the parking area; no water is available on the trail, and the climb can be hot and tiring.

You climb through low-growing coastal shrubbery and stands of alder and Douglas fir over a series of hills before topping out at the 3,283-foot summit—highest peak in the northern part of the Coast Range. Only the final ½ mile is steep. It's apt to be chilly and windy at the top, but on a clear day you can see the bridge across the Columbia at Astoria, waves breaking along a 20-mile stretch of coastline, and some high Cascade peaks.

If you have a wildflower identification book, by all means bring it along. Botanists consider Saddle Mountain an island of rare alpine flora isolated following the Ice Age. Atop the peak are small pockets of northern or high mountain flowers. Look for blooms tucked amid the rocks and crags along the steep, final climb to the summit.

Take a walk in the forest

Winding through the thickly forested Coast Range, U.S. 26 (the Sunset Highway) is a cool and pleasant route linking Portland with the coast.

If you'd like to get acquainted with the forest first-hand, take a leisurely walk along the Sunset Nature Trail; it begins 48 miles west of Portland and winds north of U.S. 26. Shielded by trees from highway noises, the path loops through woodland rich in wildlife. An interpretive brochure helps you understand what you see.

Buried treasure and kite flying

Jutting westward into the ocean, Arch Cape marks the beginning of rugged coastal scenery. U.S. 101 tunnels through the massive rock, then climbs high above the sea as it curves around Neahkahnie Mountain. Turnouts provide sweeping views of the coast. Local legends hint of buried treasure left on the mountain by the crew of a mystery ship, but so far no one has found it.

Oswald West State Park memorializes the far-sighted governor who in 1912 preserved the coastal beaches for the people of Oregon. Campers transport their gear to the walk-in campground on park-supplied wheelbarrows.

Fishing, clamming, and driftwood hunting attract visitors to Nehalem Bay, just a few miles south. Access to the state park, on the spit, is from Manzanita. Visitors are invited to stop for wine tasting at the Nehalem Bay Winery, housed in a converted cheese factory. State Highway 53 and the Nehalem River Road lead inland, through dairy lowlands and thick forests, to connect with U.S. 26.

Rockaway, largest of several beach towns between Nehalem Bay and Tillamook Bay, has a Kite Festival each spring. You can enter the competition or watch the proceedings from a wayside park along U.S. 101.

Along the shore of Tillamook Bay

Closely paralleling the northern shore of Tillamook Bay, U.S. 101 cuts through several small towns.

At Barview County Park you'll find good rock fishing and skin diving from the jetty and surf fishing from the ocean shore. Camping and picnicking facilities are available, and the park has a long sandy beach for day use. Sports fishermen can rent or charter boats at Garibaldi near the north jetty.

Back road explorers will enjoy a 14-mile drive inland, up the quiet valleys of the Miami River and Foley Creek. Steep wooded hills hem in the narrow valleys. Another scenic byway is the Kilchis River Road, heading into the foothills south of Bay City; fishermen come here for trout and steelhead.

A coastal picnic—with local cheese and fresh crab

When dairying and cheese making got started on the Oregon coast during the last century, contact between settlements was so limited by rough terrain that many pioneer valleys evolved in semi-isolation, developing their own distinctive cheeses.

Transportation barriers have long since been overcome, but the distinctive cheeses—mainly in the Cheddar family—remain. You can sample several varieties on a cheese tour that begins in Tillamook, stops in Reedsport, and ends in Bandon.

All three plants allow you to watch cheese making, sample their cheeses, make purchases, and mail gift packages.

Your selection of cheeses becomes the start of a picnic. From the abundant seafood of the coast you can add crab, shrimp, or salmon for your lunch, and then round out your menu with bread, wine, and other picnic makings. State parks and scenic waysides are so numerous along the coast you should have no difficulty spreading your feast in splendid surroundings.

Here are the cheese makers:

Tillamook County Creamery, located 1¾ miles north of Tillamook on U.S. 101. Cheese-making observation area and salesroom are open daily, 9 A.M. to 5 P.M.

Reedsport Cheese Factory, located ½ mile east of U.S. 101 on State 38 at 250 Water Avenue. Cheese-making rooms are open Monday through Friday, 7 A.M. to 3 P.M.; salesroom is open 8 A.M. to 5 P.M.

Coquille Valley Dairy Co-op, located at 680 U.S. 101 in northeast Bandon. Cheese-making rooms are open Monday through Saturday, 8 A.M. to 1 P.M.; salesroom is open 8 A.M. to 5 P.M.

Roadside stands offer fresh crab.
Ask to have it cleaned and cracked.

Picnickers spread their bounty—
cheese, crab, bread, wine, and fruit
—on a knoll above the crashing surf.

Reclaiming the Tillamook Burn

In the summer of 1933 a vast forest fire, whipped by vicious winds, turned the wooded hills of Tillamook County into a roaring inferno. More than 400 square miles—13½ billion board feet—of Oregon's finest timber was destroyed, some of it more than 400 years old. In 1939 and 1945 other forest fires broke out in the same area. Oregonians voted to tax themselves to finance the reforestation, and today the young trees of Tillamook State Forest are gradually covering the burned hills.

You can learn how the land was replanted on a self-guided auto tour (not suitable for trailers). It begins at Rogers Camp, south of State 6 near the summit. Twelve stops along the 13-mile forest road note features of the project. Most of the route follows single-lane forest roads with turnouts. A leaflet outlining the points of interest is available from the State Department of Forestry, 2600 State Street, Salem, OR 97310, or by visiting the Department office, 801 Gales Creek Road, Forest Grove.

You can camp or picnic in a number of forest parks along State 6. At Gales Creek Park, 4 miles west of Glenwood Junction, a 2-mile trail winds north along Gales Creek.

The Tillamook Valley

Large barns, grazing cows, and lush pastures identify the Tillamook Valley as dairy country. Serene and relatively uncrowded, southern Tillamook County presents dramatic contrasts: a magnificent coastline, pastoral river valleys, wooded mountains.

Many travelers stop at the Tillamook County Creamery north of town to learn how the local Cheddar-style cheese is made.

The Pioneer Museum is housed in the old county courthouse at 2nd and Pacific avenues, at the junction of U.S. 101 and State 6. This fine local museum offers an intimate glimpse of Tillamook County life and history. Here you'll find not only pioneer memorabilia and Indian artifacts but an outstanding collection of natural history exhibits; many of the 500 specimens of animals and birds are displayed in habitat settings. The free museum is open daily from 9 A.M. to 5 P.M. (1 to 5 P.M. on Sundays) from May through September, closed Mondays the rest of the year.

Craft demonstrations are featured at Tillamook's Arts and Crafts Fair in early July. County residents exhibit their local products at the Tillamook County Fair in early August.

Three Capes Loop

Travelers speeding along U.S. 101 have little hint of the magnificent coastal drive west of Tillamook. The Three Capes Loop connects a trio of rugged promontories—Cape Meares, Cape Lookout, and Cape Kiwanda—where tall forests meet the sea, waves thunder against basalt headlands, secluded beaches await the beachcomber, and tiny towns cling to the green hillsides.

You can make the drive as a 30-mile alternate to U.S. 101 or as a 50-mile loop from Tillamook.

Cape Meares. Head west from Tillamook on Third Street and follow the south shore of Tillamook Bay. Bayocean Peninsula attracts fishermen, clammers, and crabbers; you can also hunt for agates, driftwood, and glass fishing floats.

In Cape Meares State Park, you can hike through the rain forest, take a look at the Octopus Tree (a venerable and massive Sitka spruce), and stroll to the tip of the headland to see the old lighthouse (not open to visitors).

Just south of the cape, a trail leads down to Short Beach, where beachcombers explore tidepools and surf-carved caves and hunt for driftwood and agates. Offshore, look for sea lions frolicking in the waves and sea birds soaring and swooping near Three Arch Rocks, a national wildlife refuge.

Oceanside and Netarts are quiet seaside towns; in March, residents hold a Beachcombers' Fair. Anglers often hook flounder, perch, and sea trout in Netarts Bay; you can also go clamming and crabbing.

Cape Lookout. One of the most prominent headlands on the coast, Cape Lookout juts more than 2 miles into the sea. Rising some 500 feet above the surf, the rugged basalt finger—a prehistoric lava flow—is continually pounded by waves and wind.

One of the most popular coastal campgrounds, Cape Lookout State Park offers access to a broad sandy beach, many trails, clamming, and surf fishing. You can picnic overlooking the beach or beneath gnarled, moss-draped trees. A trail leads from the picnic area to the summit parking lot.

Fishermen troll for salmon on the Siletz River off State 229. Coastal rivers offer good fishing and inviting side trips into the wooded Coast Range foothills.

From the summit of the ridge, a 2½-mile trail winds through dense stands of spruce, hemlock, and cedar to the tip of the cape. Ferns, salal, and huckleberries line the forest trail, and tiny wildflowers hide in mossy crannies. You'll see the remains of a World War II plane that crashed in 1943 while on submarine patrol during foul weather. Many birds nest on the rugged walls of the headland. Check trail conditions at park headquarters —heavy rains make trails difficult to negotiate. Hiking boots are a good idea.

Sand Lake. Beach buggies take to the dunes near Sand Lake—roaring, spinning, leaping, and sliding over the sand. A natural channel breaches a low coastal berm, letting the ocean flow inland to create the small lake. Coastal plants flourish along its shore, and migrating ducks and geese winter here. Try crabbing or flounder fishing from the bridge or channel bank.

South of Sand Lake is Tierra del Mar, where attractive homes overlook a public beach.

Cape Kiwanda. Southernmost of the three headlands, Cape Kiwanda shelters the beach at Pacific City. Hang glider enthusiasts often work off the high dunes just behind the cape, and skin divers and surfers pursue their sports along the reef. You can watch spectacular wave action, and one of the finest marine gardens on the coast lies just offshore. North of the cape is Cape Kiwanda State Park, one of the newest parks in the state system.

Pacific City. With no protected harbor or boat basin, local fishermen launch their flat-bottomed dories through choppy waves in the lee of the cape. Charter trips can be arranged. It is an exciting trip as fishermen maneuver their pitching boats through the surf, then head for offshore fishing grounds. Prime quarry is the salmon, caught off the coast from June through September; bottom fishing for cod and halibut is good around Haystack Rock and off the nearby reef.

Each summer, Pacific City hosts a Dory Derby with competitive events. The Nestucca River resort offers not only deep-sea fishing but excellent surf and river fishing for salmon, trout, and steelhead. You can try your luck clamming or crabbing near the river mouth or search for driftwood along the spit curving south of Pacific City.

Along U.S. 101 to Cascade Head

Pastoral valleys and wooded mountains present restful vistas in southern Tillamook County. The highway follows the meandering Tillamook River south to Pleasant Valley, where you turn east to Munson Creek Falls, highest waterfall in the Coast Range. Forest Service campgrounds and county parks are located on side roads in the mountains.

You catch glimpses of the ocean again near the family resort of Neskowin, one of the oldest beach towns. Adults can enjoy a round of golf at either of two public courses; children can wade in the sun-warmed creek, frolic on the beach, or ride horseback on sandy trails. Surf fishing often yields good catches of sea perch, trout, and flounder.

Just south of Neskowin is Cascade Head, a wild, mountainous ridge where hills, forest, and ocean meet. Small creeks pour into the sea in sheer waterfalls. The Salmon River estuary south of Cascade Head is a haven for waterfowl and marine plants and animals. Though much of the headland is now protected as a scenic research area, hikers can sample it on the rugged, 2-mile Cascade Head Trail to Hart Cove.

To find the trailhead, look for Forest Road S61 near the ridge top and drive 4 miles west.

The scenic central coast

From Lincoln City to Coos Bay, U.S. 101 skims the ocean shore. State parks and scenic waysides come one after another. You have your pick of wide, sandy beaches—favorite destinations of agate hunters and driftwood collectors. Towns cluster at the mouths of coastal rivers and streams.

From Willamette Valley towns, a half-dozen highways head westward, cutting through the Coast Range and following rivers down to the sea.

Lincoln City is the center of the heavily promoted Twenty Miracle Miles, an oceanside strip of resorts, motels, galleries, craft and gift shops, and tourist-oriented attractions. Florence and Reedsport are gateways to the Oregon dunes, a scenic recreation area marked by miles of windswept sand dunes and a chain of fresh-water lakes. You'll discover sizable charter and commercial fishing fleets in Depoe Bay and Newport; in summer, fishermen can arrange deep-sea fishing trips in search of salmon. Other anglers cast into coastal streams for sea-run cutthroat trout or steelhead.

Elegant resorts and condominium complexes overlook the sea. Tucked into the sides of rugged cliffs, stretched along the beaches, or perched atop an ocean bluff, they offer luxury accommodations and resort facilities. A half-dozen golf courses are scattered along this stretch of shore. Numerous motels and cottages are also available; some units offer fully equipped kitchens, fireplaces, and decks overlooking an ocean view. Oceanside parks provide campsites and beach access. This area is popular in summer; plan to stop early or call ahead for reservations.

Lincoln City—five towns in one

Formed a decade ago by the consolidation of five small towns, Lincoln City is a tourist center stretching 7½ miles along U.S. 101. Built along a narrow coastal shelf between forested mountains and the sea, Lincoln City marks the center of Oregon's coastal resort area. The town's year-round population of 5,000 triples in summer.

North of town you can visit Lacey's Dollhouse and Museum (open May through September) or Pixieland, a family amusement park (open daily from mid-June through Labor Day). Both are located near the junction of U.S. 101 and State Highway 18. Numerous art galleries cater to visitors.

Center of boating and water-skiing activities is Devils Lake; sheltered picnic areas and campsites dot its tree-lined shore. You'll see rowboats, sailboats, and canoes on the lake, along with faster models—hydroplane boat races are featured each September.

Highlight of the Fourth of July celebration is a parade of decorated and lighted boats.

Residents go fishing on their lunch hour at Devils Lake or along the D River, the lake's ¼-mile-long outlet to the sea. You can rent a boat and tackle at the lake.

Fishermen of all ages have a grand time fishing off the Taft public dock at the narrow mouth of Siletz Bay. Even if the fish aren't biting, you'll meet some interesting people. Most of the action is small fish—perch, flounder, greenlings—though adult anglers often go after salmon. Heave a crab ring over the side while you fish; you might catch the fixings for a hearty seafood stew.

Along the winding Siletz

Once the homeland of the Siletz Indians and later the scene of a booming logging and sawmill industry, today the Siletz River is best known as steelhead country. Fish begin moving upriver in May.

State Highway 229 parallels the winding Siletz upriver—first through a pastoral valley and then along a narrow river canyon where forests are thick with ferns and moss-draped trees. You may see an occasional boat or fisherman, but the mean-

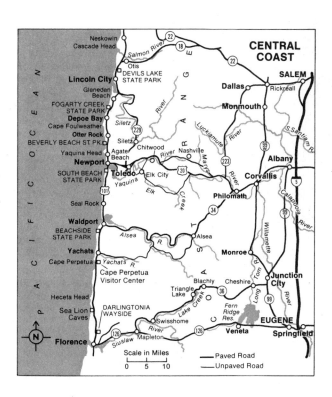

Blending with its natural surroundings, Salishan Lodge overlooks the water at Gleneden Beach. You can golf and play tennis at this popular resort.

Spectators watch deep-sea fishing and sightseeing boats thread Depoe Bay's narrow, rock-lined channel.

dering river imposes its relaxed atmosphere on the valley's scattered inhabitants. Several moorages rent boats and provide launching ramps. Small county parks are located beside the river along the 32-mile route, which intersects U.S. Highway 20 east of Newport.

Salishan and salmon fishing

Queen of the coastal resorts is Salishan Lodge, situated on a scenic promontory overlooking Siletz Bay. Renowned throughout the Northwest for its resort and conference facilities, Salishan also offers an 18-hole golf course and indoor and outdoor tennis courts.

Fogarty Creek State Park includes one of the state's most accessible ocean beaches. From wind-protected picnic sites east of U.S. 101, a path beneath the highway provides easy access to the beach. Each September an Indian-style salmon bake is held here; freshly caught fish are split and fastened onto a framework of green branches, then propped near open fires to bake.

Boiler Bay Wayside offers a fine view point and rock fishing site, but ocean breezes can be brisk. A ship's boiler that washed ashore here in 1910 can still be seen at low tide. Marine gardens are also uncovered when the tide is out.

Depoe Bay's fame rests chiefly on its scenic harbor and its colorful fleet. Experienced skippers conduct regular sightseeing and deep-sea fishing trips (several times daily in summer). Each Memorial Day, the Fleet of Flowers ceremony honors men who have lost their lives at sea.

You can stroll along the town's sea wall promenade (look for spouting horns west of the sea wall) or watch fishing and pleasure boats negotiate the narrow, rock-lined channel between harbor and sea. A salt-water aquarium exhibits sea animals and fish. Commercial fishermen unload their catch on the south side of the harbor.

Whale Cove, south of Depoe Bay, attracts surfers, skin divers, and rock hunters. Rumrunners landed cargoes of illicit whisky here during Prohibition.

A beachcomber's paradise

The central coast is a beachcomber's paradise. Agates and shells are scattered along its beaches, and intriguing pieces of bleached driftwood pile up around the mouths of creeks and rivers. At low tide, offshore rocks are uncovered, revealing tidepools filled with fascinating sea creatures.

The highway from Cape Foulweather south to Newport climbs more than 450 feet above the sea at Otter Crest (take the scenic road curving west of U.S. 101 around the headland) and hugs the coastline along Beverly and Moolack beaches. Beverly Beach State Park has good campsites.

You can watch surf fishermen at Rocky Creek, picnic at Devils Punchbowl State Park, hunt for agates near the mouths of rivers and streams, and peer into tidepools and caves north of Otter Rock and below the Yaquina Head lighthouse.

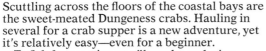

Catch your own crab in Oregon's coastal bays

Scuttling across the floors of the coastal bays are the sweet-meated Dungeness crabs. Hauling in several for a crab supper is a new adventure, yet it's relatively easy—even for a beginner.

To fish from a pier, you'll need a crab ring, a special measuring stick, and bait; equipment rental and bait cost about $3 a day at coastal sporting goods stores and tackle shops. You don't need a fishing license. For less competition, try fishing from a rented boat in calm bay waters. Rental and pier facilities vary from bay to bay; for information on specific areas, check with the Oregon Department of Fish and Wildlife, P.O. Box 3503 (1634 S.W. Alder St.), Portland, OR 97208.

Crabbing season continues the year around, but the best time is late spring through summer. Tillamook, Netarts, Yaquina, Alsea, and Coos bays offer productive crabbing.

The best crab catches are made when tidal currents are slow and the crabs can come to the bait without fighting strong currents. Pick a slack tide (either high or low) or a day when there is only a small difference between high and low tide heights. Coastal sporting goods stores have free tide tables to help you figure out the best times.

To catch a crab, fling the baited ring from the pier or boat. When it hits the bottom, the ring falls flat and crabs can crawl in to eat the bait. Wait 10 to 20 minutes—no longer, or they'll finish the bait and leave; then pull the ring up quickly and smoothly.

You are allowed to keep only male crabs at least 5¾ inches across the back, excluding spines. The V-shaped underflap tells you the crab's sex: males have narrow flaps and females broad ones.

Your enthusiasm may wane when you have to lift the crabs out of the ring. To avoid claw nips, pick up the crab from above, between its rear legs. Put freshly caught crabs in a wet burlap bag to keep them alive until cooking.

You can cook the whole crab or clean it first by forcing the shell off against something solid. Then fold the crab into separate halves, shake out the insides, and pull off the gills. Cook live or cleaned crabs for 20 minutes in boiling water with a tablespoon of salt for each crab. Some bait shops will cook crabs for you. □

The rural Yaquina Valley

Pleasant U.S. 20 winds through the Coast Range between Corvallis and Newport, paralleling the Marys River on the eastern slope and the Yaquina on the west side. A pleasant side road arcs north of the main route—between Blodgett and Eddyville—through the upper watershed.

The highway passes a rustic covered bridge at Chitwood, then continues west to the hilly mill town of Toledo and on to Yaquina Bay. Another old covered bridge lies 5 miles by gravel road south of U.S. 20 at historic Elk City.

Newport's lively waterfront

Busy capital of Lincoln County, Newport stretches along a bluff on the north shore of Yaquina Bay. Nearby beaches attract many families. Often you'll see surfers riding the waves. Sailors have also discovered windy Yaquina Bay. Fishermen cast from promontories and jetties, or you can board a boat for a day of deep-sea fishing. Yaquina tideflats have a good supply of clams, and Dungeness crabs are frequently caught off the piers.

To get acquainted with the area, take the scenic drive around town—to the Yaquina Art Center in the Nye Beach area, through Yaquina Bay State Park at the north end of the bridge, and along the colorful waterfront. Learn about the area's past at the Lincoln County Historical Museum (9th and Fall streets) or retreat into a world of make-believe in the wax museum. Undersea Gardens and the OSU Marine Science Center offer an introduction to life beneath the sea.

If you prefer, take a 4½-hour sightseeing bus tour of the Yaquina Bay area; for information, contact Dachshund Bus Lines, phone 265-5618.

Fishing boats are colorfully decorated for the Blessing of the Fleet ceremony in early April. During Newport's annual Loyalty Days Festival (on the weekend nearest May 1) you can board naval ships in the harbor and tour the lighthouse at Yaquina Head.

The old lighthouse. Overlooking Yaquina Bay from its bluff above the estuary is the Yaquina Bay lighthouse, an old harbor sentinel built in 1871. It was used for only 3 years until a more efficient beacon was built on Yaquina Head 3 miles north.

Recently refurnished with period furnishings and items typically used by local lighthouse keepers in the 1870s, it is now open to the public Friday through Sunday from noon to 4 P.M.

Along the wharf. A forest of masts and salt-water aromas lure you down to the busy mile-long waterfront. Scavenging gulls perch on piers awaiting fishy tidbits. Deep-sea trollers make regular sightseeing and fishing trips.

You can buy crabs right out of a steaming pot or enjoy seafood specialties at several popular waterfront restaurants. Undersea Gardens offers a look beneath the sea; you view marine animals, fish, and plants in a natural habitat.

Visitors can tour the *Sara*, a historic sailing vessel transformed into a maritime museum. Built in 1900, the twin-masted, gaff-rigged schooner is docked at Neptune's Wharf. As you walk her wooden decks, you can dream of the days when such ships sailed along the rugged coast.

Yaquina Bay Drive. From the Newport wharf, a paved road curves along the north shore of Yaquina Bay and estuary about 8 miles inland to Toledo. You leave the tourist waterfront behind as you head east—past the commercial fishing fleet, private cruisers, ocean freighters loading lumber, and tidal flats where clammers dig at low tide.

Marine Science Center. Oregon State University operates its outstanding coastal research center on tidelands on the south side of Yaquina Bay. Often you'll see one of the school's research vessels docked near the center.

Most visitors find this a fascinating stop. In the public area, marine fish and invertebrates are displayed in tanks designed to show the creatures' natural habitat. Displays explain various marine subjects—coastal geology, tides, estuary life, and other topics. In the handling pool, visitors can pick up and examine intertidal animals.

The center is open daily from 10 A.M. to 6 P.M. in summer, 10 to 4 the rest of the year. The summer Seatauqua program offers public mini-courses, films, and field trips about the marine environment; for information, write to Seatauqua, OSU Marine Science Center, Newport, OR 97365.

Fishing pond. Across from the Marine Science Center, the Oregon Aqua-Foods "sea ranch" (private fish hatchery) raises salmon and releases them to feed at sea. Several years later the adult fish return and are captured for marketing and spawning.

From mid-June through Labor Day, anglers of all ages can fish in a salt-water pond for coho and Chinook salmon and Donaldson rainbow trout. You need no license, and there is no limit; you pay by the pound for your catch.

South to Waldport and Yachats

On the route south to Alsea Bay, more state parks and waysides offer plenty of picnic sites and beach access for coastal travelers. Waldport, a friendly little town on the south shore of a broad estuary, is a popular fishing, crabbing, and clamming center. The Alsea River draws steelhead fishermen.

Farther south, rugged rocks jut into the crashing surf at Yachats (YAH-hots); often you'll see fishermen here, bracing themselves as they cast their lines into the incoming tide. Site of a summer smelt run, Yachats puts on a Silver Smelt Fry in July. The town also hosts an Arts and Crafts Fair in mid-March.

South of the Yachats River, a broad sandy beach invites a brisk walk or run.

Pause awhile at Cape Perpetua

This magnificent basalt headland—created by several ancient lava flows and named by Captain James Cook in 1778—is part of Siuslaw National Forest and the cornerstone of the Cape Perpetua (Per-PET-u-ah) scenic recreation area.

First stop for most travelers is the Forest Service visitor center south of the cape, just off U.S. 101. It is open daily from 9 A.M. to 6 P.M. in summer, 10 A.M. to 4 P.M. Wednesday through Sunday from mid-September to late May. A 15-minute movie and diorama introduce visitors to the plant and animal life of the area and the natural forces at work on the coastal environment.

Nature trails branch out from the visitor center to driftwood-strewn beaches, tidepools, and lush rain forest. You can picnic at Cape Perpetua Campground north of the center and at Neptune State Park about 1 mile south. Don't miss the spectacular view from atop Cape Perpetua, accessible by car and trail. Whales, seals, and porpoises are sometimes visible.

A self-conducted auto tour begins at Devils Churn, just north of the visitor center, and winds 22 miles through wooded hills and coastal valleys, returning to U.S. 101 at Yachats.

Sea lions and a landmark lighthouse

Ten miles to the south another splendid headland juts far out into the restless surf. Marked by its oft-photographed lighthouse, Heceta (Huh-SEE-ta) Head was named for Spanish sea captain Bruno Heceta, who sailed along the coast in 1775.

Though the lighthouse is not open to visitors, you can picnic in Devils Elbow State Park just below. Campers head for Washburne Memorial State Park, just north of the headland; it has a good swimming beach, surf fishing, and gravelly patches where beachcombers often find agates.

About 12 miles north of Florence, sea lions cluster around Sea Lion Point where they live the year around, mating and rearing their young pups. The barking of the sea lions resounds in the large marine cave at the base of the cliff; visitors descend through the cliff by elevator to a viewing area.

The rookery is especially interesting in spring when bull sea lions (weighing up to 2,000 pounds each) select—and sometimes battle for—their harems of 10 to 20 cows. Cubs are usually born in June. Most of the sea lions stay inside the cave during stormy weather, but when the sun comes out, they assemble on a long rocky ledge outside or frolic in the waves. Many shore birds nest on the cliffs or inside the cave.

A park for the cobra lily

One of the coast's more unusual attractions is Darlingtonia Botanical Wayside, an 18-acre state preserve 5 miles north of Florence. It has been set aside exclusively for the protection and observation of *Darlingtonia californica*, also known as cobra lily or pitcher plant, a native of boggy areas in Oregon and northern California. A wooden walkway, built above the marshy area, offers a close-up view of the plants.

Hundreds of the cobralike plants, hooded at the tops, grow in the marshy area; they flower in May and June. Insects are attracted by nectar to an opening under the hood; once inside, they are trapped and eventually converted into food for the plant.

Newport's waterfront is home port for cruisers, sailboats, and the commercial fishing fleet.

Want crab for dinner? Heave a baited crab ring off the bay pier.

Florence, rhododendron capital

Pink blooms of the coast rhododendron brighten the roads around Florence each May, providing the theme for a community-wide celebration. This friendly port town at the mouth of the Siuslaw River offers outdoorsmen a stimulating array of recreation possibilities. To the south, magnificent sand dunes rise along a 40-mile strip of shore in the Oregon Dunes National Recreation Area.

Fishermen find many nearby lakes and streams, or they can fish from jetties or surf-cast for perch, flounder, and sole. Sea-run cutthroat return to tidewater in July and August, and salmon and steelhead migrate up the Siuslaw in autumn to spawn in Lake Creek and other tributaries. Oceangoing fishing boats can be chartered.

Forested hills around the town provide logs for the sawmills and plywood plants upriver. In the port, you'll often see lumber being loaded aboard barges. A small commercial fishing fleet headquarters here, too.

From Eugene, travelers wind through pastoral hills on State Highway 126 (locally called Route F). A slower route to the coast is State Highway 36, curving around Triangle Lake and along Lake Creek to meet State 126 in Mapleton.

Florence's old town. Shopkeepers and craftsmen have revitalized Florence's old town area, a three-block stretch of Bay Street east of U.S. 101 along the Siuslaw waterfront. By-passed by the coast highway, the area languished for many years, but now merchants and artisans are preserving and refurbishing many of the old buildings, making this section a delightful place to stroll and browse.

Rhodies and huckleberries. Rhododendron Drive—lovely in May and early June—heads west from Florence along the river to Harbor Vista County Park overlooking the Siuslaw bar. Fishermen continue out to the north jetty. From the park you can drive north to Heceta Beach. Tiny blue huckleberries ripen along coastal roads in August and September.

Exploring the Oregon Dunes

Vast shifting mountains of sand, smoothed or wave-rippled by coastal winds, rim the coast for more than 40 miles between Florence and Coos Bay. Relentlessly, the wind-blown sand moves slowly eastward, creating islands of pine forest and blocking the flow of fresh-water streams to make a string of coastal lakes.

In 1972 a 41-mile stretch of this unusual region—about a tenth of Oregon's coastline—was designated the Oregon Dunes National Recreation Area, administered by Siuslaw National Forest officials. Between the Siuslaw River and Coos Bay, the dunes extend inland from 1 to 3 miles. From U.S. 101, roads and trails branch west into the dunes. Stop at the headquarters office in Reedsport for a recreation map of the area.

Recreation possibilities. You can enjoy the dunes area in a number of ways—sliding down dunes or hiking across the sand to the ocean; boating and

Sailing canoe cuts across Cleawox Lake in Honeyman State Park south of Florence. Sand dunes border the southwestern shore of this popular fresh-water lake.

canoeing on the lakes; riding dune buggies over the sandy slopes; fishing in fresh-water lakes, from jetties or piers, or casting into the surf; beachcombing for marine treasures or hunting for prized pieces of sandblasted wood.

One favorite area for hikers is the Honeyman Dunes, southeast of Cleawox Lake at Honeyman State Park, where sand dunes rise abruptly from the lake. Another is Horsfall Beach, a gentle 16-mile strand reaching north from the mouth of Coos Bay. Surf fishermen cast for perch on this beach, and clammers dig in tidelands near the jetty.

Back packers head for Threemile Lake, just north of the Umpqua River, or the Umpqua Dunes Scenic Area west of Tenmile Lake.

Many parts of the area are difficult to reach on foot. Motorized vehicles are allowed in several sections of the area, and three private operators provide dune buggy and train rides into the dunes.

Dune buggy drivers should be alert for shallow pockets of quicksand behind the foredune; vehicles can become mired easily. These areas are no special problem to hikers—though you might get a bit wet and sandy while climbing out. Beware of beach logs along the water line; waves can pick them up and toss them around like matchsticks.

Dunes wildlife. Deer and raccoon tracks can sometimes be seen near wooded areas in early morning, and beavers inhabit the lake areas. You'll see gulls and other shore birds on the beaches, and migratory waterfowl join resident birds and small animals in the marshy areas around Bluebill Lake.

A chain of coastal lakes

Just behind the dunes, a chain of several dozen coastal lakes offers a pleasant change of pace.

Some of the lakes are small, choked with lily pads, and hidden from the highway. Larger lakes—such as Woahink, Siltcoos, Tahkenitch, and Tenmile—have long fingers stretching far back into canyons and draws.

Many of the lakes have state parks or Siuslaw National Forest campgrounds along their shores. At several of the larger lakes, marinas offer boat rentals and fishing supplies. Siltcoos and Tahkenitch lakes are highly regarded by fishermen.

Sheltered from the ocean winds, lake waters are warm enough for pleasant midsummer swimming. Lakeside bathhouses are located at Cleawox and Woahink lakes (both bordering Honeyman State Park) and at Eel Lake (William M. Tugman State Park); you can swim at other lakes as well. Sailboats, bright rafts, canoes, and rowboats dot the lakes on pleasant days.

Rhododendrons, azaleas, and dogwood brighten the lake shores in spring, and huckleberries ripen in the area in late summer.

Along the lower Umpqua

From Interstate 5, State Highways 38 and 138 wend westward through rolling pastures to Elkton. From here, it is another 35 miles to Reedsport —a leisurely river route all the way. Anglers fish for steelhead, salmon, and striped bass in the riffles downstream from Elkton. The valley narrows as the Umpqua cuts through the Coast Range.

Scottsburg. Sleepy Scottsburg provides few clues to its lively past. In the early 1850s it was a rip-roaring boom town, the biggest and busiest metropolis in southern Oregon. Tall-masted schooners from San Francisco transported miners, food, and supplies up the Umpqua to Scottsburg, principal outfitting point for the Siskiyou gold mining camps.

The town's prosperity waned in the late 1850s when the gold supply was exhausted; most of the town was washed away by floods in 1861.

Parks and waysides. Riverside turnout areas beside the lower Umpqua invite travelers to picnic or stroll along the bank. If you bring your own boat, you can launch it at Scottsburg Park, at Umpqua Wayside (about 7 miles west of Scottsburg), and at Reedsport. Fields of daffodils bloom near Scottsburg in March; you can purchase a bunch at a wayside stand (payment is often on the honor system).

You can picnic at Umpqua Wayside beside the wide, murky green river or take a side trip south of State 38 to Loon Lake, a pleasant Bureau of Land Management campground in the Coast Range.

Fishing and clamming. The Umpqua has a well-deserved reputation as one of the state's best fishing streams. In tidewater areas of the Umpqua and Smith rivers, anglers pull in striped bass, Chinook salmon, and the scrappy shad. Smelt migrate upriver in February. Salmon Harbor at Winchester Bay is headquarters for salmon fishermen.

Clammers dig in the Umpqua tidelands and along coastal beaches north of the river. Crabbing is also good near the river mouth.

River towns. Logging and forest products provide the livelihood for many residents in western Douglas County; lumber, paper, and plywood mills are located in Reedsport and Gardiner.

Reedsport's Storm Festival, presented rain or shine each February, includes beach events—a crab relay race (runners use a live crab instead of a baton), sand castle building, and a driftwood hunting contest—as well as indoor activities.

Winchester Bay's prosperity is linked to its small boat marina—Salmon Harbor—liveliest in summer as Chinooks and silvers show up outside the bar and start to move upriver. Charter trips are available.

The lonely south coast

The southern third of Oregon's superb shore has fewer access highways across the Coast Range—and fewer visitors. Beach roads branch west from U.S. 101 to near-deserted beaches.

Accommodations cluster around the major towns—Coos Bay, Bandon, Port Orford, Gold Beach, and Brookings—which have become vacation and sport fishing centers.

Exploring the Coos Bay area

Coos Bay separates two entirely different types of coastal terrain. North of the bay are shifting sand dunes; from the bay entrance south to Cape Arago, rugged cliffs and rocky coves line the shoreline.

Coos Bay itself is the best natural harbor on the coast between Puget Sound and San Francisco Bay. It is a busy waterway for commerce and industry, but also a fisherman's delight. Small boats cruise its protected waters, and clammers and crabbers have their favorite grounds. A scenic tour of the bay departs from the Coos Bay waterfront.

U.S. 101 crosses the bay on mile-long McCullough Bridge, longest of the coastal bridges, to the region's twin commercial centers of North Bend and busy Coos Bay, largest town on the south coast.

Forest products dominate the south coast economy; the towns form the hub of the area's vast timber resources and the shipping point for exported forest products. Down on the waterfront, ocean-bound freighters moor close to the mills, where thousands of board feet of stacked lumber await loading and mountains of manmade wood chips will be converted into paper, particleboard, and other products. Southwestern Oregon is myrtle-wood country; you can watch this distinctive hardwood made into decorative articles by craftsmen at several area factory-shops.

Most of the area's best attractions can't be seen from the highway, which curves inland away from the coast.

North Bend's Simpson Park.

A greenery-tipped peninsula juts into the bay, greeting travelers headed south. North Bend's Simpson Park occupies the peninsula's northern end. The area's visitor information center is located here, and you'll find tables if you want to spread a picnic lunch.

Another of the park's attractions is the Coos-Curry Pioneer Museum; you can browse through its exhibits of Indian and pioneer mementos. From May through September, museum hours are 11 A.M. to 5 P.M. Tuesday through Saturday, from noon to 6 P.M. on Sunday. The rest of the year, the museum is open 1 to 5 P.M. Tuesday through Sunday. A steam-powered logging locomotive and donkey engine are displayed outside.

Coos Bay's Mall. Cornerstone of a long-range civic redevelopment program is the Coos Bay Mall, a four-block section of the town's Central Avenue between North Bayshore Drive (northbound U.S. 101) and 4th Street.

Bordered with trees and flower beds, the cobble-stoned and canopied pedestrian mall forms the heart of Coos Bay's business community. It is a pleasant place to stretch your legs, shop, or relax away from traffic. In good weather you may find flower shows, art and craft displays, or performances by local talent. At one end of the mall is the elegant City Hall, built in 1923 and modernized with covered front walkways and a fountain.

Art shows. Regional art center is the Coos Bay Art Museum at 515 Market Avenue, open daily except Monday from 1 to 4 P.M. Shows of local artists, traveling state exhibits, and art lectures are presented at the museum.

Up the Millicoma Valley

The peaceful dairy pastures and spacious old barns of the Millicoma River valley kindle images of another era. In the early days of the local dairy indus-

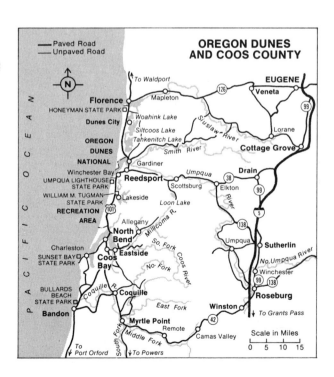

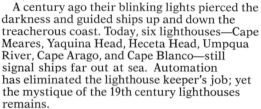

Coastal sentinels light the way for offshore ships

A century ago their blinking lights pierced the darkness and guided ships up and down the treacherous coast. Today, six lighthouses—Cape Meares, Yaquina Head, Heceta Head, Umpqua River, Cape Arago, and Cape Blanco—still signal ships far out at sea. Automation has eliminated the lighthouse keeper's job; yet the mystique of the 19th century lighthouses remains.

A walk around one of these timeless sentinels will take you back to days when shipping was a dangerous adventure. From outside a lighthouse, you can look up at its many-sided lens. As the lens turns, it focuses light from a constantly burning bulb into a bright beam. Each lighthouse has a unique light pattern—such as one flash every 20 seconds or a red and white pattern— that identifies a lighthouse to passing ships.

The Coast Guard maintains these navigational aids. Though the operating lighthouses are not generally open for tours, Cape Blanco Light— located 10 miles northwest of Port Orford—has a lighthouse display open to the public.

You can also see lighthouse furnishings of the 1870s at the old Yaquina Bay Lighthouse, now a museum, overlooking Yaquina Bay at Newport. Built in 1871, it operated only 3 years until a new lighthouse was built at Yaquina Head 3

miles north. You can drive out to see the present lighthouse, an impressive masonry-covered brick tower.

Last of the major seacoast lighthouses to be built, Heceta Head Light stands boldly on a steep bluff 13 miles north of Florence. Its 1 million-candlepower light—the Oregon coast's most powerful beacon—shines up to 21 miles out at sea. Look up at the tower from Devil's Elbow State Park beach; or for a closer look at the light and a sweeping view of the coast to the south, walk past the keeper's house and up to the lighthouse.

A small footbridge (not open to visitors) links the Cape Arago Light, 14 miles southwest of Coos Bay, with the mainland. Before construction of the bridge, keepers crossed the channel in a basket pulled along a wire cable.

The original Umpqua River Light Station, the first lighthouse on the Oregon coast, was erected in 1857 on sand dunes near the river's mouth. It fell 4 years later after the river eroded its foundation. A new lighthouse was built in 1894 on a hillside above the original site, about 6 miles south of Reedsport.

At Cape Meares Light, 10 miles west of Tillamook, a small beacon tower replaced the original light in 1963. ◻

---

try, milk boats made the run downstream to coastal settlements. In March and April, fat dairy cattle graze in pastures dotted with blossoming fruit trees. Later in the spring, newly leafed trees and wild rhododendrons brighten the coastal foothills and greenery borders the river shore. Fishermen troll the tidewaters of the Millicoma—and the north and south forks of the Coos River—for shad and bass.

In south Coos Bay, turn east off U.S. 101 on the Coos River Highway and follow signs through Eastside toward Allegany; the dairy country begins just beyond Eastside.

Beyond Allegany the paved road ends, and the gravel route narrows and worsens as you begin to climb. You can picnic in a grove of myrtle trees in Millicoma Myrtle Grove State Park 4 miles northeast of Allegany.

Six miles beyond the park a pair of 200-foot-high waterfalls make Golden and Silver Falls State Park a scenic destination. Hiking trails lead from the picnic area (no drinking water) to Golden Falls on Glenn Creek and Silver Falls on Silver Creek. The two streams converge at the picnic area.

Along the coast to Charleston

Superb state parks and other coastal attractions lure travelers west of North Bend along the south shore of the Coos estuary. From U.S. 101, head west on the Empire-Charleston Highway.

Clammers find good digging in the tideflats between Empire and South Slough; clamming is even better on the far shore (the North Spit), but you need a boat to get there. Ask at the visitor information office in North Bend for their clam digging brochure.

Dozens of sport fishermen moor their boats in the Charleston Boat Basin. Commercial and charter fishing boats also operate out of this busy marina. Peak season is mid-July through September, when deep-sea fishermen troll offshore for silver and Chinook salmon. You can have your catch smoked or canned near the docks. Rental boats and crab rings are available.

On sunny Sunday or holiday afternoons, look for the Snug Harbor Railroad. Hobbyist Leonard Hall welcomes passengers aboard his miniature train on 10-minute loop trips along the sandy river bank south of the Coos inlet. Passengers ride in small, open-top gondola cars.

Public tours are conducted at the nearby Coast Guard Station on weekdays from 1 to 3 P.M. and on weekends and holidays from 1 to 4 P.M.

A trio of splendid state parks

From Coos Head to Cape Arago, the coastline is a succession of eroding sandstone headlands, offshore reefs, and driftwood-strewn beaches. During winter storms, huge waves crash against the bluffs, sending great bursts of spray high into the air.

Three excellent state parks highlight this sea-coast's dramatic variety. Campgrounds are located west of Charleston at Sunset Bay State Park and at Bastendorff Beach County Park.

Sunset Bay State Park. Precipitous sandstone cliffs curve protectively around this miniature bay, sheltering it from ocean winds. Small children frolic safely in gentle waters near shore, while their parents enjoy the broad sandy beach for sunning or sunset watching. Hiking trails lead from the spacious campground to Cape Arago Lighthouse just north of the park. At low tide, look at the eroded troughs in the wave-cut bench rock.

Shore Acres State Park. Unique in Oregon's state park system, Shore Acres encompasses the former estate of Asa M. Simpson, a wealthy sea captain and boat builder. Simpson founded the town of North Bend in 1855 and built a flourishing sawmill business here and in several other Northwest ports. Simpson sailing ships brought many exotic plants from distant lands for the estate's garden, the only surviving part of the old estate.

The restored botanical garden still contains some of the original trees and shrubs. Spring and summer visitors enjoy wisteria trailing over a pergola; the bright blooms of rhododendrons, hydrangeas, and roses; and a Japanese garden bordering a small lily pond.

Visitors can picnic on the bluff, fish from the rocks, and watch waves crash against the sculptured sandstone bluffs during winter storms.

Cape Arago State Park. Southernmost of the three parks, Cape Arago offers a commanding view of the magnificent sea-carved coastline and offshore rocks. It is a splendid spot to watch ships entering and leaving the Coos Bay harbor.

Barking sea lions loll on wave-washed Simpson Reef, a tilted sandstone shelf just north of the cape. Students of geology and marine biology find this a rich observation area. Trails lead down the bluff to rock fishing areas, fascinating tidepools, and a pair of sheltered coves.

The rugged Seven Devils coast

Between Coos Bay and Bandon, the Seven Devils Road provides access to a trio of remote, rock-strewn beaches separated by headlands. At low tide, beachcombers can walk for 6 miles along the shore, looking for agates in the rainbow of rocks.

The hard-surfaced county road begins west of the bridge in Charleston and winds south to meet U.S. 101 about 8 miles north of Bandon; side roads lead to the beaches. Many local rockhounds prefer to take the spur road west from U.S. 101 about 9 miles south of the State Highway 42 junction.

Northernmost of the three beaches is Agate Beach, where brightly colored rocks include agate, jasper, and petrified wood. A paved access road leads to a parking area near Merchant's Beach, 2 miles south, where rockhounding is equally good. Three miles below is Whiskey Run Beach, site of a 1853 gold rush; $2 million in gold was reputedly

Eroding sandstone bluffs *indent the coast west of Coos Bay. Storm watchers come here during winter gales.*

Botanical garden *of Shore Acres State Park comes as a surprise along this coast. Many exotic plants arrived here in the sailing ships of a lumber magnate.*

Spectacular wildflower displays brighten the coastal hills and river valleys in May and June. Among the blooms you may see are (left to right) wild azalea, lavender iris, and wild cucumber vine.

taken from these sands by placer mining. Here you'll find fewer rocks but plenty of driftwood.

Along the Coquille River

South of Coos Bay, State 42 forks southeast through pleasant farms and dairy country to meet the Coquille River. Coquille (pronounced Ko-KEEL) is the shopping hub of the valley and the center of southern Oregon's myrtlewood area.

From Coquille, State 42 follows the river eastward for more than 30 miles. Fat, rounded myrtle trees decorate the coastal foothills, and you can picnic in a riverside myrtle grove at Hoffman Memorial Wayside, 3 miles south of Myrtle Point.

Another inviting stop is Camas Mountain Wayside, just east of Camas Valley. On the eastern slope of the hills, you continue through rolling farm land to Winston and Interstate 5.

Coquille back roads. Northeast of Coquille and Myrtle Point, side roads fan along the Coquille's various forks. Country routes edge the placid river, which glides smoothly between mossy banks, swirls around water-sculptured boulders, and occasionally cascades in shallow falls. Families picnic along its shores beneath maple and myrtle trees.

Forest route to the Rogue. Three miles east of Myrtle Point, a paved road leads from State 42 along the Coquille River's south fork to Powers—and ultimately to Agness, terminus of jet-boat trips on the lower Rogue. Pavement ends 11 miles south of Powers; the remaining 25 miles through Siskiyou National Forest is over a single-lane gravel road (with turnouts). Logging truck traffic is heavy during the week, but the road is closed to log hauling on Sundays and holidays.

The time to explore this river road is in spring, when ferns and blossoms decorate the banks; summer can be hot. Seven miles south of Powers, silvery Elk Creek Falls cascades down a gorge bordered in lush greenery; you can picnic here or at several Forest Service campgrounds farther south.

Bandon, Oregon's cranberry capital

Another river road—State Highway 42S—parallels the lower stretch of the Coquille River from the town of Coquille to Bandon. Salmon, trout, and steelhead are raised in the fish hatchery just east of Bandon. Rhododendrons bloom throughout the countryside in May and June.

Coquille River estuary. A mile north of Bandon, Bullards Beach State Park fronts both the Coquille River and the Pacific Ocean. Nearly 200 campsites are available here; travelers will also find a picnic area, boat launching ramp and dock, and hiking trails to the river and ocean beach.

The road through the picnic area leads to an abandoned brick lighthouse at the south end of the spit, overlooking the river's treacherous bar. Built in 1896, it was one of the few structures left standing after Bandon's disastrous 1936 fire.

Bandon's cranberry festival. Each September this friendly little town hosts a cranberry festival with a full weekend of activities, including a parade, beef barbecue, football game, dances, and crab feed. On sale in the park are breads, cakes, preserves, and beverages—all made from cranberries.

If you'd like to visit a cranberry bog, check at the chamber of commerce office. Local growers will show visitors around their properties and explain how cranberries are grown. The bright red berries are harvested in October and November.

Beach Loop Road. From U.S. 101 a loop road winds west through Bandon and along the bluff south of town. Occasional trails and stairways lead down to the beach; offshore seastacks of somber black rock add interest to the seascape. Bandon State Park provides a wind-sheltered picnic area and beach access.

Roadside attractions. Children can feed tame deer and other small animals in natural surroundings at the West Coast Deer Park about 7½ miles south of Bandon.

Indian artifacts and rocks and minerals are displayed at Stone Age Park 6 miles north of Port Orford. Children can fish in a trout pond and hand feed small animals.

Spring wildflower detours

Wildflowers brighten Oregon's coastal hills and valleys from March to August, but some of the most gorgeous displays decorate the coast from Florence south to Brookings in May and June. Florence celebrates the rhododendron season in mid-May, while Brookings honors the wild azalea during the Memorial Day weekend.

In late spring the golden flowers of Scotch broom and spiny gorse cover hillsides and line sections of U.S. 101. Blossoms of blue and yellow lupine swell in the spring sunshine, wild cucumber vines clamber along fences, and clumps of lavender iris bloom perkily beside the roads.

Short detours from the highway yield rich rewards to flower lovers. South of Florence, pink rhododendron blossoms festoon side roads, and water lilies bloom atop fresh-water ponds. The drive from Coos Bay up the Millicoma River (see page 57) passes banks of wildflowers.

Try the short spur roads, too, like the one from Langlois up Floras Creek or the Elk River Road that winds through dairy country beside a fine salmon and steelhead stream. An outstanding seasonal display of iris and other wildflowers lines the route to Cape Blanco.

You can see fine clumps of Oregon's golden iris on the forest route from Wedderburn up the north bank of the Rogue River to Lobster Creek, and more grow along the Hunter Creek road that heads east from the highway 3 miles south of Gold Beach. Hillsides glow with the blue blossoms of ceanothus along the ridge road southeast of Port Orford and beside Cape Sebastian trails.

Visit a century-old lighthouse

Occupying Oregon's windy westernmost tip is the Cape Blanco Lighthouse, the only one of Oregon's coastal beacons that has regular visiting hours. The access road wanders 6 miles northwest from its junction with U.S. 101 north of Port Orford. You can visit the lighthouse between 1 and 3 P.M. on weekdays, 1 to 4 P.M. on weekends. No tours are conducted when the light is in operation.

Built in 1870 and in continuous operation since that time, the brick lighthouse has walls 6 feet thick at the base. A Coast Guardsman guide will show you the 1000-watt bulb that lights the beacon.

Cape Blanco's rugged shoreline has interesting rock outcroppings offshore. The state park has wind-protected camping and picnic facilities, and you can hike down a trail to the driftwood-littered beach; after winter storms, beachcombers look here for glass fishing floats. At low tide you can explore tidepools near the tip of the cape.

Giant salmon and historic Battle Rock

Port Orford is a sportsmen's center, busiest in fall when fishermen congregate along the Elk and Sixes rivers. Migrating salmon and steelhead make a big splash here—up to 30 pounds and sometimes more—as they swim upriver to spawning grounds. Tours are available at the state fish hatchery, where salmon lunge up the fish ladders in season.

Garrison Lake attracts both coast birds and trout fishermen. Garrison Lake State Wayside offers access to coastal dunes and—at low tide—good hunting for blue agates and glass floats.

Buffington Memorial Park, west of U.S. 101 in town, has a picnic area, playground, sports facilities, lake fishing dock, and horse arena.

Harbor activity. Be sure to visit the local harbor to see activity in a working fishing village. In season, you can purchase fresh Dungeness crab, shrimp, bottom fish, and salmon. Boats have no bar to cross to get to the open sea; both commercial and sport boats are launched by means of a converted log loading boom. A paved ramp is also available.

Port Orford Heads State Wayside, southwest of town, offers sweeping coastal views from Cape Blanco south to Humbug Mountain. Migrating whales pass offshore, and you'll often see fishing boats trolling for salmon or checking crab pots.

Historic Battle Rock. Rising above Port Orford's sandy beach like a giant mossy-backed serpent,

Driftwood *rims the beach at Battle Rock. In 1851 settlers used the rock as a fortress during Indian attack.*

Battle Rock was the site of a historic conflict in June, 1851. A party of hostile Indians besieged a group of white settlers who took refuge on the rock. Armed with a small cannon, the settlers fought off their attackers and finally escaped north along the coast. The battle is reenacted on the Fourth of July during the city's Jetty Jubilee.

At low tide you can walk out to the rock and follow a winding trail to its tree-covered crest or explore a tunnel. Battle Rock becomes an island at high tide, when waves surge around it.

Other attractions. Surfers head for a pair of excellent surfing beaches south of town at Battle Rock Wayside and Hubbard Creek Bridge.

About 13 miles south of Port Orford, life-size replicas of dinosaurs and other extinct animals lurk in a fern-filled forest setting at Prehistoric Gardens.

South to the Rogue

From Bandon south to the California border, no paved roads link the coast with interior cities. Today a fine, fast highway parallels the coast. But a generation ago, cautious drivers maneuvered a curve-filled road around coastal headlands—and more than one terrified passenger made the trip on the floorboards rather than regard the hazy oblivion just a few feet away.

Most of Humbug Mountain State Park lies on the sheltered inland side of the mountain, but on the north slope, trails lead down to a sandy beach cut by a pleasant creek.

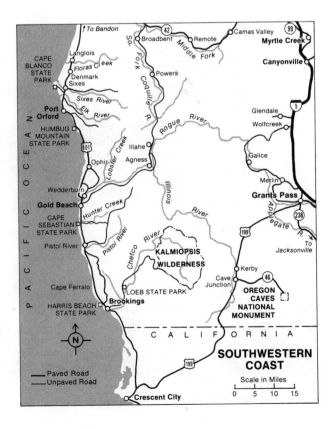

Vacationing at Gold Beach

The twin towns of Gold Beach and Wedderburn flank the mouth of the Rogue River, famous for its salmon and steelhead fishing and jet-boat trips.

Fishermen come here the year around. Depending on the season, they cast for Chinook, silvers, or steelhead from bank, boat, or ocean. In Gold Beach you can rent tackle and boats and arrange for fishing guides. Good clamming areas are along Bailey Beach and Myers Creek.

Saddle horses are available for scenic trail rides in the Wedderburn hills. The long beach below town provides good pickings for agate hunters and beachcombers. Rogue Arts, a mile north of the Rogue River bridge, is the work and retail center for local artists and craftsmen.

Jet-boat trips up the lower Rogue

One of the best side trips on the coast is the jet-boat trip up the Rogue River. From docks in Gold Beach and neighboring Wedderburn, three boat operators transport passengers and mail upriver in open boats powered by hydro-jets. Travelers have a choice of excursions: a 32-mile trip upstream to Agness or a 52-mile ride up to Paradise Gorge in the "wild river" section of the canyon.

Daily excursions are available from May through October; in winter the mail boat travels upriver three times a week. For current information on fares and schedules, write to the Gold Beach Chamber of Commerce.

Boats depart about 8:30 A.M. for the upriver trip, pause 2 hours for a hearty, family-style lunch at one of the Rogue riverside lodges, and return to Gold Beach in the afternoon. You can arrange to stay overnight in one of the rustic lodges, renowned for home cooking and unbroken solitude; confirmed reservations are essential.

Thick forests cover the hills above the rocky canyon. Passengers often see blacktail deer and other wild animals along the river; birds swoop overhead, and clumps of wildflowers add bright touches to the shore. Often the boat's pilot will point out interesting geological features or recount tales of river life.

Above Agness the canyon narrows and deepens. White-water rapids come one after the other. You might see hikers on the Rogue River hiking trail, which parallels this roadless section.

Riverside trails

A forest road, paved part of the way, now follows the south bank of the winding Rogue upstream to meet the Powers-Agness road (see page 60). Hikers can branch off on trails along the Rogue or Illinois rivers in the Siskiyou National Forest.

Illahe marks the western end of the 40-mile Rogue River hiking trail (see page 85) along the roadless stretch of the river.

A primitive forest road branches south from the Rogue River road along the scenic Illinois River, known for its clear water, rugged canyon, and excellent steelhead fishing (fall through spring). The hiking trail begins above Lawson Creek.

Rugged panoramas

Some of Oregon's finest coastal scenery is concentrated along U.S. 101 between Gold Beach and Brookings. Rugged and wild, it begins at Cape Sebastian with its magnificent ocean views.

The highway dips to meet the sea at Pistol River, then climbs another bluff to enter Samuel H. Boardman Park. If you'd like to drive a stretch of the twisty old highway, take the road southeast of Pistol River which climbs to Carpenterville; it offers splendid views and little traffic.

Samuel H. Boardman Park. Named for the father of Oregon's state park system, this 11-mile stretch of parkland offers three picnic sites in addition to its splendid seascapes.

U.S. 101 crosses 345-foot-high Thomas Creek Bridge. Beachcombers look for driftwood near the Whale's Head picnic area, or you can try surf casting or clamming at Lone Ranch picnic area.

Short access roads lead to spectacular view points at House Rock and Cape Ferrelo. Hiking trails descend to Natural Bridges Cove, a series of rock arches carved by the surf, and to Indian Sands, where the rust-crusted, sculptured dunes extend to the edge of the bluff.

Harris Beach State Park. Southernmost of Oregon's state campgrounds, Harris Beach State Park combines sandy beach and rocky shoreline. Located 2 miles north of Brookings, the park attracts surf fishermen, hardy swimmers (on incoming tides), and beachcombers. Offshore rocks add drama to ocean views. Goat Island is a refuge for numerous sea birds.

South of the parking lot, a trail winds over the knobby little headland to a tiny cove that becomes one enormous tidepool at low tide. Wildflowers, native azaleas, and other flowering shrubs brighten park trails in summer.

Azaleas and lilies at Brookings

Just north of the California border, Brookings marks the mouth of the Chetco River. Timber, commercial fishing, and flower bulb raising dominate the economy.

Blooming wild azaleas attract visitors for the Azalea Festival on Memorial Day weekend; the best display is in Azalea State Park, a 26-acre natural park east of U.S. 101. The town's unusually mild climate encourages a year-round display of flowers. Acres of snowy lilies bloom in July, scenting the air with delicate fragrance, and fields of golden daffodils blossom in February and March.

The productive waters of the Chetco River offer trout in spring, steelhead and salmon in fall; you can arrange to have your catch smoked or canned. Licensed guides are available for either stream or ocean fishing, and charter boats set out from

Jet-boat operators transport visitors from Gold Beach up the forest-bordered Rogue River. You'll pause for a hearty lunch at a riverside lodge.

Brookings during salmon season. Other anglers enjoy rock fishing, surf casting, or fishing off the jetty at the mouth of the river. The Brookings-Harbor Chamber of Commerce can direct visitors to good crabbing and clamming areas.

Up the Chetco River

Inland from the coast, myrtle trees and redwood groves are scattered amid heavy stands of Douglas fir. Rhododendrons, azaleas, wild lilacs, and Sadler oaks grow profusely. Siskiyou National Forest also contains some unusual trees and plants, including the rare Port Orford cedar, the Brewer's weeping spruce, and Oregon's few groves of coast redwoods (*Sequoia sempervirens*). Rarest of all is the kalmiopsis, a small rhododendronlike plant protected in the Kalmiopsis Wilderness (see page 89).

The well-maintained Chetco River Road offers access to several attractions. For information, check the Chetco Ranger Station in Brookings.

About 6 miles inland, a side road branches north to Palmer Butte Overlook. You climb along a ridge to the 2,074-foot view point and BLM picnic area.

Eight miles east of Brookings, a riverside grove of virgin myrtle trees provides the setting for Loeb State Park. Picnic tables are scattered beneath the rounded, widespreading trees.

The river road leads to stands of redwood trees ½ mile east of the park and farther upriver near Little Redwood Campground; more redwoods are located along Wheeler Creek, about 20 miles east of Brookings.

Forest Road 3917 branches off from the river road to climb toward Vulcan Peak and the western trailhead for hiking in the Kalmiopsis Wilderness.

The Willamette Valley

Historic towns dot Oregon's fertile heartland

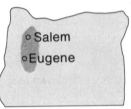
Salem
Eugene

Sturdy old Benton County Court House, built in 1888, is topped by a square clock tower.

Covered bridges dot Willamette Valley back roads. Linn County's Shimanek Bridge, rebuilt in 1966 northeast of Scio, is one of about 60 in existence.

The broad and bountiful Willamette Valley extends some 125 miles south of Portland, cradled between the fir-clad slopes of the Coast Range on the west and the Cascade Mountains on the east. Still essentially rural, it contains most of the state's large cities and industries and (including Portland) roughly two-thirds of the population. The flat lowland has just enough rolling hills and buttes to make it interesting. Numerous tributary streams meander down from the hills to join the main river.

Interstate Highway 5 cuts through the valley, by-passing the cities. Older north-south routes are State Highways 99W and 99E, which link valley towns west and east of the river. Main intersecting routes are State Highway 22 at Salem, U.S. Highway 20 at Corvallis and Albany, and State Highway 126 at Eugene and Springfield.

Oregon's heartland

The Willamette Valley was the wellspring of civilization in the Pacific Northwest. In terms of influencing history, the Willamette was to its valley what the Mississippi and Ohio rivers were to mid-America. The history of the valley is really the history of Oregon, for it was the destination of fur

Golden Pioneer statue *gleams atop the white marble capitol building in Salem. In summer, tours depart from the rotunda; you can climb to the tower.*

Fountain *and brick-paved plaza highlight Eugene's attractive downtown mall.*

trappers and homesteaders from the earliest days.

From the arrival of fur trappers and traders until railroads were completed in the 1870s, the river was the primary carrier of commerce. Towns grew up around the river's ferry landings, shipping points, and mill sites. Steamboats traveled up the Willamette as far as Springfield—and on tributaries such as the Yamhill and Tualatin—transporting passengers and cargo between riverside settlements.

From its early days, the Willamette Valley was Oregon's center of agriculture, commerce, culture, and social activity. It still is.

Some outsiders mispronounce the name of the valley and river; as one exasperated old-timer told a visitor, "it's Will-LAMB-it, dammit!"

The pioneers' promised land

The journey west was a long and difficult one. Some early travelers sailed around Cape Horn, but most made the tiring journey overland by wagon train along the Oregon Trail.

Settlement in the Willamette Valley meant isolation, hardship mixed with pleasure, and even prosperity for some; but life was generally uneventful. Most of the settlers were Americans; Oregon had little of the cosmopolitan influence that peppered the development of other western states.

The discovery of gold in California in 1848 had a profound influence on the settlement of the valley. It turned the majority of overland migrants southward, away from the Oregon Trail that had previously led most pioneers to the Willamette Valley.

Many Oregon men traveled south to the diggings. Farmers who stayed behind made big money supplying the California merchants who supplied the miners. Many Oregonians who left for the mines returned with gold, and more than a few valley stores, farms, and businesses were financed by gold removed from the ground in California.

Rich farm land and thick forests

The fertile lands of the Willamette Valley attracted settlers in the 1840s, and this rich farm land still yields an impressive array of crops.

As you travel rural roads you can discover strawberries, caneberries, hops, peppermint, wheat, flax, beans, corn, bulbs, holly, and nut and fruit crops (filberts, walnuts, peaches, prunes, and cherries). At harvest time, many Willamette Valley residents head for the fields and food processing plants, though mechanized equipment now handles a sizable amount of the harvesting.

Most of the nation's northern-climate lawn grass seed is grown in the Willamette Valley. In late spring, grass fields are high, green, and billowing. Then during the short, delightful dry season, the grass turns gold or brown. Harvesting machines come through and cut the grass, taking the seed and leaving the straw.

Logs are cut on the surrounding hills and mountains, but most of the processing takes place in the valley. The Eugene-Springfield area, at the southern end of the valley, is recognized as the lumber capital of Oregon—and as one veteran lumberman put it, "You might as well call it the lumber capital of the world." Sawmills, plywood plants, and paper factories have been joined by a host of forest products industries that process bark and wood chips into many useful products.

A river parkway

The Willamette winds through Oregon's most populous region, yet in many stretches it retains a sense of the untouched wild. Most people get only glimpses of this splendid waterway; the most enjoyable way to explore it is by boat.

Since 1967 the Willamette has been the focus of an innovative river parkway plan—known as the Willamette River Greenway—that is enhancing its ecology, history, and recreational uses. Eventually a public recreation belt will extend for more than 100 miles along both banks of the river—from south of Eugene to the river's mouth northwest of Portland. It will include a chain of parks, campsites, trails, drives, and marinas.

Reservoirs near the river's headwaters have tamed the Willamette's rampaging floods, and much has been done to clean up the river. The state park system and various cities and counties now hold many miles of river bank. Boaters can go ashore or camp on a sandy beach or gravel bar almost anywhere along the river, except where owners have posted it private.

Canoeing and cruising. The upper Willamette froths and gambols like a mountain stream until it begins its long meander north through the valley beyond Eugene and Springfield. Essentially a lazy river, it still offers canoeists and kayakers plenty of fast chutes and white water all the way to Corvallis, but with long, lazy stretches in between. Lush banks lined by cottonwoods and willows invite campers up from the river's sand and gravel bars.

Below Corvallis the river widens, gathering tributaries and dignity as it flows northward. Water activity increases—as do boat launching ramps and marinas—especially around Corvallis, Albany, Salem, and Wilsonville. You can hunt for rough agates and jasper pebbles in gravel bars exposed by summer's low water.

At Oregon City boaters by-pass Willamette Falls by means of locks along the west bank of the river, behind the paper mill. Passage through the locks is free; they operate 7 days a week from 8 A.M. to midnight. Once a boat enters, it takes about 45 minutes to pass through the series of locks.

As the Willamette passes through Portland, it becomes a broad canal, most of its shoreline straightened and sea-walled. Several marinas operate along this stretch of the urban river, and it is exhilarating to be part of the downtown Willamette River traffic.

Cruising in an open boat on the river can be unexpectedly hot; you'll probably want sun lotion and a hat. Besides food, carry drinking water.

Boating on the Willamette has increased in recent years. You'll often see wildlife in the river's natural areas, and numerous waterside parks dot the river banks.

Wildlife. Great blue herons fish in the river's quiet reaches, wild canaries dart among wildflowers on the banks, and crayfish scuttle out of sight in the clear shallows. Occasionally you'll see a beaver in his natural habitat.

Fish are thriving again in the Willamette. Salmon and steelhead attract great crowds of anglers as the fish migrate upstream. Trout, bass, and other fresh-water fish await the fisherman's lure.

Boat rentals. If you don't have your own boat, you'll find limited boat rental opportunities, but if you search in the larger cities, you can rent canoes and other small craft.

Ferrying across the Willamette

Many roads and highways cross or touch the Willamette, but no scenic routes follow the river for extended stretches; early road builders avoided the muddy lowlands and sought higher ground.

Motorists can get acquainted with the Willamette in its various moods at numerous parks along the river. Another pleasant prospect is a short ferry ride across the Willamette on any of three free county-operated ferries that transport traffic across the river. Each ferry accommodates four to six cars—and an occasional cyclist or two—per trip, making continuous crossings during daylight hours. Electrically powered cables operate the ferries.

Canby. North Holly Street runs about 3 miles north from Canby on State 99E to the ferry landing. A county park north of the crossing provides picnic facilities and a boat launching ramp.

Wheatland. This ferry crosses the Willamette 12 miles north of Salem. In river boat days, vast amounts of grain were shipped from a settlement here.

Buena Vista. Located midway between Albany and Salem, this river crossing has had ferry service since 1851. To reach it from Interstate 5, drive about 4 miles west from the Talbot turnoff. In the 1860s, pottery was manufactured here and shipped throughout the Northwest; artists still occasionally use the clay deposit on the bank.

The joy of shunpiking

To see the best of the Willamette Valley, you must leave the main roads and explore the network of country roads that wind through small towns and farm lands, up tributary rivers and creeks, and into foothills overlooking the valley. You can explore simply for the fun of it, or you may select your route with a definite destination in mind. On nearly any summer weekend, you can find a valley fair or festival.

If you prefer to pick your route, obtain county-issued recreation maps showing lakes and reservoirs, picnic and camping areas, covered bridges, and other points of interest. Use these in combination with the state highway map and other materials providing detailed road and recreation information.

Canby Ferry transports motorists and cyclists across the Willamette River north of Canby. Other ferries operate upriver at Wheatland and Buena Vista crossings.

Map in hand, you can explore country roads that play hide-and-seek with streams. Your route may cross covered bridges or pass 19th century churches. On byways through farm lands, you see spacious old farmhouses and barns and farmers working in the fields. In summer, many farmers sell their produce at roadside stands or invite you to pick on their land (check local newspapers). If you've brought picnic supplies, you'll have no problem finding a pleasant spot to spread your lunch.

Most country routes are two-lane paved roads with little traffic, winding through valley farm lands. Occasional stretches of graded gravel road are no problem for passenger vehicles.

Birthplace of Oregon

The lower Willamette Valley was the birthplace of American government in the Oregon country. It was here that pioneers settled to farm the rich lands and, in a historic vote at Champoeg, that a majority of settlers voted to cast their lot with the United States.

Oregon City, which grew along the Willamette River at the site of an impressive waterfall, became the center of government west of the Rockies. Settlements grew up along the territorial roads; many of these towns are now linked by State 99W and 99E west and east of the river.

Oregon City, territorial capital

In the 1840s, Oregon City was the Northwest's major city and capital of the vast Oregon Territory.

The town grew up near the base of Willamette Falls, a 41-foot drop that provided power for mills (it still does). A transportation industry grew, since it was necessary to portage cargo and passengers around the falls.

Oregon City is 12 miles south of Portland near the confluence of the Clackamas and Willamette rivers. The town's business district borders the river; its residential area is atop the high bluff east of the Willamette.

Municipal elevator. Pedestrians find a unique form of public utility in Oregon City; a free elevator transports some 1,800 passengers each day between the town's upper and lower levels. The 130-foot-tall structure rises at 7th Street and Railroad Avenue. The elevator operates 7 days a week, and the 90-foot ride takes 15 seconds. On the upper level, a glass-enclosed viewing area offers a fine panorama of the river and falls.

Downtown attractions. You can see the original plat for the city of San Francisco in the County Clerk's office in the Clackamas County Court House at 8th and Main streets. Now framed and hanging on the wall, the historic document was filed in the District Court office of the territorial government on February 1, 1850; at that time Oregon City was the seat of the only organized government west of the Rockies.

Clackamas County Historical Society operates a museum in a house at 6th and Washington streets near the City Hall.

CENTRAL WILLAMETTE VALLEY

Riverside parks. Good sites for river-oriented recreation are Clackamette Park, at the confluence of the Clackamas and Willamette rivers, and West Linn's fine Willamette Park. You can picnic, swim, launch a boat, fish from shore or craft, or water-ski at both parks. Willamette Park also has a playground.

Industrial tours. Inquire at the Tri-City Chamber of Commerce in Oregon City for information on guided tours of Oregon City's paper mills.

Home of "the father of Oregon"

On the bluff east of the river, the former home of Dr. John McLoughlin stands as a monument to the man who has been called "the father of Oregon."

Factor (chief agent) and superintendent of Hudson's Bay Company at Fort Vancouver, Dr. McLoughlin encouraged the American emigrants to settle in the fertile Willamette Valley. He found it difficult to ignore their needs, so he supplied many settlers with food, seed, milk cows, and farm implements.

In 1828 he and British Governor Simpson chose the falls of the Willamette as the site for a sawmill to process timber for Pacific markets. In 1842 the town by the falls was surveyed and named Oregon City; it became the capital of the provisional government and the seat of the vast Oregon Territory.

As the volume of new settlers increased, Dr. McLoughlin's loyalty to Britain wavered. In 1845 he resigned his position with Hudson's Bay Company and settled at Oregon City, where he lived until his death in 1857.

His compact, two-story, white clapboard house is now open to visitors. Located atop the bluff at 713 Center Street, it has been carefully restored and refurnished with items from the territorial period, including many of Dr. McLoughlin's personal articles. It is open daily except Monday from 10 A.M. to 5 P.M. in summer, from 10 A.M. to 4 P.M. in winter. The graves of Dr. McLoughlin and his wife are now located just north of the house.

Next door is another historic house—the former residence of Dr. Forbes Barclay, a civic leader from 1850 to 1872.

Willamette Falls and its locks

Approximately 26 miles above the mouth of the Willamette, the river plunges 41 feet over a rocky, horseshoe-shaped reef. When the salmon migrate upriver in spring, fishermen in boats congregate near the base of the foaming falls.

Between 1870 and 1872, a series of locks were built along the west side of the river to facilitate transportation. The government purchased the locks from private owners in 1915, and they have since been operated by the U.S. Army Corps of Engineers. The locks handle more than a million tons of traffic each year; rafted logs and paper and paper products make up most of the commercial traffic. Pleasure boats and other small craft also pass through the locks. Passage is free to all craft.

When salmon migrate upstream in spring, fishermen congregate near the base of Willamette Falls near Oregon City.

Catalogs in hand, gardeners note their daffodil selections at a commercial bulb farm northeast of Canby.

To see the locks in operation (daily between 8 A.M. and midnight) cross the bridge from Oregon City to West Linn and turn left. A walkway down to the river leads to the lockmaster's office and several good view points.

West Linn's Camassia Natural Area

An island of rare plants occupies a 22½-acre site atop West Linn's high basalt bluff. You'll find the small Camassia Natural Area immediately east of West Linn High School.

Isolated by the glacial Missoula Flood at the end of the Ice Age, the small natural area contains more than 300 species of plants rare to this part of the Northwest. Groups of students come here to study the plants and wildflowers, but the area is open to other visitors as well. The flood also deposited several erratic boulders and gouged ponds in the meadows.

A historic loop

From Oregon City or Portland, you can make a day's loop trip including a stop at the Aurora Colony in Aurora, a free ride across the Willamette on the Canby ferry, and a visit to historic Champoeg State Park.

Canby's flower fields. One of Oregon's horticultural centers, Canby is a commercial growing area for many types of flowers—including dahlias, irises, daffodils, gladioluses, pansies, lilies, and perennials —as well as shrubs and trees for wholesale and retail nurseries and evergreen seedlings for reforestation. New varieties of horticultural and agricultural products are grown and tested at Oregon State University's North Willamette Experiment Station northwest of Canby. In spring and summer you can see blooming flower fields from rural roads east and west of State 99E.

From Canby, North Holly Street heads north to the Willamette.

Each August Canby hosts the Clackamas County Fair—an old-fashioned county fair with modern trimmings.

Communal living in Aurora. The small town of Aurora, 13 miles southwest of Oregon City, was the site of the Aurora Colony, an unusual experiment in Christian communal living. Dedicated to living by the golden rule, the nondenominational religious community was established here in 1856 and thrived for almost 25 years. Its citizens pursued interests in music, literature, and philosophy, and the colony's highly skilled craftsmen fashioned furniture and household articles that have become "Colony-style" collectors' items.

Several of the colony buildings have been restored by people who appreciate the life style of this pioneer society. At Aurora's Ox Barn Museum —housed in one of the original buildings—you can see examples of the furniture, household articles, and crafts familiar to members of the colony. Several other buildings of the 1860s have been restored nearby.

Visitors are guided on informal tours of the colony buildings Wednesday through Sunday from

1 to 5 P.M. (closed January); groups should make advance arrangements.

Each April the Aurora Colony Historical Society serves a family-style sausage dinner at the Ox Barn Museum. All buildings are open during the day, and you can see demonstrations of colony crafts.

Historic Champoeg

Twenty miles upriver from Oregon City is Champoeg (pronounced Sham-POO-ig), one of the most historically significant sites in the Pacific Northwest. Several important meetings were held here in the early 1840s, resulting in the formation of the Oregon provisional government.

With its natural boat landing on the river and the rich prairie land nearby, Champoeg attracted white men from the start. Many trappers settled here permanently to farm after retiring from Hudson's Bay Company.

A decisive vote. By 1843, settlers in the Willamette Valley felt the need of a civil government, though Hudson's Bay Company ruled the land at the time. At the Champoeg meeting, they voted to decide whether they should write their own constitution or continue under the rules of the British company. By a vote of 52 to 50, the Willamette settlers decided to write their own document.

The provisional government of Oregon was followed by territorial status in 1848 and statehood (for Oregon, not the entire territory) in 1859.

Champoeg became a fair-sized town, but in the winter of 1861-62, the Willamette's greatest flood swept away most of its buildings.

Oregon's winemakers invite you to visit

A tour through an Oregon winery can be a casual, relaxed visit with a winemaker who loves tending his vineyards and making his wine.

Oregon wineries are small-scale operations with an air of informality that allows you a close look at the winemaking process, from the growing of grapes to the labeling of bottles. Your guide—who may be the winemaker himself —will show you wine presses, wooden aging barrels, perhaps a hand corking machine. Most wineries combine traditional methods with modern equipment. And when you get to the tasting room, you'll discover why Oregon wines are getting increased attention.

Oregonians made wine before Prohibition, but the winemaking revival didn't begin until 1961, when 20 acres were planted near Roseburg. Now hundreds of acres of vineyards are under cultivation.

Most of Oregon's table wine grapes are grown in the Willamette Valley in the north and the Umpqua Valley in the south, but numerous small vineyards are found throughout the state. Winemakers credit the even temperatures of the summer and fall growing season with producing premium grapes; climate and growing factors resemble those of prime northern European growing areas.

The following seven wineries make dry table wines from vinifera grapes (varieties grown only for wine). Before you set out to visit any of these country wineries, call for directions.

Each winery has one or two wines it considers special—among them Riesling, Chardonnay, Gewürztraminer, Cabernet Sauvignon, and Pinot Noir. To learn of a winery's new bottlings, ask to be put on the mailing list.

Charles Coury Vineyards, P.O. Box 372, Forest Grove, OR 97116; phone 357-7602. Located off David Hill Road, the winery and part of the vineyard stand on a knoll known as Wine Hill. Visitors are welcome from 1 to 5 P.M. daily.

The Eyrie Vineyards, P.O. Box 204, Dundee, OR 97115; phone 864-2410 or 472-6315. You can visit the winery at 935 E. 10th Street, McMinnville, on most weekends for tours, tasting, and purchases, but call ahead for an appointment.

Knudsen-Erath Winery, Rt. 1, Box 368, Dundee OR 97115; phone 538-3318. Touring and tasting are by appointment. The winery is located off Worden Hill Road behind Crabtree Park.

Ponzi Vineyards, Rt. 1, Box 842, Beaverton, OR 97005; phone 628-1227. This small, family owned winery is striving to maintain traditional winemaking techniques. It is located 15 miles south of Portland, 4½ miles south of Washington Square on State 210. Tour and tasting by appointment.

Tualatin Vineyards, Rt. 1, Box 339, Forest Grove, OR 97116; phone 357-5005. You can tour the winery—on Seavy Road northwest of town— and taste wines on weekends from noon to 6 P.M. and by appointment.

Bjelland Vineyards, Rt. 4, Box 931, Roseburg, OR 97470; phone 679-6950 or 679-5288. Bjelland is open from 11 A.M. to 5 P.M. daily except Tuesday. To reach the winery, turn off State 42 on Reston Road near Tenmile.

Hillcrest Vineyard, Rt. 3, Box 3095, Roseburg, OR 97470; phone 673-3709. This winery, oldest now producing in Oregon, offers tours and tasting daily from 10 A.M. to 5 P.M. To reach it, drive west from Interstate 5 on Garden Valley Road and follow signs northwest of Melrose to Elgarose Road.

Two other Oregon wineries are better known for the production of fruit wines: Honeywood Winery (see page 74) and Oak Knoll Winery, Rt. 4, Box 185B, Hillsboro, OR 97123 (phone 648-8198).

Vintners and the wine-loving public gather to celebrate the grape at festivals in Milwaukie (in mid-July) and Roseburg (late September). A harvest tour of the Willamette Valley wineries is held in October.

For more information on Oregon wines and wineries, write to the Wine Growers Council of Oregon, 816 S.W. First St., Portland, OR 97204; or the Oregon Wine Growers Association, P.O. Box 367, Roseburg, OR 97470. □

Champoeg today. Except on busy summer weekends, Champoeg State Park is a quiet place. You can study the historic monument, walk down to the river's edge, and wander through a garden of native trees and plants. You'll find camping and picnicking areas in the park.

A state museum contains an extensive collection of items from early statehood days, emphasizing the role of river transportation.

Two other museums trace the history of the settlement. The Pioneer Mother's Home is a replica of a settler's log cabin, furnished with period furniture and household items. Adjacent to the park, the two-story clapboard Robert Newell residence is a restoration of a Champoeg house built in 1852. Both private museums are open daily except Mondays.

The state park has its own bicycle trail—a pleasant 3-mile route meandering southward from the park to the rural hamlet of Butteville.

The rural charms of French Prairie

In pioneer days, the grassy undulating plain south of Champoeg was known as French Prairie, named for the French-Canadians who settled here—most of them former trappers. Bounded on the west and east by the Willamette and Pudding rivers and on the south by Salem, this fertile wedge became a wheat-growing area in the 1830s and '40s.

Several streams cut north across the plain to meet the Willamette. Country roads crisscross the area. From Newberg, State Highway 219 goes south to St. Paul, noted for its 1846 church and the annual St. Paul Rodeo in July. Many early settlers are buried in the local cemetery, one of several historic burial sites in the region.

Partisans of early farm machinery gather in Brooks each August for the Antique Powerland Farm Fair (also known as the Great Oregon Steamup). Among the entries that parade and perform are steam-powered tractors, threshing machines, and traction engines.

Woodburn, past and present

Woodburn's pioneer father was Jesse Settlemier, who arrived here in 1863 with his bride. In 1889, after the town's growth was assured, he built a showcase house on Boones Ferry Road. A triumph of carpenter's artistry, the restored Settlemier house is a Woodburn landmark, a community activity center for meetings and social events, and a museum of French Prairie memorabilia.

Woodburn—home of more than 2,000 Spanish-speaking residents—hosts a Mexican Fiesta in early August. Other local events include a Mardi Gras celebration in February and a Chuck Wagon Breakfast on the Fourth of July.

In the early 1960s, Russian immigrants seeking religious freedom established a small colony of farms southeast of Woodburn. They dress in conservative garb and follow fundamentalist religious practices. Men are not allowed to shave their beards nor women to cut their hair.

Combine a winery tour with a picnic. This family chooses an attractive hillside spot overlooking vineyards of the Tualatin Valley near Forest Grove.

Newberg, Herbert Hoover's boyhood home

Motorists traveling on State 99W between Portland and McMinnville pass within a block of the boyhood home of former President Herbert Hoover.

After the death of his parents, the 10-year-old boy came to Newberg in 1884 to live with his aunt and uncle, Dr. and Mrs. Henry Minthorn. The house where he lived for 5 years is now a museum. Located at S. River and E. Second streets, it is open Tuesday through Saturday from 10 A.M. to noon and 1 to 4 P.M., on Sunday from 2 to 5 P.M.

The two-story white frame house is furnished in the style of the 1880s; it has a neatly kept garden and a well near the back door. In Hoover's small bedroom you'll see some of his schoolboy treasures.

During his stay in Newberg, Hoover attended Pacific Academy, now George Fox College, a liberal arts school still run by the Society of Friends.

Yamhill County byways

Southwest of Tigard, State 99W passes quickly into farming country. West of the river, roads wind through rolling hills covered by neat orchards and fields planted with strawberries, wheat, grapes, beans, and other vegetables. In late summer, you may see roadside stands offering locally grown produce for sale.

Largest of the towns are McMinnville, dominated by Linfield College, and Newberg, home of George Fox College.

Nearly every community has its ties with valley history—old houses and stores, a grange or coun-

Cyclists pedal leisurely through Willamette Valley farm lands. Level terrain, minimum traffic, and interesting way points make pastoral roads inviting.

try school, perhaps a pioneer church or cemetery.

Dayton has a number of 19th century buildings; Fort Yamhill blockhouse stands in the city park. The Yamhill County Historical Museum in Lafayette is housed in an 1890 church.

Among parks of special interest are Bald Peak State Park, northwest of Newberg off State 219, where you have wonderful views and can picnic beneath Douglas firs; Erratic Rock Wayside southwest of McMinnville, resting site of a massive boulder rafted here by a glacier during the Ice Age; and Yamhill Locks County Park, southwest of Dayton, on the Yamhill River.

South of Dayton, State Highway 221 parallels the Willamette. A side road leads to quiet Grand Island, encircled by the river. Maud Williamson State Park offers a pleasant spot to picnic. You can cross the Willamette on the Wheatland ferry (see page 67) or continue south to Salem.

Northwest of Salem

In the pastoral countryside north of Silverton, creeks wind down from the foothills to join the Pudding and Molalla rivers. State 213, 211, and 214 can be combined with country roads to discover placid settlements, 19th century churches, and pioneer cemeteries.

From State 213 you can detour to rustic Scotts Mills, then return to the highway to continue north to Molalla. On the return journey, you'll pass through Mount Angel.

Molalla Buckeroo. Since 1913, this outstanding rodeo has been a feature of Molalla's July 4 celebration. Members of the Warm Springs Confederated tribes participate in the festivities, which include a parade, picnic, and Indian dances. An old-fashioned beef barbecue with "all the fixings"—irreverently dubbed the Holy Cow Barbecue—is served at the Molalla Methodist Church on July 4. Fireworks follow the evening rodeo performance.

Mount Angel. From the parking area of the Mount Angel Abbey, the valley is a tapestry of green and gold fields stretching to the foothills of the Cascades. The Abbey Bach Festival is held here in July.

In September the community turns into a Bavarian-style village during the 4-day Oktoberfest celebration. Residents dressed in traditional costumes celebrate the community's German-Swiss ancestry with a biergarten, Bavarian-style foods and crafts, folk dancing, and strolling musicians.

The central valley

The heart of the Willamette Valley boasts a rich and diversified agriculture. Country roads cut through fields planted in row crops and berries, orchards of fruit and nut trees, pasture lands for dairy and beef cattle, and broad acreages where much of the nation's grass seed is harvested.

Salem, the state capital, lies at the center of the valley. Other major towns are Corvallis, home of Oregon State University, and Albany, center of the grass seed industry and rare metals manufacturing.

Salem, the state capital

Oregon's capital city marks the heart of the fertile valley some 50 miles south of the Columbia.

One of the valley's oldest cities, Salem was settled by the Reverend Jason Lee and his small group of Methodist missionaries who arrived in the Willamette Valley in 1834. The churchmen established an Indian mission and founded the Oregon Institute (now Willamette University). The men of the mission were influential in the settlement and orderly development of the Oregon country by American citizens.

Visiting the capitol. Heading the list of Salem's attractions is the white marble capitol, topped by a 24-foot Pioneer statue covered in gold leaf. Marble sculptures flank the Court Street entrance; they honor the Lewis and Clark Expedition and the pioneers who traveled along the Oregon Trail.

In the capitol rotunda, the polished bronze state seal gleams on the floor directly beneath the dome. Murals on the rotunda walls—and in the Senate and House chambers on the second floor—depict historic events in Oregon's early years.

At the rear of the rotunda, you can obtain maps and travel information in a visitors' information lounge, open from 8 A.M. to 5 P.M. Monday through Saturday (in summer, also from noon to 5 P.M. on Sundays and holidays).

Capitol tours. From June 15 through August, tours depart from the rotunda at 9, 10, and 11 A.M. and 2, 3 and 4 P.M. Winter tours for groups are by appointment. Tour groups visit the Senate and House chambers and the Governor's office. Oregon's legislature convenes on the second Monday in January in odd-numbered years.

If you want to climb the 121 spiral steps of the

tower, trips depart every half hour from 9 to 11:30 A.M. and 1 to 3:30 P.M. The tower is closed on days when temperatures exceed 90°.

Park areas. Several inviting park areas border the capitol. To the west is Willson Park, an attractive landscaped strip with a fountain. The capitol mall extends north of Court Street. An arboretum of labeled trees is located east of the capitol.

Other Salem highlights

Though the state capitol attracts most of the visitors, Salem has a number of other attractions as well. Like many other Oregon towns, Salem is rejuvenating its downtown area. The new Civic Center and gracious old Bush Pasture Park offer inviting places to stroll.

Civic Center. In 1972 Salem's city offices and public library moved to an attractive civic complex between Commercial and Liberty streets—a delight of modern architecture, landscaped plazas, fountains, sculpture, and art. The main entrance is at 533 Liberty Street S.E.

East of the city buildings, landscaped bike trails and footpaths follow Mill and Pringle Creeks. A five-block area along Trade Street is being transformed into the Pringle Park Plaza. Landscaping, walkways, and benches enhance the natural attraction of the Mill Race and its waterfalls and bridges.

Downtown landmarks. The old Reed's Opera House, center of Salem's cultural and social life during the Victorian era, has been transformed into a shopping complex in the heart of the business district. Built in 1871 at N.E. Court and Liberty streets, the old building now houses specialty shops on its ground and basement levels.

Another pioneer building with a new lease on life is the Ladd and Bush Bank, now a branch of the U.S. National Bank of Oregon at 302 State Street. Its ornate cast-iron moldings were popular for store fronts during the 1860s.

Willamette University. A gracious tree-shaded campus and sturdy red brick buildings testify to the New England heritage of its founders. Located behind the capitol, the university is known for its colleges of liberal arts, music, and law, and the graduate school of administration.

Bush Pasture Park. Salem's favorite park was once the country estate of Asahel Bush, one of Salem's civic leaders in the 1870s. He built his Victorian country mansion at the edge of the city in 1878; now Salem surrounds the farm. The garden and grounds contain some of the west's oldest tree plantings.

The Salem Art Association maintains the 2-story, 13-room Bush house as a museum. Many of the family's original furnishings give the Victorian building a lived-in feeling. Elegant as well as utilitarian, the mansion has many innovations and comforts unusual in the gaslight era. The house is open daily except Mondays from 2 to 5 P.M. (in summer from noon to 5 P.M. Tuesday through Saturday and 2 to 5 P.M. Sundays).

Behind the house, the farm's barn has been remodeled as an art center and gallery. The Art Association schedules exhibits featuring the work of local and Northwest artists and craftsmen and maintains a year-round program of classes. Bush Barn is open from 9:30 A.M. to 5 P.M. Tuesday through Friday, 1 to 5 P.M. Saturday and Sunday.

Each July, art combines with a "Sunday in the park" atmosphere during the annual art festival. Paintings, sculpture, pottery, and crafts are displayed in the barn and on the grounds.

Mission Mill Museum. Historic buildings of Salem's early days have been assembled at Thomas Kay Historical Park southeast of the capitol.

Restoration has been completed on the Jason Lee house and the parsonage of the Methodist Mission, both built in 1841, and the John D. Boon house, built in 1847. Currently undergoing restoration are buildings of the Thomas Kay Woolen Mill, which operated here in the 1890s.

From June through August the museum is open from 10 A.M. to 5 P.M. Tuesday through Saturday, 1:30 to 4:30 P.M. on Sunday. The rest of the year, hours are 1:30 to 4:30 P.M. daily except Mondays.

Other favorite parks. Southeast of Salem on Turner Road is Cascade Gateway Park, a 100-acre area oriented to family recreation.

Salem's main riverside park is Wallace Marine Park, on the west bank of the Willamette River at the end of Musgrave Lane. You'll find picnic tables, a boat ramp, and horseshoe pits.

Salem's modern civic center complex offers simple benches, landscaped plazas, and cool fountains. Cyclists find landscaped bike trails along nearby creeks.

Classic lines distinguish the Memorial Union at Oregon State University. You can park nearby and stroll around part of the campus. Don't miss the Horner Museum.

Wine tasting. Oregon's oldest winery—Honeywood Winery, founded in 1933—welcomes visitors to stop and taste its fruit and berry wines. Located at 501 14th Street S.E., it is open from 9 A.M. to 4 P.M. on weekdays, and 10 A.M. to 4 P.M. on Saturdays.

Oregon State Fair. The state's agriculture, industries, and natural resources are on display during the 10-day run of the Oregon State Fair, which climaxes on Labor Day weekend. The fairgrounds are located northeast of Salem's central district at 17th Street N.E. and Silverton Road. Though agricultural and commercial displays are a major part of the fair, people still exhibit their prize animals, pickles, and quilts and compete for awards.

Enchanted Forest. Wooded trails lead into a world of fantasy and make-believe in this woodland setting 7 miles south of Salem near Interstate 5. Storybook scenes are depicted in larger-than-life replicas. The attraction is open from May through October from 9:30 A.M. until dusk.

Waterfalls in abundance

If the sight and sound of falling water soothes and revives your spirit, head for Silver Falls State Park in the Cascade foothills east of Salem. Located on State Highway 214 about 26 miles east of the capital, the park offers waterfalls in abundance in a pair of lovely wooded canyons cut by the North and South forks of Silver Creek.

You hike from waterfall to waterfall on a 7-mile loop through Silver Creek Canyon; the trail passes 9 of the park's 14 waterfalls—5 of them plunging 100 feet or more. Spur trails allow you to shorten your route if you wish. Ferns and wildflowers mark the trails. Tributary streams tumble in misty veils of spray or form quiet pools. Rustic footbridges span the creeks, and trailside benches invite you to linger at scenic points. The park also has a 4-mile bike path and an additional 13-mile network of hiking and horse trails.

A day-use lodge and picnic facilities are located near the trailhead to South Falls. Camping facilities for families and groups are also available.

Meandering Polk County byways

Southwest of Salem, you can follow a meandering road west of the Willamette or explore old logging settlements near the base of the foothills.

Rickreall, at the crossroads of State 22, 99W, and 223, is known for its Christmas pageant. Dallas is the seat of Polk County. The campus of Oregon College of Education is located in Monmouth, and nearby Independence is renovating some of its downtown facades to emphasize the town's historic buildings.

Midway between Salem and Albany, you'll enjoy a detour to the Buena Vista ferry, one of three that cross the Willamette (see page 67).

State 223 loops near the base of the thickly forested Coast Range. Side roads branch west from the main road to small logging settlements. The historic Ritner Creek covered bridge, long a Polk County landmark, has been moved a stone's throw from its former site and will become part of a wayside park along State 223.

Corvallis, home of Oregon State University

West of the Willamette, Corvallis marks the intersection of U.S. 20 and State 99W. It is the seat of Benton County and the home of Oregon State University.

Downtown, take a look at the fine old Benton County Court House. Built in 1888, the classically simple main building and its clock tower contrast with the modern wing.

Avery Park, a 75-acre recreation area south of U.S. 20, has plenty of picnicking sites, broad lawns, a pleasant rose garden, and children's play area.

Headquarters for the community's art groups is the Corvallis Art Center, housed in a renovated 1889 church building at 7th and Madison streets. Visitors browse through art exhibits, a sales-rental gallery, and a gift gallery; hours are noon to 5 P.M. daily except Mondays. The main gallery, marked by wood-beamed ceilings and arched windows, also serves as a theater and concert hall.

Stroll on the Oregon State campus

Dominating and enriching the town of Corvallis is Oregon State University, home-away-from-home for some 16,000 students. Downtown signs direct you to the 500-acre campus in the western part of town.

Visitors can obtain courtesy parking permits at campus information centers.

For a look at the heart of the campus, drive west on Jefferson and park in the visitors' area east of Memorial Union; you can stroll around the older part of the campus.

Sports fans can watch OSU teams compete

against Pacific Eight Conference rivals and other top college teams. Football and track teams compete in 41,000-seat Parker Stadium, while basketball contests are held in Gill Coliseum.

The Horner Museum in Gill Coliseum contains an excellent array of pioneer items, Indian artifacts, and exhibits depicting features of Oregon's natural history—including minerals, fossils, and birds. The museum is open daily except Monday from October to June, weekdays only in summer. Inquire about the museum's summer folk festival.

Albany's Timber Carnival

Bordering the river's east bank, Albany sits 70 miles south of Portland at the hub of the valley's prime agricultural lands; the town is a leading producer of rye grass seed and mint.

The town is best known for its World Championship Timber Carnival, a 3-day celebration saluting the Northwest timber industry. Burly loggers gather here over the July 4 holiday to compete in championship log chopping, bucking, speed climbing, tree topping, log birling, ax throwing, and jousting. Competition is held outdoors at Timber Linn Lake east of Interstate 5. Spectators also enjoy a big parade and fireworks display on the 4th.

City parks are scattered throughout Albany; favorite ones are the centrally located Swanson Park with its municipal swimming pool, Waverly Lake Park at Pacific Boulevard and Salem Road, and Bryant Park bordering the Willamette near downtown Albany.

Oregon's newest incorporated town is Millersburg, formerly an industrial park in the northeast part of Albany. The new community is an important manufacturing center of rare metals.

Exploring Linn County back roads

The pastoral countryside east of Albany invites leisurely exploration of back roads and country settlements. Small streams meander down from the foothills toward the Willamette. You'll discover historic settlements, covered bridges, and scenic spots for a picnic. Stop at the Albany Area Chamber of Commerce for a county recreation map.

You can take a look at Jefferson, once a river boat town on the South Santiam; Scio, gateway to a cluster of covered bridges; Stayton, an agricultural center on the Marion-Linn county border; Lebanon, which celebrates its local strawberries with a civic festival; historic Brownsville; and Sweet Home, a favorite area for rockhounds.

Covered bridges. If searching out covered bridges strikes your fancy, you'll find five along Thomas Creek: two south of the Jefferson-Scio road, the red Shimanek bridge northeast of Scio, and two more east of Scio just south of State Highway 226.

Two more covered bridges cross Crabtree Creek east of Crabtree, and you'll find another—now unused—at Crawfordsville.

Strawberry shortcake. Highlight of Lebanon's annual June Strawberry Festival is the world's largest shortcake—an 8-foot-tall pyramid using some 3,000 pounds of fresh strawberries. It is served to over 16,000 festival guests after the Saturday parade.

Historic Brownsville. Founded in 1846, this town bordering State Highway 228 looks toward the past. Business facades create the look of the 1890s to blend with the town's numerous fine old homes.

Mementos of the past are displayed in the Linn County Historical Museum, open afternoons daily except Monday from May through September, weekend afternoons in winter. You can also visit the restored Moyer House, an elegant mansion erected by one of the city's founders; it is open from 2 to 5 P.M. daily except Monday.

Oregon's oldest continuing community festival—begun in 1887—is the Linn County Pioneer Picnic, celebrated here each June with 3 days of festivities. Among the traditional events are a flower show, spelling bee, loggers' jamboree, and a tug of war across the river.

Rockhounding near Sweet Home. Rock hunters look for petrified wood and Holley blue agate in the Holley-Sweet Home area near State 228. The local Chamber of Commerce can direct you to good digging areas. Sweet Home hosts a rock and mineral show in late March.

Sweet Home is the gateway to recreation on the South Santiam River and its tributary reservoirs. In July the Sportsmen's Holiday celebration features speedboat racing, a water carnival, and a logging contest.

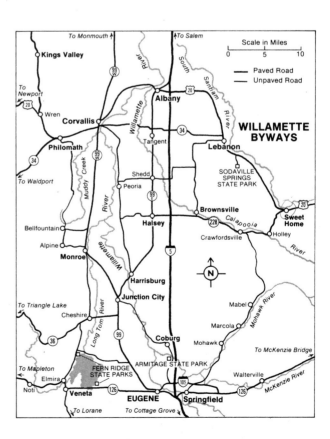

University of Oregon landmark is vine-covered Deady Hall, built in 1876; the 3-story building housed the school's first classes and is still in daily use.

The Emerald Empire

Lane County calls itself the Emerald Empire — a spacious region stretching from the ocean beaches to the crest of the Cascades. Forests cover many valley foothills, and in a matter of minutes, Eugene and Springfield residents can journey to wooded glades far removed from urban bustle. Numerous lumber mills and forest products industries dot the area.

Dominating the region is Eugene, the state's second largest city (95,000) and home of the University of Oregon. Neighboring Springfield adds another 35,000 to the metropolitan population.

Getting acquainted with Eugene

A landscaped pedestrian mall brightens the heart of Eugene's downtown business district. Trees, flowers, a fountain, benches, and children's play areas transform Willamette Street—between 7th and 11th avenues—and intersecting streets into an attractive shopping and rendezvous area.

Several blocks east is the civic center. The Lane County Court House and Eugene City Hall occupy modern quarters between East 7th and 8th avenues; across the street is a downtown park.

Downtown renewal has triggered the restoration of several old buildings. A popular shopping area is the Smeede Hotel at 767 Willamette, now filled with three floors of shops, boutiques, and restaurants. The recently renovated Quackenbush's Hardware Store, located at 160 E. Broadway, has been a downtown institution since 1903; employees ring up sales on hand-cranked cash registers for items ranging from kerosene lamps and pickle crocks to gourmet foods and hardware supplies.

You'll see joggers and cyclists everywhere, and canoeing is a fast-growing local sport. Sailors and water-skiers head for Fern Ridge Reservoir west of Eugene; this vast lake on the Long Tom River is the site of many sailing competitions. Parks and boat ramps dot the shoreline.

Downtown markets. Area craftsmen and vendors display their hand-produced or home-grown wares for sale at the Saturday Market, held each weekend from April until Christmas at 7th and Oak. The open-air bazaar now operates every Saturday and Sunday from 10 A.M. to 5 P.M. on the upper deck of the parking structure west of the Court House.

New in 1976, the Fifth Street Public Market at Fifth and High is open daily except Monday. Local farmers, home gardeners, and area craftsmen offer home-grown or hand-prepared foods and craft items.

Museums and art. Similar in concept to its parent organization in Portland, the Southwest Oregon Museum of Science and Industry offers an intriguing array of exhibits and scientific experiments. Currently located at 27 E. 5th Avenue, it plans to move to new quarters in Alton Baker Park in late 1977 or early 1978. The museum is open from 10 A.M. to 6 P.M. Tuesday through Saturday.

The Lane County Pioneer Museum offers a look at 19th century Lane County—photographs, household and agricultural tools, and vehicles including an authentic covered wagon. Located at 740 W. 13th Avenue, the museum is open 9 A.M. to 5 P.M. Monday through Thursday, 1 to 5 P.M. Saturday and Sunday. Museum personnel can direct you to some of Eugene's fine pre-1900 houses.

Indian crafts and culture of more than 100 North American tribes provide the theme of the Butler Museum of American Indian Art at 1155 W. 1st Avenue. The museum is open daily except Monday from 10 A.M. to 5 P.M.

The Maude I. Kerns Art Center at 1910 E. 15th Avenue coordinates Eugene's art activities. Open daily except Friday from 1 to 5 P.M., it sponsors classes in various art forms for adults and children. On the premises you'll find varied exhibits, a sales-rental gallery, and a gift shop.

Eugene's outstanding parks. The city utilizes its river and surrounding wooded slopes as parklands for its residents. Numerous neighborhood parks dot the residential areas.

Bordering the Willamette's north bank is Alton Baker Park, the city's showcase project. You reach it from the city center by the Ferry Street Bridge or by log footbridge across the river from the University campus. Winding through this wooded, 500-acre regional park are a 4-mile riverside bike path (connecting Springfield, Eugene, and Valley River Center) and a 5-mile European-style jogging trail and parcourse. You can paddle a canoe or kayak along a 3-mile manmade canal, which winds lazily through a quiet landscape of green fields and tall trees. Canoes can be rented at the park in summer.

Well-used Skinner Butte Park borders the Willamette just north of the downtown area. Picnic areas, bike paths and foot trails, and a rose garden make this an enjoyable spot. A road leads to the view point atop the high, forested butte.

The city's oldest park area is Hendricks Park, a large natural forest on the slopes southeast of the university. You can picnic beneath the trees or follow trails through the conifer forest. The park's large garden of native rhododendrons and azaleas is a splendid sight in late spring.

Undeveloped Spencer Butte, 20 minutes south of the downtown area, offers a wooded hiking trail to Eugene's highest overlook.

Other points of interest. Several local industries welcome visitors. For information on companies offering tours, inquire at the Chamber of Commerce.

You can arrange a guided tour of the attractive Lane Community College campus in southeastern Eugene by phoning 747-4501, ext. 340.

The area's primary suburban shopping center is Valley River Center, bordering the Willamette River north of Eugene. Numerous stores and shops face an enclosed, climate-controlled mall.

Local events. Lean and tanned cowboys test their mettle against ornery rodeo stock during the Emerald Empire Roundup in July.

Area residents gather for old-fashioned fun during the Lane County Fair in August.

A look at the University of Oregon

The University of Oregon adds depth and cultural stimulation to the Eugene area. Founded in 1876,

the liberal arts school encompasses a 250-acre campus south of Franklin Boulevard in the eastern part of the city. Enrollment is about 17,000.

Visitors will find a guest parking lot at E. 13th and Agate and a metered parking area south of the Erb Memorial Union (EMU) at E. 13th and University. Permits are needed for parking in campus lots.

Guided 1-hour tours of the campus depart at 10:30 A.M. and 2:30 P.M. on weekdays from Oregon Hall at E. 13th and Agate. Free campus maps are available at the Information Booth here.

Center of student activity, the EMU is worth a look. The main building recently added an interesting new three-level wing.

Vine-covered buildings a block northwest of the EMU mark the oldest part of the campus. Deady Hall, completed in 1876, housed the school's first classrooms. Villard Hall was built in 1885 and Friendly Hall in 1893. The area surrounding Villard and Deady halls contains an exotic collection of trees from around the world.

The UO Geology Department has prepared an eight-page campus guide and map emphasizing the interesting geologic origins of many buildings. You can obtain a free copy from the Geology Department in the Science Complex (or by mail if you include a stamped, self-addressed envelope).

Recorded information on the day's university activities—including lectures, concerts, plays, and movies—is available by phoning 686-4636.

Museum of Natural History. Located on the west side of the Science Complex courtyard (facing E. 13th), this fascinating museum includes exhibits on

Covered bridges—reminders of a gentler era

Covered bridges add an enjoyable and nostalgic touch to the rural landscape of western Oregon. Most of them are found in wooded country, built from timber felled near the site. But the bridges are disappearing fast—victims of the easy transportation they helped to make possible.

Though designed for the era of horse and buggy transportation and Model Ts, many of the bridges still bear the traffic of everyday commerce on country routes. Some have been by-passed by newer spans, but preserved by local groups as reminders of a quieter day. The remaining bridges have become objects of affection, cherished even by persons who may never use or see them.

Oregon's first recorded covered bridge was built in 1851 at Oregon City. In the early days, builders felled big trees and prepared hand-hewn timbers near the crossing. Travelers were charged tolls to cross private bridges. Over the years, many covered spans were swept downstream by capricious flood waters.

Why covered bridges? Because the trusses and plank decking last longer when protected from the weather. The sheltered timbers even strengthen with age.

It is not deterioration that is bringing about

the replacement of covered bridges, but traffic far heavier than was foreseen when they were built. Yet even under today's heavy loads, the wooden spans hold up well.

A number of covered bridges are mentioned in this book. You can obtain additional information from local chambers of commerce or recreation officials. Several counties issue recreation maps noting the location of covered bridges as well as parks and other points of interest.

If you look at the bridges with a discerning eye, you'll note design differences varying from county to county. Portals may be rounded, square, or angled. Walls may be solid—except for slit windows just beneath the roof—or cut by eye-level "daylighting" windows, which enable drivers to glimpse oncoming traffic when the road curves beyond the bridge.

Open-sided, white bridges showing exposed trusses mark most of Linn County's bridges; a notable exception is the rebuilt Shimanek Bridge east of Scio with its barn red walls and attractive white trim. Many of Lane County's bridges have daylighting windows. Lincoln County's covered bridges can be recognized by their curved portals and flaring, windowless sidewalls. □

fossils, rocks and minerals, birds and animals, and plant life. It is open Monday through Friday from 8 A.M. to 4:30 P.M.

Museum of Art. A red brick, Moorish-influenced building north of the university library houses the university's art museum. Guided tours are available by appointment. A splendid collection of oriental art is augmented by works of contemporary Northwest and American artists and works from Pacific countries. Open daily except Monday from noon to 5 P.M., the museum features changing exhibits, a sales-rental gallery, and a gift shop.

Sports activities. The university is a member of the Pacific Eight Conference and competes in major and minor sports. Autzen Stadium (football) is located north of the Willamette; McArthur Court (basketball), Hayward Field (track), and other sports areas are located in the southern part of the campus. Eugene's intense interest in track and field attracts top athletes to locally hosted and national meets.

Students continue an old campus tradition as they paddle canoes along the meandering Mill Race in the northern part of the campus. On sunny days, canoes may be rented at the canoe shack north of Franklin Boulevard.

Springfield, gateway to the McKenzie River

East of the Willamette, Springfield is the gateway to the McKenzie River and a major center of Oregon's forest products industry.

Spacious Willamalane Park contains a large indoor swimming pool, a children's play area, and tennis courts. Each July the scent of barbecued chicken wafts over the park during Springfield's annual Broiler Festival; racks of chickens grill on outdoor barbecues during the 2-day community celebration. Downtown Springfield is the scene of a Christmas Parade in early December.

Tall trees shade the green lawns of Island Park along the broad Willamette at the western edge of Springfield's business district. The park offers inviting spots for riverside picnicking.

Logging and the varied wood products industry dominate the local economy. In addition to mills producing lumber, plywood, and veneer, local manufacturers market products ranging from shingles and kraft paper to fencing and agricultural mulch. For information on summer mill tours, stop at the Springfield Chamber of Commerce.

Seek out some covered bridges

Lane County is the heart of western Oregon's covered bridge country; about 20 covered bridges—some in use, some by-passed by newer roads—are still standing. Ask at the Eugene Chamber of Commerce for the Lane County parks map folder showing exact locations.

You'll find a concentration of old bridges near State Highway 58 (south of Dexter, and north of the highway on a Lowell-Fall Creek-Jasper route).

Three more are located up the McKenzie near State Highway 126 (see page 106).

Near Cottage Grove, two bridges cross the Row River and three more span Mosby Creek.

North of Springfield, the Mohawk River road passes near two more: the Wendling Bridge reached by a side road, another north of Marcola.

Give in to the wanderlust urge

When sunny weather awakens the wanderlust urge, Eugene and Springfield residents find a number of interesting roads fanning out from the urban area.

Coburg Road heads north from Eugene to attractive Armitage State Park on the south bank of the McKenzie. The road becomes Coburg's tree-lined main street, then continues another 12 miles through orchards and farm lands to meet State 99E.

From Harrisburg you can continue north to Corvallis on the Peoria Road, paralleling the meandering Willamette River.

Fall Creek Road follows the north shore of the reservoir to woodsy campgrounds. You can park just west of Dolly Varden Bridge and follow a level 4-mile trail along the south side of the creek. Or stroll along the 1-mile nature trail that begins at the north side of the parking area at Clark Creek Organization Camp.

A stretch of the old West Side Territorial Road—once a stagecoach route—winds through rolling hills west of Interstate 5 from Anlauf to Monroe. It passes through several farming communities, skirts the west side of Fern Ridge Reservoir, jogs 1½ miles east on State Highway 36 at Cheshire, and continues north to meet State 99W at Monroe.

A pleasant route follows the meandering Siuslaw

UPPER WILLAMETTE VALLEY

Paved Road
Unpaved Road

Scale in Miles
0   5   10

River northwest from Lorane for some 45 miles to meet State 126. Several parks along the way invite picnicking and fishing.

Scandinavian days in Junction City

Each August Junction City salutes its Scandinavian heritage and revives interest in its old-world roots during a 4-day community-wide celebration. Many local residents are descendants of the Danish farmers and Norwegian, Swedish, and Finnish lumbermen who settled here decades ago.

Residents dress in costume, prepare Scandinavian foods, demonstrate old-country handicrafts and folk dancing, and arrange cultural exhibits. Each day's festivities focus on a different country.

Originally planned as a railroad junction point, Junction City is now a busy farming center north of Eugene and the point where State 99 forks into 99E and 99W to connect midvalley towns east and west of the Willamette.

Cottage Grove salutes its past

South of Eugene, the town of Cottage Grove sits beside the Coast Fork of the Willamette just above its confluence with the Row (rhymes with cow) River. Southeast of town, parks border a pair of impoundments—Cottage Grove Reservoir on the Coast Fork and Dorena Reservoir on the Row River. Families come here to picnic, camp, launch a boat, fish, swim, or go water-skiing.

Items from the area's pioneer and mining days are housed in the Cottage Grove Historical Museum at Birch Avenue and H Street. It occupies an octagonal-shaped former church built in 1897.

Ride the "Goose." The hissing and chugging of a steam-powered train still resounds in the Row River valley. In summer, passengers depart from the Village Green complex on a leisurely 2½ hour, 35-mile trip into the timber and mining country of the Cascade foothills. A steam engine pulls the train on weekends, a diesel engine on weekdays.

From mid-May through September trains depart on weekends and holidays at 10 A.M. and 2 P.M.; from July through Labor Day, weekday excursions also depart at 2 P.M. daily. A railroad museum adjacent to the station (open all year) displays railroad articles from the steam era.

The Goose—short for the Galloping Goose—got its nickname in pre-World War I days when it lurched and bucked over rough track hauling loads of logs. The track goes 18 miles up the Row River, past Dorena Lake and into the foothills of the Calapooya Mountains.

Bohemia Mining Days. In the early 1890s James "Bohemia" Johnson struck gold in the hills just southeast of Cottage Grove. Each July old mining traditions are revived for the 4-day Bohemia Mining Days. The town salutes this era with a rodeo, parade, fast-draw contest, and guided tours of the Bohemia country.

Lumber mills and wood products industries dominate the Lane County economy; you'll see many of them around Eugene and Springfield. Inquire locally about summer tours.

An adventurous loop to the Bohemia mines

The Bohemia mining district southeast of Cottage Grove has been called the richest mining area of the Cascades. After gold was discovered here in 1863, the area boomed then declined. New discoveries in the 1890s triggered a burst of shaft mining activity, which continued through the World War I period. Weathered buildings and half-hidden shafts mark these old mining sites.

Narrow dirt roads climb the flanks of the Calapooya Mountains to the old mines. Experienced mountain drivers can make a 70-mile loop from Cottage Grove to the mines, or if you don't want to drive your own car, inquire about guided tours of the mining district. The road is generally open from late June through October.

Before starting out, make sure your car radiator is full so the engine won't overheat on the steep grades. Obtain a copy of the Umpqua National Forest brochure outlining interesting sites along the way, and bring along a picnic lunch.

A rugged route. To reach the district, head southeast from Cottage Grove along the paved Row River road through Dorena. Beyond Culp Creek, turn right over the bridge and head up Sharps Creek.

The narrow and twisting mountain roads demand a driver's full attention. In many places the dirt road has a hair-raising dropoff on one side; sound your horn on blind curves. Use low gear on the steep and rough climb up Hardscrabble Grade.

You return along Champion and Brice creeks to meet the paved road at Disston.

The mining country. The mountain loop winds past more than a dozen mines, marked by rotting old mine buildings and a maze of holes and shafts. You follow county roads, but the mines themselves are on private land and off limits to visitors. Overgrown bushes often hide vertical shafts, and old timbers and equipment should not be trusted.

Southwestern Oregon

Come here for Shakespeare and river recreation

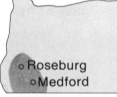

Roseburg
Medford

Fishing *on the Umpqua, angler shows off his handsome catch of striped bass.*

Oar-powered drift boats *float a placid stretch of the Rogue. Local river guides conduct groups on fishing and sightseeing trips.*

The Umpqua River marks the dividing line between northern and southern Oregon. Cradled between the Coast Range and the Cascade Mountains, the southwestern corner is one of Oregon's most enjoyable regions—a center of culture as well as outdoor recreation.

Whatever your interest, you can pursue it here. Ashland's famed Shakespearean Festival rates national acclaim, and art and music thrive in Jacksonville and other southern Oregon towns. If it's pioneer history you want, you can learn about Indian conflicts, frontier towns, Applegate Trail lore, or the gold strikes at Jacksonville and other Siskiyou sites.

Here you'll find two of the best fishing rivers in the world—the Umpqua and the Rogue. Heart of southern Oregon is the valley of the Rogue River. This famous stream flows westward through one of the wildest and most scenic canyons in the United States. White-water boaters, fishermen, and hikers can enjoy its primitive beauty. If you want lake fishing you're in luck, for numerous trout-filled lakes dot the Cascade slopes, most of them within an hour's drive of Medford.

The Siskiyou Range has its own unique plants, including the rare rhododendronlike *Kalmiopsis leachiana* preserved in the rugged Kalmiopsis Wilderness. The Oregon Caves National Monument preserves an unusual geologic site on the slopes of the Siskiyous.

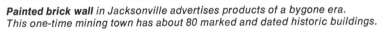

Painted brick wall in Jacksonville advertises products of a bygone era. This one-time mining town has about 80 marked and dated historic buildings.

First a picnic, then they will enjoy a Shakespeare play in Ashland.

The Umpqua Valley

South of Cottage Grove, you leave the Willamette River and its tributaries and enter the land of the Umpqua. Small communities—Oakland, Sutherlin, Wilbur, Winchester—lie east of the freeway along State Highway 99, the main north-south route until completion of Interstate Highway 5 in the 1960s.

Take the Winchester exit from Interstate 5 to reach the North Umpqua River. At Winchester Dam you can watch migrating salmon and steelhead climb the fish ladder, then view them close-up through underwater viewing windows. Families picnic nearby at popular Amacher Park.

Umpqua Community College, facing the North Umpqua River about 7 miles northeast of Roseburg, is the center of Douglas County's cultural and educational activities—including lectures, films, and community music, art, and theater programs.

Fishing on the Umpqua. To many fly fishermen, the North Umpqua is "The River." One of the nation's most famous fly-fishing streams, it flows over ledges and deepens into clear green pools. Multitudes of anglers congregate on the rocky promontories when spring Chinook and summer steelhead make their way upstream. For information on Umpqua fishing, write to the Roseburg Chamber of Commerce.

Zane Grey, the prolific writer of western books,

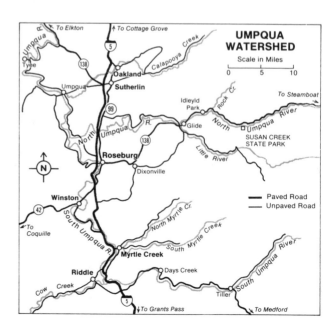

Gazing down their noses at motorists, stately camels regard the passing scene at Wildlife Safari near Winston.

did much to popularize the Umpqua and Rogue rivers in the years before World War I.

Local events. Douglas County hosts a number of annual events. Glide's Wildflower Show in late April displays some 350 plant species from all over southern Oregon. White-water boaters race in the North Umpqua Aquacade between Steamboat and Glide each spring. Scottsburg hosts a Daffodil Festival in May. June marks Lamb Show time and the Umpqua Valley Roundup, both held at Roseburg's Douglas County Fairgrounds, and Oakland's Old-Time Days.

In early July local artists display and sell their art in Riverside Park during Roseburg's Arts and Crafts Festival. August activities include Sutherlin's Timber Days, Canyonville's Pioneer Days, and the Douglas County Fair.

You can savor locally grown melons at the Winston-Dillard Melon Festival in mid-September. Roseburg's Wine Festival in late September salutes the local wine industry with tours, tasting, and German foods and entertainment. The Veterans Day Parade always attracts a good Roseburg crowd.

Roseburg, timber town on the Umpqua

Now a town of 16,700, Roseburg got its start in 1851 when Aaron Rose and his family settled in the Umpqua Valley; their home became a stopping place for travelers along the old Oregon-California trail. Settlers arrived to farm the rich land, and the timbered hills reverberated with the sounds of ax and saw. The area's rich timber resources still provide the region's main livelihood.

A complex of strikingly modern wooden buildings east of Interstate 5 preserves and displays the county's historical heritage. Exhibits at the Douglas County Museum show how the pioneers lived

and worked; other displays include artifacts of Indians and fur trappers, pioneer agricultural tools, and early logging equipment. The museum is open daily except holidays from 9 A.M. to 5 P.M.; to reach it, take the Fairgrounds exit off Interstate 5.

You can see the home of General Joseph Lane, Oregon's first territorial governor, at 544 S.E. Douglas Street on Saturday and Sunday afternoons; view the work of local artists at Roseburg Art Gallery, 247 S.E. Jackson from Monday through Saturday; or detour to Riverside Park in downtown Roseburg (between the bridges) to picnic or enjoy spring displays of azaleas and rhododendrons.

Riverside parks along the Umpqua

Pastoral roads allow you to get acquainted with the Umpqua River. The North Umpqua Highway parallels the scenic stream for many miles east from Winchester. Another delightful route is State Highway 138, following the river northwest to Elkton.

Several fine Douglas County parks border the Umpqua, offering pleasant spots to spread a picnic, camp overnight, or fish from the shore.

River Forks Park lies 6½ miles west of Roseburg at the junction of the North and South Umpqua rivers; children clamber over a western-style fort in the play area. Along the North Umpqua northeast of Roseburg are Amacher Park, marked by a grove of myrtlewood trees, and Whistler's Bend, where a children's ghost town is under construction. Bordering the South Umpqua River, sports facilities are found at Stewart Park, and Umpqua Park features a pleasant picnic and play area.

A drive-through wild animal park

Zebras, elephants, lions, tigers, gazelles, ostriches, and about 60 other species of African and Asian animals roam a 600-acre wooded preserve southwest of Roseburg. In late summer, the rolling hills of Wildlife Safari are dry and tawny, taking on the appearance of an African savanna.

To reach Wildlife Safari from Interstate 5, take the Winston-Coos Bay exit and drive 3 miles west on State Highway 42; a marked secondary road leads northwest to the park. Wildlife Safari is now open to visitors the year around; hours are 9 A.M. to 6 P.M. (9:30 or 10 A.M. to dusk in winter).

In your own car you set out on a sightseeing safari over a graded 5-mile road that winds through the park. Some 450 animals roam free through the preserve. Your admission fee includes a tape-recorded commentary that guides you through the park and helps you identify unfamiliar animals.

Morning is the best time to visit, when the animals are grazing in the open fields. By midday, temperatures climb and the animals retreat to the shade under the trees.

Children enjoy the *m'toto* (Swahili for baby) petting area, where they can pet and feed young llamas, goats, sheep, and other animals.

Along the Applegate Trail

Much of the route followed by Interstate 5 and State 99 closely parallels the Applegate Trail, a southern route to the Willamette Valley blazed by brothers Lindsay and Jesse Applegate and their pioneer party in 1846.

These highways also follow the old territorial road that linked California's capital city of Sacramento with the territorial capital of Oregon City.

Historic Wolf Creek Tavern. For more than a century, travelers have stopped at Wolf Creek Tavern. Located just south of Stage Road Pass, the old inn opened as a stagecoach station in 1857 and has remained in use, little changed through the years.

Believed to be Oregon's oldest hostelry, it stands west of Interstate 5 (on old Highway 99) about 21 miles north of Grants Pass. A piazza decorates the front of the long, two-story building. Among celeb-

rities reputedly enjoying the inn's hospitality were President Rutherford B. Hayes and his entourage and writer Jack London.

The historic inn was recently acquired by Oregon's state parks department, which plans to restore the building's original design and furnishings and reopen it for meals and tours of the interior.

A covered bridge. Josephine County's only remaining covered bridge crosses Grave Creek east of Interstate 5 just north of Sunny Valley, about 15 miles north of Grants Pass. A young girl traveling with the Applegate party died and was buried beneath an oak tree near the stream.

The fabled Rogue River

Fishermen and boaters rave about the splendid Rogue River—that scenic ribbon cutting across Oregon's southwestern corner. From snowy Cascade slopes west of Crater Lake, it plunges in a kaleidoscope of changing moods on its 200-mile journey to the sea. You can experience it as a tumbling mountain stream, a quiet-flowing river deepening into a pensive pool, or in crashing whitewater rapids.

The Rogue is one of only a few federally designated wild and scenic rivers, the only one in Oregon. Greenery borders its banks for much of the route. Below Grave Creek, you can explore the ruggedly scenic canyon of the wild Rogue on whitewater boat trips or on foot along a riverside hiking trail. Persons planning a trip along this section should obtain a copy of the Rogue River recreational map from Siskiyou National Forest officials or from the Bureau of Land Management office in Medford.

Grants Pass is the departure point for most guided fishing and boating trips. The Grants Pass and Josephine County Chamber of Commerce can provide information on local guide service, various boat trips, and lodge and motel accommodations.

A herd of wild goats forecasts Roseburg's weather

When Roseburg residents want to predict the day's weather, they don't rely on the U.S. Weather Bureau; they look toward Mount Nebo to see where the goats are grazing.

Years ago a local rancher allowed his herd of goats to forage on the grassy slopes of Mount Nebo, which rises above the South Umpqua River and is visible from most Roseburg homes. Over the years, residents noted that during good weather, the goats ranged near the top of the hill; when the animals grazed low on the hill or were out of sight, weather was generally changeable or stormy.

After the U.S. Weather Bureau closed its Roseburg station, residents began to notice that the goats were more accurate in predicting the

weather than the official weather forecast prepared in Portland, nearly 200 miles away— the score was reckoned as 90 percent for the goats, 65 percent for the bureau.

Twice each morning Roseburg radio station KRSB broadcasts its "official goat weather forecast." Local spotters belong to a Goat Observation Corps and call in goat sightings on the mountain.

At one time nearly 30 goats ranged Mount Nebo, but now the number is believed to be seven. The best place to see the goats "in person" is from downtown Roseburg, along the east bank of the South Umpqua River. Look west toward Mount Nebo; the goats range the entire length of the mountain. ◻

Grants Pass, gateway to the Rogue

Rogue-oriented recreation dominates Grants Pass life; the river flows through town, adding a pleasant ambience to the community.

Riverside Park, bordering the south bank of the Rogue, offers a pleasant picnic spot and fine river views. Children clamber over playground equipment, and their elders head for the park's sports areas. During July and August, outdoor band concerts are performed here on Thursday evenings.

The Boatnik Festival on Memorial Day weekend features a 35-mile white-water race from Grants Pass downriver to Hellgate Canyon and back—open to all comers—and a square-dance festival. In August local artists display their work at the Southern Oregon Art Show, and residents gather for the Josephine County Fair and Horse Races.

A magnet for fishermen

The Rogue is a fisherman's river. Its legendary runs of steelhead and salmon rate most of the enthusiasm, but the Rogue and its main tributaries offer good rainbow trout fishing as well. You can fish by yourself along the bank or arrange for a guide and a drift boat.

Fishing is best from September to May. Summer days can be blistering hot in the canyon, when river waters warm to swimming temperatures. Many fishermen plan trips here after the first autumn rains have cooled the canyon and hungry steelhead have begun to move upriver.

The Rogue has fall, winter, and spring steelhead runs; peak seasons vary a great deal up and down the river.

Schools of salmon migrate upstream to spawn in spring and fall; you can watch them jumping the falls along the Rogue or the ladders at Savage Rapids Dam. The best fishing on the middle river is between April and mid-July. Most of the fall salmon action is near the mouth of the river.

June, July, and August belong to trout fishermen, who cast into deep holes and into the slick waters above and below riffles; best fishing in summer is along the upper river and its main tributaries.

Sightseeing trips on the middle Rogue

The Rogue has a well-deserved reputation as a classic river run. Many white-water boaters confront its challenging rapids each summer. Day visitors can take a 2-hour round-trip jet-boat ride from Grants Pass downriver to Hellgate Canyon. For information, write to the Grants Pass and Josephine County Chamber of Commerce.

White-water excursions. Experienced local guides and a number of commercial operators conduct a variety of Rogue trips by rubber raft, wooden drift boat, and inflatable canoe. Some groups camp along the river; others stay in rustic riverside lodges. The white-water boating season extends from May through September; most trips last 2 to 4 days.

Jet-boat trips. If you have time for only a short excursion, you can take a sightseeing trip through pastoral country downstream from Grants Pass. Your destination is Hellgate Canyon, a narrow, deep cleft where rock walls rise some 250 feet above the water. Jet boats make the 35-mile round trip daily from May 15 through September.

Downstream to Grave Creek Bridge

A half-dozen county parks and an equal number of boat launching sites dot the river banks downstream from Grants Pass. Largest campground is at Indian Mary Park, 16 miles northwest of town.

The river road heads northwest from Grants Pass; or you can turn off Interstate 5 toward Merlin to reach the Rogue above Hellgate Canyon.

Attractive Indian Mary Park nestles in a curve of the river 2 miles below Hellgate Canyon. Broad lawns slope down to the Rogue, where anglers cast their lines and children splash in sun-warmed water. The park overflows with camping families on weekends. This was once the smallest Indian reservation in the United States, given to Indian Mary in memory of her father, Indian Joe, for his aid to white settlers during the Indian wars of 1855-56.

Gold was first discovered on the Rogue in 1859; you'll see evidence of mining in mounds of rocks along tributary stream beds, scars of hydraulic mining, and occasional abandoned shafts and equipment.

Galice was an early-day mining town, and dirt roads lead up nearby gulches to abandoned mines. About 4 miles downriver, look across to the far shore to see the remains of the Almeda Mine, in operation from 1908 to 1916.

Almeda Bridge at the mouth of Grave Creek marks the start of the wild river and of a 39-mile hiking trail along the roadless Rogue. To sample this trail, pack a lunch and hike 2-miles downstream to Rainie Falls for superb views of the turbulent river.

Motorists can return to Grants Pass over the same road or take the winding gravel road along Grave Creek (and later, Wolf Creek) east to meet Interstate 5.

Riding the white-water Rogue

Below the bridge at Grave Creek you enter the rugged and rock-studded Rogue canyon for an adventurous and memorable wilderness journey. The river flows through towering canyons, splashes over riffles, and crashes in foaming fury over boulder-strewn cascades.

In quieter stretches you can absorb the canyon's beauty and listen to the stillness. Streams tumble in from side canyons. Wildflowers grow along the banks, and deer and bear inhabit the forest.

Two miles downstream from the bridge, boats are lined through hazardous Rainie Falls, which drops 10 feet over large boulders. You then dive through graphically named white-water areas: Wildcat Rapids, the Washboard, Windy Chute

Oars "at the ready," drift boats chug up the tree-bordered Rogue canyon.

Paddling her inflatable kayak, girl heads into white water on the Rogue.

Creek. Downstream from Kelsey Falls you pass Winkle Bar, where the weathered, tumble-down remains of Zane Grey's cabin kindle memories of this writer who loved the outdoors.

Below Marial you ride through Mule Creek Canyon with its sheer walls that pinch the river into a swirling maelstrom only 15 feet wide. Beyond Stair Creek Falls is Blossom Bar, considered by most river men as the most treacherous stretch of the canyon.

The final part of the trip follows the curving canyon from Paradise Bar downstream to Illahe.

Riverside diversions. The trip isn't all white-water excitement. Along the way you'll enjoy majestic scenery and glimpse wild animals and birds. At the end of the day's voyage, you can go for a swim in the river, cast your fishing line into a shady pool, try gold panning, or hunt for interesting rocks.

Rustic lodges. Several simple but comfortable lodges are located along the river. Blending with their settings, they offer comfortable beds and family-style cooking to enhance this splendid but rigorous trip. Some white-water excursions include these accommodations or offer them as an option. Space permitting, fishermen and hikers can make advance reservations to stay at the lodges.

Hiking the Rogue River Trail

For nearly 40 miles the Rogue River churns a rugged, twisting route downstream from Grave Creek Bridge to Illahe. On the cliff beside it is an equally twisting hiking trail. Blazed by Indians and prospectors, it follows the steep, timbered north shoulder of the river canyon.

Early summer and early autumn are the best seasons to hike this route; days are pleasantly warm and wildflowers or fall foliage brighten the trail. Hot temperatures prevail in summer.

Heavy winter rains often cause slides and bridge washouts. The Forest Service and Bureau of Land Management share trail maintenance; check on current conditions in Grants Pass before you start.

This is a trail for veteran hikers. Back packers should carry provisions for the entire trip—no supplies are available along the route. Wear long pants and hiking shoes and carry rain gear. Bring water purification tablets and a snakebite kit. Be alert for rattlesnakes and poison oak. Wood ticks are numerous in spring and summer.

Most hikers take about 5 days to cover the entire distance. This allows time to enjoy the scenery and study trailside plants, wildlife, and geology. If you prefer a shorter trip, a dirt road approaches the river at Marial.

Primitive campsites are located along the trail between Grave Creek and Marial; downstream, hikers can camp on or near the many river bars. Drinking water is available at Big Slide, Tucker Flat, and Illahe, but not at other campsites.

Upstream from Grants Pass

Before the pioneers arrived, the broad valley above Grants Pass was the homeland of the Takelma Indians (also called the Rogue River Indians). Seeing their country invaded by newcomers, the game driven away, and the land plowed, they fought fiercely against the white settlers. An 1853 treaty was broken by renegade bands, culminating in the Indian war of 1855-56. After the treaty of 1856 was signed, the Indians were moved to reservations.

At Savage Rapids Dam, salmon stage a seasonal show as they fight their way to upstream spawning beds. Water sports enthusiasts enjoy the reservoir.

Bisected by Interstate 5, the town of Rogue River is the site of a Rooster Crowing Contest each June; prizes go to owners of roosters crowing the most times in 30 minutes. East of town, a county road follows the north bank to Rock Point Stage Station, built in 1863, and to Rock Point Bridge, named for a formation in the river bed below.

Gold Hill's main attraction is the House of Mystery (also called the Oregon Vortex), where puzzling phenomena lure visitors. Guides tell groups that normal perspectives are distorted by unusual magnetic force fields and demonstrate experiments to show the phenomena. The site is open daily from March to mid-October.

Back road exploring. From the town of Rogue River, drive north on Pine Street (which becomes East Evans Creek Road) through the pastoral valley. Nine miles north at Wimer is one of Jackson County's few covered bridges. To return to Rogue River, backtrack 2 miles to Minthorn Lane and turn south onto West Evans Road, which closely follows the stream. Palmerton Park has a small arboretum of native and imported plants.

If you want a longer excursion, continue northeast from the covered bridge up Evans Creek Road; you curve south and take Meadows Road to meet State Highway 234.

State 234 heads northeast from Interstate 5 at Gold Hill, cutting through Sam's Valley to connect with State Highway 62 north of Eagle Point. The beautiful valley was named for Chief Sam of the Upper Takelma tribe. The 1853 peace treaty between the Indians and the federal government was signed on the north side of Table Rock, just below the cliff, near Sam's Valley.

The historic south bank. State 99 follows the route of the 1846 Applegate party and later wagon trains along the river's south bank.

West of Gold Hill, a highway bridge crosses to the Rogue's south bank. Many campers make Valley of the Rogue State Park their headquarters while exploring southern Oregon. The large and attractive riverside park is open the year around.

A historic marker notes the site of Fort Birdseye, a stockade during the Indian wars. Nearby is the oldest structure in southern Oregon still in use —the David Birdseye home, built in 1855. Privately owned and occupied, the house is not open to the public. Many of its dovetailed, hand-hewn logs were originally used in the construction of the fort.

Bear Creek to Lost Creek Dam

A half-dozen small parks—most of them merely a few picnic tables and a boat ramp—dot the Rogue from Bear Creek upstream to the site of Lost Creek Dam near McLeod, about 30 miles northeast of Medford.

Scheduled for completion in 1977, the dam will mark the upriver migration limit for salmon and steelhead; Cole River Fish Hatchery is being built downstream from the dam. Travelers can watch dam construction from a view point on State 62.

The upper Rogue

Above Lost Creek Reservoir, the upper Rogue has the characteristics of a mountain stream. From its Cascade headwaters, it tumbles in rushing torrents and cataracts, carving its way through rocky canyons bordered in greenery.

Southeast of Prospect, a pleasant side road arcs briefly away from State 62 to parallel the river; you can take a short walk to a view point of falls near Prospect. Farther north the highway becomes a tree-lined avenue through Rogue River National Forest. You can stretch your legs at Natural Bridge, where the Rogue vanishes into underground lava tubes, and at the Rogue River Gorge, where it crashes through a narrow chasm.

Recreation areas. Visitors find a variety of accommodations in the Union Creek area. Campers find good facilities at Farewell Bend Campground, and a resort offers food and lodging.

Early-day sightseers enjoyed a cool rest stop at Farewell Bend before starting the long, rugged climb by horse and wagon over exposed pumice flats to Crater Lake. Farewell Bend Campground has a play area of natural wood attractions, including a tree house.

Hiking trails. Many pleasant hiking routes wind through the northern part of Rogue River National Forest. Inquire at the Prospect Ranger Station for trail information and additional suggestions.

The 5¼-mile Union Creek Trail appeals to both fishermen and hikers. From forest roads, short trails lead to National Creek Falls and to midsummer wildflowers in Hummingbird Meadow. The

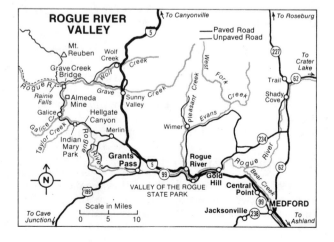

ROGUE RIVER VALLEY

7½-mile Buck Canyon Trail can be hiked in a day or combined with other forest routes for a weekend trip.

Now under construction along the upper Rogue is a 60-mile hiking trail—a joint effort of the Forest Service, Corps of Engineers, the State of Oregon, several private companies, and volunteer groups. When completed in the late 1970s, it will link the Pacific Crest Trail (from the Crater Lake National Park boundary) and Lost Creek Reservoir. You can now hike several stretches, viewing and studying the river in a variety of moods and settings. Fall color is brilliant along the route.

The Siskiyou Mountains

South of Grants Pass, U.S. Highway 199 curves southwest through the heart of the Siskiyou Mountains, site of Oregon's first gold discoveries; it reaches the ocean at Crescent City, California.

From Selma, a gravel road heads west down the Illinois Valley. East of Selma is Lake Selmac, a trout-stocked, manmade lake in a wooded setting. Boat rentals, fishing supplies, horses, and bicycles are available in summer at the lake resort.

At Cave Junction, State Highway 46 branches east to Oregon Caves National Monument.

The State of Jefferson

Since gold rush days, settlers of southwestern Oregon and northwestern California have been an independent breed. Feeling both far removed and neglected by their state governments, residents of the coastal border counties revolted—first in the 1880s and again in 1941.

Claiming that elected state officials were insensitive to their needs, they "seceded" and organized the State of Jefferson. In the second rebellion, organizers set up a series of carefully staged events to call attention to their act. Newsreel companies recorded the inauguration of a governor, parades, and demonstrations for simultaneous release in theaters all over the country. That release date—unfortunately—was December 8, 1941.

Kerby's pioneer museum

During the early years of the gold rush, Kerbyville (now Kerby) was a mushrooming trading center of tents and crude log shacks; in 1858 it supplanted Waldo as the county seat.

Josephine County's pioneer days are recalled in the well-organized Kerbyville Museum, administered and maintained by the county. Housed in a restored two-story frame dwelling of an 1870s Kerbyville merchant, the museum is furnished with possessions of many pioneer Josephine County families.

A wing adjacent to the house contains many fine exhibits, including a section of the old Waldo post office and collections of Indian artifacts and antique

Several riverside trails offer hikers a chance to enjoy vistas of the rugged Rogue Canyon and white-water rapids. Back packer surveys Mule Creek Gorge below Marial.

guns. Many displays relate to the mining era at Waldo (see page 88), and early farming and mining equipment are displayed on the grounds. A one-room log schoolhouse built in 1898 has also been reassembled here. The museum is open daily from May through October, the rest of the year by appointment (phone 592-2076 or 592-2736).

Oregon Caves National Monument

Deep in the Siskiyous, a spectacular underground cavern has been transformed by mineral deposits into a subterranean wonderland. Poet Joaquin Miller, who visited it in 1907, called it the "Marble Halls of Oregon."

Though known as the Oregon Caves, it is a single cavern with a mazelike system of connected corridors and chambers. With a guide, you walk through winding passageways into subtly lighted chambers bearing such descriptive names as Dante's Inferno, Ghost Chamber, King's Palace, Banana Grove, and Paradise Lost.

The cave was discovered in 1874 by Elijah Davidson while he was deer hunting with his dog Bruno. Scenting a bear, the dog led his master to a dark opening in the rocks. By the flickering light of sulphur matches, Davidson gazed upon the spectacular cavern.

Local adventurers explored parts of the cave, but for many years few visitors made the difficult journey. After his visit, Miller publicized the site through his writings, and in 1909 President William Howard Taft proclaimed it a national monument. The winding road to the caves was opened in 1922.

The Oregon Caves National Monument is 20 miles east of Cave Junction by way of State 46.

Oregon Caves landmark is the six-story Chateau, a 1930s-era wooden hotel rising from the canyon floor. A mountain stream runs through its dining room.

The curving road climbs nearly 3,000 feet through a beautiful forest of mixed conifers.

The Marble Halls. Some 200 million years ago, an ancient sea covered this area; it deposited a thick layer of calcium carbonate that later hardened into limestone. Heat and pressure fused the limestone into marble. Then an upward thrust occurred, making the region a part of a mountain range.

Over millions of years, water seeped into fractures in the submerged marble, combining with minerals to dissolve the stone. Gradually small fractures were enlarged to the size of the cave. The drip, flow, and evaporation of countless droplets of dissolved carbonate formed stalactites hanging from the cave's ceiling; falling to the floor, the droplets gradually built up stalagmites.

Some of the deposits are graceful; others are odd or fanciful. You'll see miniature stone waterfalls, limestone canopies, rock chandeliers, and fluted columns.

Guided tours. Trips through the cave are guided, usually in groups of 16; average time of a tour is 1¼ hours. It is a strenuous trip, not recommended for persons with heart or breathing problems or walking difficulties. Children under 6 years old are not permitted in the caves, but a child-sitting service is available. Fees are charged for both the tour and nursery care.

Wear good walking shoes and a warm jacket; average temperature inside the cave is about 45°. It's drippy in spots (that's what builds up the formations); you can rent boots and coveralls.

During your tour you'll walk, crouch, and climb through the cave's many marbled chambers, ducking low ceilings and dodging protruding stalactites.

Metal steps and handrails ease your passage in difficult stretches.

From May through September, guided trips depart frequently between 9 A.M. and 5 P.M.; between mid-June and September 10, hours are expanded—8 A.M. to 7 P.M. In winter, trips depart at 10:30 A.M. and 12:30 and 3:30 P.M., or more frequently as parties of 12 to 16 visitors assemble and guides are available.

Facilities and other activities. From Memorial Day to Labor Day, you can obtain meals and lodging in the Chateau, a six-story wooden hotel rising in rustic grandeur from the floor of the canyon. Opened in 1934, this spacious lodge was constructed with huge wooden beams, peeled tree trunks, and local stone. A mountain creek gurgles through the dining room.

In other seasons, only light refreshments are available at the monument.

Rangers can direct you to several trails beginning near the cave entrance. No camping or picnicking areas are located within the monument; the nearest area is Cave Creek Campground, 4 miles northwest on State 46.

The Illinois Valley

From headwaters near the crest of the Siskiyou Range, the two forks of the Illinois River flow north, merging near Cave Junction. You can picnic near the junction at Illinois River State Park. The river continues northwest, carving a deep canyon on its journey toward the Rogue.

From Selma, a rough gravel road parallels the Illinois for more than 20 miles into Siskiyou National Forest. Downstream from Selma, the river is a state-designated scenic waterway—wild and turbulent for much of its route, hard to boat except in spring.

Cave Junction. The main town along U.S. 199 is Cave Junction, gateway to the Oregon Caves. On July 4, Siskiyou area residents gather in Jubilee Park for fun and fireworks; Labor Day weekend signals the Illinois Valley Jubilee, highlighted by a loggers' carnival and a parade.

About 1½ miles south, the Woodland Deer Park features tame deer (which children can feed and pet), other animals, and picnic and play areas.

Gold discoveries. Gold was first discovered in Oregon in the spring of 1851 on Josephine Creek; a few months later, new discoveries in the Applegate Valley attracted gold seekers toward Jacksonville.

In 1852 a group of British sailors—who had deserted their ship at Crescent City to head for the Jacksonville gold fields—hit pay dirt in the Illinois Valley. Sailor Diggins (later called Waldo), Althouse, and Browntown became important mining centers. The richest gold producing area was along Democrat Gulch and Althouse Creek. Little remains today of these mining towns, but you can drive to their sites: Browntown and Althouse bordered Althouse Creek, south of Holland; Waldo's site lies about 4 miles east of O'Brien.

The rugged Kalmiopsis Wilderness

Of primary interest to botanists, this federal pre-serve harbors a number of rare plants and trees, including the *Kalmiopsis leachiana*, a small low-growing rhododendronlike shrub that is considered a relic of the pre-Ice Age.

Wilderness terrain is wild and rugged, and trails are extremely primitive. Hikers should plan to be completely self-sufficient. Rattlesnakes abound, and yellow jackets and hornets are numerous.

Three routes lead to the wilderness border: best maintained is the Chetco River Road (see page 63) from the coast; from U.S. 199 unpaved roads lead west from Selma and Kerby. Persons planning to enter the wilderness should consult Siskiyou National Forest officials in Grants Pass or Brookings for detailed information.

Through the Applegate Valley

The peaceful Applegate Valley is a route for history buffs, who can spend days investigating mining sites, old cemeteries, and back-country roads. For half of the 40-mile drive, State Highway 238 follows the river, passing through small farm settlements.

Your major destination on this route is Jacksonville, a boom town that refused to die. Today this one-time mining camp is a thriving historic landmark and cultural center; its August music festival draws visitors from throughout the state.

Jacksonville, Oregon's first boom town

Richest and best known of the Siskiyou mining camps was Jacksonville, which mushroomed along Jackson Creek in the early 1850s. Now a National Historic Landmark, Jacksonville lies 5 miles west of Medford on State 238.

Many of the town's 19th century wooden and brick structures have been restored, and about 80 old homes and buildings have been marked and dated. The old courthouse has been transformed into a historical museum. Jacksonville celebrates its lively past each June on Pioneer Day.

A number of artists and craftsmen have settled here, and several galleries and antique shops are housed in restored century-old buildings.

A golden past. Late in 1851, two pack train drivers traveling between the Willamette Valley and California discovered gold on Daisy Creek. Within a matter of days, a boom town sprouted as hundreds of prospectors streamed north from the California gold fields and south from the Willamette Valley.

In the 1850s and '60s, Jacksonville lived the fast-paced life of a lusty frontier mining town. Unlike most, it survived as a community when homesteading families settled in the Applegate Valley.

Both the railroad and the main highway by-passed Jacksonville, and the community's importance was further diminished after the county seat was moved to Medford in 1927. For more than 30

years Jacksonville slumbered, nearly a ghost town. Its resurgence began in the early 1950s, and today this town is enjoying new prosperity.

Peter Britt Festival. For 2 weeks each August, professional musicians from around the United States gather in Jacksonville for a series of classical concerts and recitals.

Orchestral and youth-oriented concerts are performed outdoors in a tree-shaded garden. Recitals and chamber music concerts are presented in the upstairs ballroom of the restored United States Hotel building. For information, write to the Britt Music Festival Association, P.O. Box 669, Jacksonville, OR 97530.

Originated in 1963, the festival honors Peter Britt, a Swiss immigrant who photographically recorded the history of Jackson County from 1853 to the early 1890s. Britt's hobby was horticulture, and in his garden he planted many semitropical shrubs and trees.

Outside the festival period, you can visit the Britt gardens on 1st Street south of California.

Pioneer Village. On Jacksonville's eastern outskirts, you can see a collection of relocated historic buildings that show pioneer life in southern Oregon. The century-old structures have been furnished with items typical of the era. You can also see an extensive display of early-day farm implements, wagons, buggies, and mining equipment.

In summer, outdoor melodrama and olios are performed each Friday and Sunday night, and silent movies are screened on Saturday nights.

Touring 19th century Jacksonville

Jacksonville is a town that invites strolling. Balustraded brick and frame buildings cut by narrow, high-arched entries and windows line the main street. Tall trees shade the side streets, where clapboard dwellings and steepled churches stand, having survived a pair of fires in the 1870s.

Begin your tour at the Jacksonville Museum, where you can obtain a map showing the town's main points of interest.

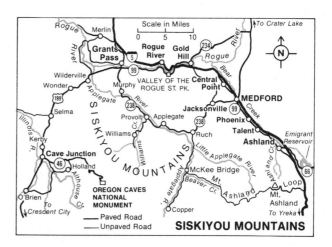

SISKIYOU MOUNTAINS

Jacksonville Museum. The monumental old Jackson County Courthouse, on 5th Street a block north of the business area, houses Jacksonville's outstanding free historical museum. Built in 1883, the courthouse was the center of county government until 1927.

One of the most extensive and fascinating historical displays in the state, the museum's collection demands more than a casual look. It is open daily from 9 A.M. to 5 P.M. Monday through Saturday, noon to 5 P.M. on Sunday (closed Mondays from Labor Day through May).

Exhibits bring alive the daily life of Jacksonville's early residents—Indians, miners, gamblers, law men, Wells Fargo agents, teachers, circuit riders, farmers. You'll see pioneer firearms and 19th century money among the exhibits. One room displays the early photographic equipment, oil paintings, and home furnishings of Peter Britt. His photographs of Jacksonville in the 1850s and '60s show buildings still visible today.

Beekman Bank. Cornelius C. Beekman, another of Jacksonville's prominent early residents, was the town's first Wells Fargo express agent and banker. The bank at the corner of 3rd and California streets was the most important financial institution in southern Oregon from 1853 to 1880. About $31 million in gold dust crossed its counter to await safe transport by Wells Fargo. Furnishings remain much as they were in the 1860s; you'll see gold scales in a glass case.

Other buildings. Handsome 19th century period furnishings decorate the stately Beekman residence on Stage Road South; it is open daily from June through Labor Day.

The large brick United States Hotel on Califor-nia Street hosted President Rutherford B. Hayes and his party in 1880; it now houses a local bank.

The historic McCully House, built by a Jackson County physician in 1860, has been completely restored and furnished with antiques. Located near 5th and California streets, it is open to visitors.

Jacksonville Inn, constructed in 1863, has been renovated as a hotel and restaurant; its 8 rooms are furnished with antiques.

The Rogue River Valley Railway depot, built in 1891 near Oregon and C streets, now houses exhibits and is open to the public without charge. The rail line linked Jacksonville and Medford until 1925.

19th century churches. Jacksonville's Methodist-Episcopal church at 5th and D streets was built in 1854 with substantial contributions by local gamblers and other citizens. The Catholic church, located at 4th and D, was built 2 years later.

The Presbyterian church at 6th and California streets was constructed in 1881. Built of native sugar pine, it contains Gothic stained-glass windows imported from Italy. A local tale relates that the varnish on the pews failed to dry completely before the first service, and for some years the bustles and trouser seats of a number of worshippers decorated the benches.

Jacksonville cemetery. Headstones in the cemetery northwest of town provide a glimpse of frontier hardships. Among the graves are victims of Indian attacks and smallpox, men who died of "lead poisoning" or hanging, even one killed by a grizzly bear. The cemetery contains graves of several prominent pioneers including Beekman, Britt, Indian fighter John Ross, and William Green T'Vault.

To reach the cemetery, drive out E Street, cross Jackson Creek, and take the gravel road uphill.

Gold discovery marker. A monument commemorating the 1851 gold discovery site is on the south bank of Daisy Creek south of town. From California, take Oregon Street about 3 blocks south and turn on Sterling Road. The actual discovery site was several hundred yards southwest of the marker, up Rich Gulch.

Historic byways

If you want to explore some of the old mining sites, maps are available at the Jacksonville Museum for a nominal fee. Additional information is available from the Greater Medford Chamber of Commerce or Star Ranger Station south of Ruch, where you can purchase a Rogue River National Forest map.

Among sites you can visit are the Logtown Cemetery, containing graves of many valley residents who died during the smallpox and diptheria epidemics of the 1860s and '70s, and the sites of the old mining settlements of Sterlingville and Buncom along Sterling Creek.

If you head south from State 238 at Ruch, toward the headwaters of the Applegate River, you'll discover an old covered bridge, picnic area, and swimming hole at McKee Bridge.

Restored brick buildings in Jacksonville now house a bank, galleries and gift shops, and a hotel-restaurant.

Sea of pear blossoms transforms the countryside surrounding Medford in mid-April.
Pears are picked in late summer, washed and packed, and shipped to points all over the nation.

Forest roads wind northwest from Copper along Carberry Creek past old mining claims and a small cemetery at Steamboat.

Along Bear Creek

Bear Creek, a main tributary of the upper Rogue, meanders north from Emigrant Reservoir to join the Rogue River near Central Point. On its way it passes or bisects Ashland, Medford, and several smaller towns.

A. linear parkway now under development—the Bear Creek Greenway—is enhancing the stream's natural assets and offering new possibilities for recreational use. A number of small creekside parks will dot its banks.

Partially cradled by forested mountains, Medford lies in the center of seemingly endless fruit orchards. Ashland is the home of the Oregon Shakespearean Festival and Southern Oregon College.

Pear orchards surround Medford

Largest town in southern Oregon, with a population of about 34,000, Medford is renowned for its setting amid vast pear orchards that cover the valley and climb the gently sloping foothills. In mid-April pear blossoms turn the valley into a marvelous garden, and a Pear Blossom Festival in Medford heralds the occasion.

After the riches of the Jacksonville gold fields diminished and the Indian troubles were resolved, many prospectors settled in the fertile Bear Creek Valley. With the arrival of the railroad in the late 19th century, Medford prospered, and in 1927 the Jackson County government was moved from Jacksonville to Medford.

Downtown. City and county buildings are clustered along West 8th Street near South Oakdale Avenue. The imposing Jackson County Courthouse was completed in 1932. Nearby are the Medford City Hall, library, and post office. The city park has an attractive central fountain.

Well-planned from its early days, Medford enjoys wide streets shaded by mature native trees that give it a parklike appearance.

Originally designed to cover scars left by a downtown fire, Mini Park—at the corner of East Main Street and Central Avenue—has become a much enjoyed oasis surrounded by business buildings. People come here to eat lunch or lounge in the sun.

In summer, a Saturday market is held at the K-Mart Plaza.

Along the creek. About 10 miles south of its confluence with the Rogue, Bear Creek flows through Medford, bisecting the town; a half-dozen bridges connect the east and west sections of the city.

Bicyclists and pedestrians enjoy a delightful bike and nature trail along Bear Creek. The 3½-mile bikeway begins at Barnett Road and extends north to McAndrews Road. The nature trail begins at Bear Creek Park; a descriptive brochure, available

Cycling—a great way to enjoy the scenery

If you prefer touring on two wheels rather than four, climb on your bicycle and go for a ride on one of Oregon's bikeways. It's a relaxing way to see the countryside, and new cycling routes are freeing riders of the highway hassle.

You can cycle leisurely along the Willamette and other streams or pedal along level valley roads through farm lands. Several state parks—among them Fort Stevens, Tryon Creek, Mary S. Young, Champoeg, and Silver Falls—feature bike trails. The Eugene-Springfield area has more than a dozen posted bike routes.

In recent years, Oregon has taken a strong stand in favor of bike trails and footpaths. By law, 1 percent of state gasoline tax revenues goes for bikeway development and construction.

Most of the bike routes are located near the population centers of the Willamette Valley and southern Oregon, but you'll also find them along the coast, near central Oregon's main towns, and in northeastern Oregon. For a list of Oregon's bikeways, write to the state Travel Information office (address on page 11).

Bicyclists must follow the same rules as drivers of motor vehicles. You can cycle along any state highway unless otherwise posted (in the Portland metropolitan area). Pedestrians have the right-of-way on sidewalks, and cyclists must give audible signals before overtaking and passing them. □

---

at City Hall, notes 25 trailside points of interest.

Families relax and picnic in Bear Creek Park along the east bank, near Highland Drive and Siskiyou Boulevard. In summer, outdoor band concerts are held here and tennis players rally on lighted tennis courts.

Fruit and roses. The valley is one big orchard. Some 11,000 acres are planted in pears, with additional land in apple, peach, and other fruit and nut trees.

South of town on State 99 is the headquarters of Harry and David, a major mail-order firm offering fruit and food gifts. From August 15 to December 15, you can tour the plant on weekdays; at other times, tours are by arrangement. From late October to mid-December you'll see holiday gifts being packaged. A Jackson & Perkins test and display rose garden is nearby.

Other nearby destinations. To picnic with a view of the valley, drive to the top of Roxy Ann Peak east of Medford; you'll find tables near the summit.

Rockhounds will enjoy a stop at the Crater Rock Museum in Central Point. Located at 2002 Scenic Avenue, the museum contains exhibits of cut and polished rocks and regional Indian arrowheads.

Getting acquainted with Ashland

Known throughout the nation for its outstanding Shakespearean repertory theater, Ashland is a charming town of 13,000 tucked into a mountain-ringed bowl. Green slopes climb steeply into the Siskiyou's wooded foothills.

The Elizabethan atmosphere spills over into the community for some downtown buildings; recent years have brought Elizabethan facades or shop names adapted to an olde English motif. Center of activity is the Plaza. Craft shops are thriving, and food shops invite picnicking.

The city's jewel is Lithia Park, bordering the downtown district and extending about a mile up Ashland Creek. An integral part of the community, it is the site of community picnics and outdoor concerts and classes. Within its 99 acres are lawns and picnic areas, duck ponds, children's playground, nature trails, tennis courts, band shell, and other features.

At the southern end of town is Southern Oregon State College, one of the state 4-year schools. Its 4,500 students play an important role in Ashland's cultural and economic life.

Ashland celebrates an old-fashioned Fourth of July with a parade, fiddlers' contest, and other entertainment in Lithia Park, followed by a fireworks display and dance at Emigrant Reservoir.

Inquire at the Ashland Ranger Station on State Highway 66 for directions to the Ashland Nature Trail south of town.

Ashland's Shakespearean Festival

A classic example of community pride and cooperation is the Oregon Shakespearean Festival; it has grown from a small community event to a nationally recognized repertory theater attracting more than 210,000 people each year.

It all began in 1935 when a small group of Ashland residents decided to present a 3-day Fourth of July celebration including fireworks, boxing, and Shakespeare. Two plays were performed in Lithia Park's old chautauqua shell by inexperienced actors using makeshift costumes and simple staging in the style of 16th century London. Sponsors figured profit from the boxing matches would underwrite the cost of the plays; instead, Shakespeare subsidized the boxing expenses. Attendance doubled the following year, and the rest is history.

The original 3-day venture now extends from mid-February through September with spring and summer seasons; the educational repertory theater also offers an array of lectures, tours, concerts, and college-level classes. Schedule and ticket information is available by contacting Shakespeare, Ashland, OR 97520 (box office phone 482-4331). Some performances are sold out far in advance.

Angus Bowmer Theatre, new in 1970, seats 600 viewers for indoor performances in spring and summer.

Backstage tour at festival allows children to wear crowns, heft scepters.

Elizabethan staging. Ashland's outdoor stage (see back cover of this book) is patterned after and built to the known dimensions of the Fortune Theater of 16th century London. Plays are staged in the lively, human, often bawdy manner of Shakespeare's time with elaborate costuming, little scenery, and Elizabethan-style dancing and singing. No intermissions disturb the flow of action.

Completion of the 600-seat Angus Bowmer Theater in 1970 permitted expansion of the summer program and a second festival season in the spring. Plays performed from mid-February to mid-April are drawn from all theatrical periods and are also presented in repertory. Both theaters are constructed without aisles, but with wide walkways between the rows.

Persons attending outdoor performances should bring coats or heavy jackets—a lap robe, if you like —as evenings can be quite cool. You can rent a cushion at nominal charge to ease the hardness of wooden seats.

Other diversions. A number of spin-off activities from the main summer program are open to the public, many of them taking place in Lithia Park.

Costumed dancers and strolling troubadours entertain in the theater gardens before outdoor performances, setting the Elizabethan mood.

Backstage tours lasting 1½ to 2 hours are conducted by members of the festival company on Monday through Saturday at 10 A.M. Purchase reserved tickets in advance at the central box office.

In one room, visitors can heft swords and scepters, sit on a throne, and see costumes at close range.

Members of the staff and company offer informal noontime talks in Lithia Park several days each week in summer; bring a picnic lunch.

Special events during the season include the opening night Feast of the Tribe of Will, the annual Renaissance Feast featuring Elizabethan foods, a midnight Renaissance Ball, and a Tudor Guild Festival and Handcraft Fair.

Forty years of festival history are recalled in displays at historic Swedenburg House on the Southern Oregon State College campus. The museum is open Monday through Saturday from 10 A.M. to 3 P.M., Sunday from noon to 3 P.M.

Workshop courses allow college students to earn course credit based on the festival program. For information, write to Renaissance Institute, Box 605, Ashland, OR 97520.

Up Mount Ashland

In winter or summer, Mount Ashland invites skiers and festival-goers. Located southwest of Ashland in the Siskiyou Range, it lies 10 miles west of Interstate 5 just north of the California border.

Rustic ski resort. Awaiting skiers each winter are 10 miles of wooded ski trails, four open slopes, and a snowy bowl. The ski area perches on the north slope of the 7,523-foot peak; four lifts transport skiers up the mountain. Cross-country skiers use

Sailboat slips past the boat dock at Howard Prairie Reservoir. Several regattas are held here each year.

the resort as a base. The season lasts from November to April.

Popular with families and students at nearby Southern Oregon State College, this low-key ski area has a cozy charm. In the day lodge you'll find a cafeteria and cheery lounge; other facilities include a ski shop with rental equipment and a ski school. On weekends, bus service transports skiers from Medford and Ashland to the ski area.

Summer picnic site. If you want to picnic with a panoramic view, drive to the top of Mount Ashland. Summer flowers bloom in July, and you'll find picnic tables atop the mountain.

The paved road ends at the ski area, but a good graveled road continues along the Siskiyou Mountains crest. A steep rocky road climbs the final steep mile to the mountaintop, but if you prefer, you can picnic at Mount Ashland Campground about 2 miles below the summit.

Mount Ashland Loop. If driving remote gravel mountain roads doesn't faze you, consider the 75-mile Mount Ashland Loop Drive that winds along the summit of the Siskiyous. It follows the high bare ridges to Jackson Gap, drops down to the Applegate River, and returns to Ashland through Jacksonville. Summer wildflowers and mountain panoramas make this a striking trip.

Detour a mile off the route to the Dutchman's Peak Lookout; its unusual cupola-style building—now rare—is typical of Forest Service structures of 50 years ago.

The mountain road is generally open from early July to mid-October; it is usually well marked, but inquire at Rogue River National Forest offices in Medford or Ashland for detailed directions and current road conditions.

Water sports on reservoir lakes

Three lakes east of Ashland attract sailors and fishermen. County parks are located at Emigrant

and Howard Prairie reservoirs; Hyatt Reservoir has a BLM recreation area.

Emigrant Reservoir. Located 5 miles southeast of Ashland off State Highway 66, Emigrant Lake is the site of Ashland's Fourth of July fireworks display. Boat ramps, camping and picnic areas, and good fishing and swimming make this lake a family favorite.

Howard Prairie Reservoir. Largest of the three areas, this lake lies 22 miles northeast of Ashland by way of Dead Indian Road. Cradled between two mountain ridges, the 6-mile-long lake covers a former meadow surrounded by pines and fir trees. Popular with southern Oregon families, it offers more than 325 campsites in addition to a picnic area.

On summer weekends you'll see sailboats and canoes gliding across the lake; several regattas are held here each year. At the south end of the lake, water-skiers sweep in foaming arcs. Fishermen cast in quiet inlets for trout and catfish, and children splash near shore. Fishing supplies and boat rentals are available at the lake marina.

Hyatt Reservoir. Continue 5 miles southwest of Howard Prairie Reservoir to Hyatt Reservoir (or you can reach it by spur road from State 66). It has a year-round resort and small camping and picnic areas. The lake is stocked with rainbow trout; boat rentals are available. In winter, families go snowmobiling, cross-country skiing, and sledding near the lake—and ice-skating if conditions permit.

Mountain lakes

South of Crater Lake, the Cascades are a wonderland of mountain lakes—some large, many small—sprinkled along the alpine crest and slopes. A few large lakes have highway access and simple resort amenities, but most are in remote areas and are accessible only by trail.

Most visitors explore this high country in July and August, but a number of Oregonians prefer these lakes during the long, unhurried days of early autumn—when days are warm, nights crisp, and the crowds have departed.

State Highway 140 is the main route across the southern Cascades. Another enjoyable route linking Interstate 5 and U.S. Highway 97 is State 66, a scenic drive winding some 64 miles between Ashland and Klamath Falls.

A trio of popular lakes

When residents of southern Oregon head for the mountains, the destination is often one of three Cascade lakes—Fish Lake, Lake of the Woods, or Fourmile Lake.

State 140—part of the Winnemucca to the Sea Highway (see page 129)—veers east from State 62 north of Medford and climbs through Rogue River National Forest to Fish Lake. East of the summit, you pass Lake of the Woods and descend through

Winema National Forest, skirting the southwest shore of Upper Klamath Lake to Klamath Falls.

Ashland families drive northeast on Dead Indian Road to connect with State 140 just east of Lake of the Woods.

Each of these lakes has a resort and at least one public campground. The Pacific Crest Trail winds north across the slopes of Brown Mountain, crossing State 140 near Fish Lake, and entering the Sky Lakes Wilderness Study Area on the eastern slope of Mount McLoughlin.

Fish Lake. Rainbow and eastern brook trout thrive in this mountain lake at the foot of Mount McLoughlin; fishing is the primary activity here. Boat rentals and supplies are available at the resort. The Forest Service provides two campgrounds and a boat launching ramp.

Lake of the Woods. Summer homes, youth camps, and several Forest Service campgrounds border the shore of this lovely lake southeast of Mount McLoughlin. The lake resort operates year round, but its dining room is open May through October.

Boating, water-skiing, and swimming are popular summer sports, but the fishing is good, too. Anglers haul in rainbow and eastern brook trout and kokanee salmon. You can obtain rental boats and tackle at the resort. Horses and guides are available in summer for day rides or longer trips, or you can take off on several mountain climbs or hiking trails.

Winter visitors go cross-country skiing or snowmobiling, fish through the ice, or skate on the lake.

Fourmile Lake. Forest roads lead north of State 140 to this reservoir, most remote of the three major lakes. The campground is a popular departure point for hikers following the Pacific Crest Trail north to the Sky Lakes Wilderness Study Area and Crater Lake National Park.

You can fish for rainbow trout and kokanee salmon at Fourmile Lake; in summer, boat rentals and fishing supplies are available at the resort. Nearby mountain trails offer good hiking.

Mountain Lakes Wilderness

One of Oregon's original wilderness areas, the Mountain Lakes region is a 6-mile-square tract some 20 miles northwest of Klamath Falls. Known for its rugged topography and dozens of high lakes, it is reached by primitive roads and forest trails south of State 140.

Heart of the wilderness is a large glacial cirque surrounded by eight peaks, all topping 7,700 feet. A loop trail enables hikers and horseback riders to visit the main trout-stocked lakes. From the summit of 8,208-foot Aspen Butte and other high points, you can look east over Upper Klamath Lake, west to Lake of the Woods and Mount McLoughlin, and south to Mount Shasta.

Most of the area lies above the 6,000-foot elevation. Trails are generally blocked by snow until late June, and weather turns brisk by September.

Only a few dirt roads approach the wilderness boundary. Horseback riders generally prefer the Mountain Lakes Trail, winding into the basin from the northwest. The easiest approach for back packers is over the Varney Creek Trail; from the trailhead, it is a good 4-mile hike to the first of the fishing lakes.

Other trails enter the wilderness from the east and south. You can obtain trail information at the Winema National Forest office in Klamath Falls.

The Sky Lakes area

Straddling the crest of the Cascades south of Crater Lake National Park, the Sky Lakes area is one of several in Oregon under consideration for wilderness status. The Pacific Crest Trail traverses this lake-studded high plateau, and a network of trails connects the lakes. The area is closed to motorized vehicles.

Many small lakes and ponds are scattered across the timbered glacial basins. Rocky ridges and sharp peaks break the terrain. Water is abundant in the southern part of the area, but hikers should carry water when traveling north of Ranger Spring through the area known as Oregon Desert.

Main access trails for hikers and horseback riders begin at Fourmile Lake and Cold Spring Campground on the south, Seven Lakes Trail or Blue Rock Saddle on the west, and Cherry Creek and Sevenmile Marsh on the east. Trails are open from July through October. Bring warm clothing and rain gear; though summer days are warm, night temperatures can drop to freezing. Sudden rain or snow storms can occur at any time of year. Bring mosquito repellent.

Trail information is available from offices of Rogue River and Winema national forests which jointly administer the Cascade forest area.

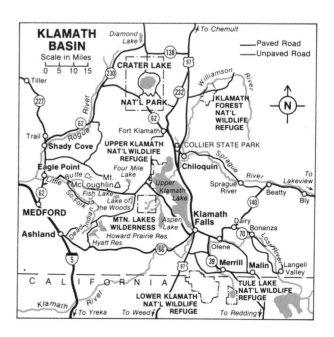

Cascade vacationland

Hike through the forest or fish alpine lakes

Hiking trail *follows Pamelia Creek deep in the Mount Jefferson Wilderness.*

Cross-country skiers *make their way across the McKenzie Pass (closed by snow in winter) during the annual John Craig ski race.*

Oregon's backbone is the Cascade Range, a chain of massive dormant volcanoes dividing the state into west and east. Snowy cones tower above the lesser mountains, and vast, dark green forests carpet the Cascade slopes.

The lofty and serene peaks we see today belie their violent origin. Formed by quiet outpourings of lava and fiery volcanic eruptions, their slopes gouged by glaciers, the Cascades marked the final rugged barrier for early travelers. Many places bear names reminiscent of the area's Indian heritage or names bestowed by pioneers, prospectors, and stockmen. Portions of today's trans-Cascade highways still follow old Indian trails, emigrant routes, and pioneer wagon roads.

Oregon's dense forests not only yield a substantial portion of the nation's timber but also provide a vast, year-round mountain playground.

In spring you'll enjoy the tender shades of new growth and the first wildflowers; pink rhododendrons bloom along forest roads. Summer brings the temptations of the high country—shady forest trails, tumbling mountain streams, and blossoming alpine meadows. Autumn splashes the foothills and valleys with vibrant shades of scarlet and gold. Winter snows cloak the trees, and ski slopes glisten in the frosty sun.

Campers, hikers, fishermen, boaters, mountain

Framed by tall pines, snowy Mount Jefferson forms a scenic backdrop for the meandering Metolius River and its meadow. Many campgrounds border the river.

Secluded mountain lakes high in the Cascades lure fishermen.

climbers, hunters, and skiers can choose from dozens of destinations on the forested flanks of the Cascades. You can explore the moist, lush valleys on the western slope, the drier, open pine country east of the mountains, or the alpine wilderness along the Cascade crest.

Oregon's highest peak

Monarch of the Oregon Cascades, snow-capped Mount Hood towers over its empire. The 11,235-foot peak dominates Mount Hood National Forest,

more than a million acres spreading from the Columbia River south along the mountain spine to Mount Jefferson, and from the foothills east of Portland to the central Oregon plateau.

Once a landmark for pioneers seeking the green valleys west of the mountains, today Mount Hood is probably the most accessible peak in the Cascades. Skiers throng to its slopes, climbers ascend its glaciers, and hikers tramp its trails. The mountain's northwestern slopes have been preserved as Mount Hood Wilderness.

In forested lands surrounding the peak you can camp at popular sites or in secluded campgrounds, go fishing or boating or skiing, picnic by

Cascade vacationland **97**

Snow tractor transports skiers to Mount Hood's high slopes. Sea of clouds blots out forests below.

Massive timbers, a soaring central fireplace, and the work of Oregon artists and craftsmen of the 1930s add grandeur to famous Timberline Lodge.

a stream or waterfall, swim in a lake or bathe in hot spring waters, spend a day on the golf course, hike forest trails or climb mountains, ride a chairlift or a snow-cat up the glacier, or laze away a summer afternoon in a flowery meadow.

Campgrounds in Mount Hood National Forest range from the big drive-in areas at Timothy Lake and Lost Lake to isolated back-country sites accessible only by forest road or trail. Motorboats are not permitted on some of the lakes, including Frog, Trillium, Lost, and Olallie lakes.

Information on camping and other forest activities is available from the forest supervisor's office in Portland or from local ranger stations at Troutdale (Columbia Gorge), Estacada and Ripplebrook (Clackamas River), Zigzag (Mount Hood Highway), Parkdale (Hood River Valley), Bear Springs (State Highway 216), and Dufur (U. S. Highway 197).

Mount Hood Loop

A favorite drive of Portland families—particularly if they're entertaining out-of-state visitors—is the circuit called the Mount Hood Loop. The 170-mile excursion east of Portland traverses some of Oregon's best scenery. The route climbs through Cascade forests to Mount Hood, winds through the fruit orchards of the Hood River Valley, and returns to Portland along the famed Columbia River Highway.

From downtown Portland, you drive east on U. S. Highway 26. Farm land gradually gives way to wooded hills as you ascend the western slope of the Cascades. Beyond Sandy the snow-covered peak of Mount Hood looms ahead. Much of the route parallels the Barlow Road, the pioneer wagon road across the mountains. At Mount Hood, you'll detour up the mountain to famed Timberline Lodge for a sweeping view of the Cascades.

The route swings around Mount Hood's southeastern flank onto State Highway 35, through mountain meadows and past foaming cascades along the East Fork of the Hood River. After winter snows melt, you can explore some interesting dirt roads—south from State 35 along a stretch of the old Barlow Road or north from the highway to Sahalie Falls and Hood River Meadows. Another side trip climbs to rustic Cloud Cap Inn (no public facilities) on the northeast slope for a different view of the mountain.

Continuing northward on State 35, you leave the forest and descend into the rich Hood River Valley, then follow the Columbia downstream through the spectacular Columbia Gorge. For a brochure describing points of interest, write to the state Travel Information office (address on page 11).

Winter fun at Mount Hood

Winter sports fans approach Mount Hood with enthusiasm. The exciting freedom of its slopes, a dependable snowfall (averaging 21 feet), and a concentration of excellent ski facilities little more

Timberline Lodge—a craftsmen's showcase

High on the south slope of Mount Hood perches Timberline Lodge, the pride of Oregon's best known ski area. The unique lodge, an ambitious project of the Works Progress Administration in the 1930s, utilized the state's native materials and the diverse skills of many Oregon craftsmen.

The building's massive timbers, as well as carvings and pictures, depict features of the Cascade mountains. Painters and stonecutters, woodcarvers and weavers, carpenters and metal workers all contributed to the construction and furnishing of the great lodge. The result is a unique showcase of Oregon arts and crafts.

Throughout the lodge, the craftsmen emphasized three major themes: the pioneers, the Indian influence, and plants and wildlife in Oregon.

Begun in 1935, Timberline Lodge was dedicated by President Franklin D. Roosevelt in 1937. It is still federally owned, and privately operated under a concession from the U.S. Forest Service.

The visitor is often so overwhelmed with the massive building's distinctive rugged architecture that he may miss the carefully executed detail of the finishing and furnishing. Each piece of furniture, each lamp and lamp shade, each door hinge was hand-crafted especially for the building.

Elaborate woodcarvings, painted murals, intricate mosaics of wood or stone, and numerous original paintings contribute to the art heritage of the lodge. The stonework of the great hexagonal fireplace, the beautiful pegged oak floors, and the massive exposed beams of the lobby testify to the talents of the many artisans.

Although the lodge's great scale might seem like an extravagance for the "hard times" of the 1930s, the building and furnishing of Timberline Lodge was actually a curious study in thrift. The lodge is built entirely of native Oregon materials, and when possible, used the talents of local craftsmen. The handwoven rugs are made from scraps of old Civilian Conservation Corps uniforms; the elaborately carved newel posts were once discarded telephone poles; and the beautifully worked andirons of the lobby's great fireplace were handwrought from old railroad tracks. □

---

than an hour's drive from Portland attract a profusion of skiers, from beginners to experts.

Advanced skiers head for the mountain's three major areas—Timberline, Mount Hood Meadows, and the Multorpor-Ski Bowl complex near Government Camp. Skiers can choose from more than 100 miles of challenging runs—including an 8-mile course from Mount Hood's upper slopes all the way down-mountain to Government Camp. Several areas offer nighttime skiing.

Families enjoy the gentler slopes and children's play areas at Summit ski area and Snowbunny Lodge, both near Government Camp, and Cooper Spur ski area on the northeastern slope. The countryside offers miles of uncrowded trails for cross-country skiers and snowshoe hikers.

Ski season. If there's enough snow, the ski areas open by Thanksgiving weekend, and by mid-December activities are usually in full swing. Facilities around Government Camp usually shut down in March, but you can ski on the high slopes above Timberline as late as July.

Access and accommodations. Most skiers drive up for the day, but overnight accommodations are available at Timberline Lodge, Government Camp, and Wemme. Space is limited and reservations are advised. Snowplows clear the roads constantly, but carry chains and a pressure can of deicer for your windshield.

Other winter activities. Ski touring trails begin at Timberline Lodge, Mount Hood Meadows, and Multorpor-Ski Bowl. Trail information is available at the Forest Service district office at Zigzag.

Unplowed forest roads provide wintry trails for snowshoers, cross-country skiers, snowmobilers, and dogsledders. Some routes are restricted; check with a forest ranger for suggestions and a map before starting your trip. Snowmobile loop trips on marked trails are popular in the Trillium Lake Basin and in the Frog Lake area.

From Timberline Lodge at 6,000 feet elevation, skiers and sightseers can take the "magic mile" chairlift up to the 7,000-foot level. Snow-cats take passengers up to an elevation of 9,000 feet. At Timberline Lodge you can swim—even in a snowstorm —in the heated outdoor swimming pool.

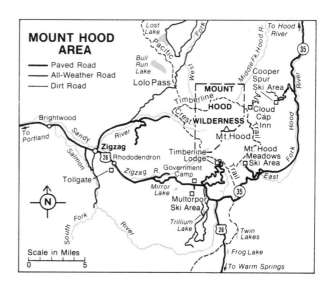

Summer activities on the mountain

When snow melts at the lower elevations, skiers head for Mount Hood's upper slopes, where skiing lasts until July. Climbers look toward the mountain's glaciers, and hikers take to the trails.

Summer skiing. High on the mountain, a succession of afternoon thaws and nighttime freezes creates good corn snow conditions for skiers who just won't pack their equipment away. But toward afternoon the snow turns mushy and they call it a day, retiring to lower elevations to hike, fish, or swim. Summer racing schools operate in June and early July. Skiers are transported to the high snow fields by double chairlift, Poma lift, and snow vehicles.

Sightseeing rides. From Timberline Lodge you can take the "magic mile" double chairlift above timberline to the 7,000-foot level. The lift operates daily during the summer season, weekends only during late spring and fall. (Many hikers follow the chairlift route up the mountain to alpine meadows.) Snow-cat trips up the mountain provide spectacular views and a chance to see the mountain's glaciers at close range.

The climb to the summit. Several thousand people climb Mount Hood annually. Novice climbers with guides and rented equipment can reach the summit in summer, but only experienced mountaineers should attempt to scale the peak in winter, as weather conditions can change quickly at high altitudes. Mountaineering clubs and schools provide good instruction for those new to the sport.

Many climbers leave from Timberline Lodge, ascending the southern slope; other groups leave from Cloud Cap Inn or Tilly Jane Forest Camp to climb the more difficult north face. March to mid-June is the best climbing period. Mountaineers usually start by 4 A.M., making the 6 to 7-hour climb in the cool morning hours before the sun has softened the snow. Climbers should register before departure and check out on return at Timberline Lodge, Cooper Spur, or the district ranger station at Parkdale.

High on Mount Hood, fumaroles still emit gas and steam, evidence that the ancient volcano is not yet extinct.

And what do you see when you reach the top? On overcast days, a sea of cottony clouds often blots out the forests; only the snowy tip of Mount Jefferson—50 miles away—pierces them. But on a clear day, the view from the summit is magnificent. To the south you see Mount Jefferson and the Three Sisters looming above a dark green forest. Eastward lie the wheat fields and plateau of central Oregon; westward, the Willamette Valley and Coast Range. To the north the snowy peaks of Adams, St. Helens, and Rainier break the horizon; much nearer is the deep Columbia River Gorge, and just below, silvery tree-rimmed Lost Lake.

Hiking the Timberline Trail

Encircling Mount Hood is the Timberline Trail, a rugged 37½-mile alpine mountain path. The entire trail is usually open by July 15, with the best weather conditions in July and August.

Most of the trail follows the 5,000 to 6,000-foot level, but it descends to 3,000 feet along Ramona Creek and climbs above 7,300 feet crossing Lamberson Spur. Most hikers cover only a section of the Timberline Trail at a time, entering by one of a dozen side trails.

If you plan to travel within the Mount Hood Wilderness, inquire at a Forest Service office regarding wilderness regulations. You'll need to obtain a free wilderness permit (see page 8). Pack and saddle animals are prohibited on a number of trails, and campers are restricted in some areas. No campfires may be built above 5,500 feet.

Trail conditions. Seldom an easy trail to hike, Timberline is often steep, with the grade continuing for miles. Some sections are in blazing sun, some deep in sand. As the snow melts on hot summer afternoons, glacier-fed creeks rise, making crossings difficult. Carry drinking water, and purify any stream water you use for drinking or cooking. Wood is practically nonexistent above timberline.

Stone shelters were built along the trail during its construction in the 1930s, but 40 years of heavy snows have taken their toll; some are merely ruins.

Around Mount Hood. From Timberline Lodge, the trail ascends northeast through forests and meadows, curves around Gnarl Ridge, climbs across Lamberson Spur, and reaches Cloud Cap Inn, which perches on the slope at the end of an ac-

MOUNT HOOD NATIONAL FOREST

To Estacada
Clackamas River
Roaring River
So. Fork
Frazier Fork
Trail
River
Rock Lakes Basin
Oak Grove Fork
224
Ripplebrook
Clackamas River
Collawash River
Springs Fk.
Hot Fork
Bagby Hot Springs
Bull of the Woods
Elk Lake
Breitenbush Springs
To Salem
North
Breitenbush River
22
Detroit
Santiam River
22
Detroit Reservoir
To U.S. 20
MOUNT JEFFERSON WILDERNESS
North Fork
South Fork
Skyline Road
Pacific Crest
Crest Trail
Timothy Lake
To Mount Hood
Clear Lake
26
To Warm Springs
WARM
SPRINGS
INDIAN
RESERVATION
Olallie Meadow
Olallie Butte
Olallie Lake
Monon Lake
Breitenbush Lake

Scale in Miles
0   5

—— Paved Road
—— All-Weather Road
—— Dirt Road

Youngsters stop to fish along the Hot Springs Fork of Clackamas River on the way to Bagby Hot Springs.

cess road just below Eliot Glacier. Opened in 1889, the rustic hotel is anchored to the mountain by cables to resist winter storms. The inn is headquarters for a mountaineering group.

Beyond Cloud Cap Inn, you enter Mount Hood Wilderness. The trail winds through forests to Elk Cove and Eden Park. It continues west around Bald Mountain, linking up with the Pacific Crest Trail, curves around Yocum Ridge, and then follows greenery-lined Ramona Creek up to the falls.

The final section along the southern flank cuts across the rocky, alpine meadow of Paradise Park and continues to Timberline Lodge.

Wildflowers. The colorful wildflowers carpeting high alpine meadows such as Eden and Paradise parks are a special delight from mid-July to late August. Among the varieties you may see are lupine, Indian paintbrush, avalanche lilies, blue gentian, red heather, and beargrass.

Day hikers can enjoy wildflowers around Hood River Meadows on the southeastern slope.

Sampling Mount Hood's forest trails

The varied terrain of the Cascades provides forest and alpine scenery to delight any hiker. You'll find no shortage of destinations for day hikes, weekend trips, or longer excursions. Here are a few suggestions; for trail information, inquire at ranger stations (see page 98).

A favorite day hike is the 4½-mile Ramona Falls Loop. You follow the Sandy River Trail up to the falls, where a sparkling stream cascades over mossy ledges, then return along Ramona Creek. Another short day trip is the 1½-mile climb to Mirror Lake, south of U.S. 26. Popular Bagby Hot Springs is crowded in summer, but it's a lovely site in spring or fall; underground hot springs have been channeled to a rustic bathhouse and into long cedar tubs.

If you want a longer trip and some back-country solitude, consider the 14-mile Salmon River Trail beginning south of Trillium Lake; you pass several waterfalls and enjoy excellent fishing in the canyon's remote sections. Relatively few hikers venture into the Rock Lakes Basin, but it offers trout-stocked lakes, good mountain trails, and huckleberries (along Indian Ridge) in late August and September. Back packers and fishermen hike to the mountain lakes of the roadless Bull of the Woods area near the headwaters of the Collawash River; high trails may be blocked by snow until late June or July.

River route along the Clackamas

A favorite loop trip of many Willamette Valley residents links Portland and Salem with a scenic route along the Clackamas River.

From Portland you follow State 224 to Estacada and southeast along the river into Mount Hood National Forest. Beyond Ripplebrook, paved forest roads parallel the Clackamas River up toward its headwaters in the high Cascades. Campgrounds are located along the way, and fishermen find good river access.

The Clackamas route links up with the forest road along the Breitenbush River where travelers turn west toward Detroit and State Highway 22.

The Olallie Lakes area

More than 100 solitary mountain lakes are tucked away amid the rocky buttes and virgin forests in the Olallie Lakes district north of Mount Jefferson. Even on a midsummer weekend, you won't find many people here. Access roads are rugged and are usually not passable until late June or early July. Heavy rains also make travel difficult.

Only about 6 miles square, the area rests atop the crest of the Cascades in the southernmost part of Mount Hood National Forest. A winding dirt road connects the main lakes—Olallie, Monon, Horseshoe, and Breitenbush—but most of the lakes are reached by hiking trails.

A half-dozen forest campgrounds are located near the road, and a small resort at the north end of Olallie Lake has groceries, fishing tackle, and rowboat rentals. No motorboats are permitted on the lakes. From the camps, trails lead to literally dozens of back-country lakes where you can fish for brook, rainbow, and cutthroat trout.

Skyline Road. Routes leading into the Olallie Lakes area are adventures in themselves, particularly the Skyline Road (Forest Road S42)—a winding, one-lane, dirt road with many turnouts, clinging to the Cascade crest. You'll find the driving slow, though the route is neither rocky nor precipitous. It leaves U.S. 26 near Clear Lake, crossing and recrossing the crest on its southward trek. Take your time and enjoy the scenery — flower-filled meadows, stands of pine and mountain hemlock, barren cinder cones—along the 35-mile drive to the lakes. Deer and elk frequently wander near the road, and you might see a bear or beaver.

North of Olallie Meadow, a spur road connects the Skyline Road with the Clackamas River Road.

Up the Breitenbush River. The southern approach to the lakes is by the 25-mile Breitenbush River Road, which branches northeast off State 22 at Detroit. You drive fewer miles over unpaved roads, but they're rougher and steeper. Inquire at the Detroit Ranger Station about current road conditions.

The first 11 miles of the route—to Breitenbush Campground—is now paved, but the remaining stretch is dusty, rocky, and steep (the road climbs 2,500 feet in 4 miles). If your car tends to overheat, it probably will happen here. Though not a route for people in a hurry, the road is passable to passenger cars, and you'll have some magnificent views of Mount Jefferson. From Breitenbush Lake Campground, the Pacific Crest Trail goes south into Mount Jefferson Wilderness.

Along Santiam routes

From the central Willamette Valley, highways follow the North and South Santiam rivers upstream into the Cascades, where the two routes intersect near Santiam Pass. The roads pass reservoirs— popular for water sports—and forest campgrounds.

The Santiam Loop makes a fine day trip from valley points. Fall foliage is colorful.

From Santiam routes you can hike into Mount Jefferson Wilderness, go skiing at Hoodoo Bowl, or—on the eastern slope—cast your fishing line into the famed Metolius River (fly fishing only for its first 10 miles). U.S. Highway 20 parallels the route of the old Santiam Wagon Road, a pioneer toll road that crossed the Cascades just north of Mount Washington.

The North Santiam

Southeast of Salem, State 22 follows the North Santiam River east and south into the Cascades to a highway junction with U.S. 20.

From Mehama, west of Mill City, a side road follows the Little North Santiam River northeast through the Elkhorn Valley. You can still see evidence of old mines.

Boaters head for Detroit Reservoir, about 46 miles east of Salem, where state and Forest Service campgrounds await travelers. For information on campsites and trails, stop at the Detroit Ranger Station. Piety Island Campground, on a knobby island in the middle of the lake, can be reached only by boat. Tackle, supplies, and boat rentals are available in Detroit.

Forest roads throughout Willamette National Forest lead to lakes and trailheads; some trails are closed by snow from late autumn until June.

Mount Jefferson Wilderness

In the shadows of 10,497-foot Mount Jefferson stretch nearly 100,000 acres of alpine wilderness—

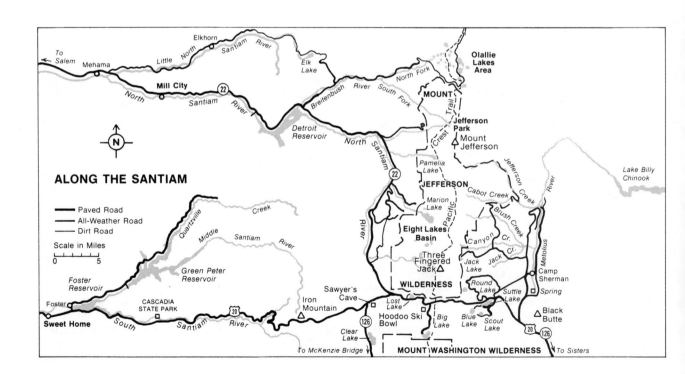

tranquil lakes, swift streams, mountain meadows, and dense conifer forests. On the eastern slope, long narrow lava flows follow Jefferson and Cabot creeks.

From State 22 forest roads climb eastward to trailheads near the wilderness border. East of the Santiam summit, forest roads north of Suttle Lake lead to east side trails.

Hiking and climbing. Hikers relish more than 160 miles of wilderness trails, including a 36-mile stretch of the Pacific Crest Trail. You pass waterfalls and small lakes shimmering like scattered jewels, cross rushing creeks on rustic bridges, and traverse snowfields shaded by evergreens or glistening in the sun.

Experienced mountaineers pit their climbing skills against both Mount Jefferson and Three Fingered Jack, whose three rock needles thrust up against the skyline.

Alpine lakes. Many of the area's 150 lakes are fishermen's favorites.

Clustered in a rocky basin just north of Mount Jefferson are the Jefferson Park lakes, a series of alpine tarns stocked with golden trout. From mid-July through mid-September, mountaineers make base camp here before starting their all-day assault up the slopes.

Only a 2-mile hike from its access road, tree-rimmed Pamelia Lake is skirted by the Pacific Crest Trail. You can fish here for cutthroat trout the year around—through the ice in winter. In late summer the shallow lake warms enough for an afternoon swim.

About 3 very steep miles south of Pamelia Lake, Hunt's Cove is one of several delightful lake-studded valleys and a favorite starting point for a climb up Mount Jefferson's south slope.

Shimmering under the mountain rim, mile-long Marion Lake contains rainbow, brook, and cutthroat trout. On the road to the trailhead, you can detour to climb Independence Rock or stop to enjoy several waterfalls. On the easy 2-mile hike into the lake you'll pass Lake Ann.

Trails lead south from Marion Lake into Eight Lakes Basin, where more than 30 mountain tarns have long attracted fishermen and hikers. From Jorn Lake, trails to the southwest take you to Mowich and Duffy lakes.

Along the South Santiam

From Albany, U.S. 20 parallels the South Santiam River upstream, through Lebanon and Sweet Home, into the Willamette National Forest. Inquire at the Sweet Home ranger station about campgrounds and picnic sites near U.S. 20.

Water sports and old mines. In the Cascade foothills, two dams—Foster and Green Peter—hold the Santiam waters in check. Reservoir lakes behind the dams are well used by boaters and other water sports enthusiasts.

U.S. 20 follows the south shore of Foster

Party of horseback riders pack deep into the mountains of Mount Jefferson Wilderness along the Cascade crest.

Reservoir. Recreation facilities—camping and picnic areas, boat ramps and docks, and a swimming area—are found along the north side of the lake.

The Quartzville Road climbs above the northern shoreline of Green Peter Dam on the Middle Santiam River. You'll find similar recreation facilities here. If you continue up Quartzville Creek, you're on your way to the Quartzville gold mines. Miners flocked here during Civil War days.

Mineral springs. Cascadia was once a mineral springs resort along U.S. 20; today it's the site of an attractive state park. The river flows through a narrow, rocky corridor. Campers and picnickers can fish or swim in the river or hike nearby trails.

Two easy hikes. If you want to stretch your legs, try one of these short trails just off U.S. 20.

From House Rock Campground, 24 miles east of Sweet Home, take the trail starting at the footbridge. You cross the river, follow it to a pretty waterfall, and return to the campground on the old Santiam Wagon Road.

Thirty-four miles east of Sweet Home, the Iron Mountain Trail follows an easy 1½-mile route through old-growth Douglas fir and mountain meadows to a lookout; your view extends from the Coast Range to the high Cascades.

Sawyer's Cave. Just west of its junction with State 22, the Santiam Highway (U.S. 20, State 126) crosses a lava field and passes near Sawyer's Cave. A small sign on the south side of the highway marks the short trail to the cave.

Formed by a volcanic gas bubble in the crust as

Big Lake attracts water sports enthusiasts. Hikers head south into the Mount Washington Wilderness.

molten lava cooled, Sawyer's Cave is a fine place to cool off on a hot summer day; a sheet of ice usually covers the floor. You can picnic on rocks near the cave entrance.

Lost Lake. No longer lost, this small lake lies in a pleasant meadow about 4 miles west of the Santiam summit. A small campground, popular with boat fishermen, is located on the western shore. Though a creek flows into the lake, no outlet is visible as the water disappears into underground channels.

Winter sports at Hoodoo Bowl

When winter snows arrive, skiers, snowmobilers, and snowshoers congregate at Hoodoo Ski Bowl just west of the Santiam Pass, about 92 miles southeast of Salem. Activities center around the day lodge, cafeteria, and ski shop. From December through April the area is open Wednesday through Sunday, on holidays, and during spring vacation.

Three double chairlifts take skiers up Hoodoo's broad open bowl. Even on weekends, lift lines are usually short and slopes relatively uncrowded. Beginners find gentle slopes near the lodge.

A favorite trail for cross-country skiers and snowshoers is the 2-mile unplowed road south from Hoodoo Bowl to Big Lake, where you can camp and go boating in summer. You ski over gentle terrain, passing beneath the rough cliffs of Hayrick Butte. In clear weather you'll see Mount Washington to the south. (Summer hikers can follow a stretch of the old Santiam Wagon Road, which intersects the Big Lake Road; the pioneer route heads east toward Cache Mountain and Sisters, west past Sand Mountain and Fish Lake.)

Snowmobilers have a separate parking area at

Hoodoo Bowl near the start of a marked 9-mile snowmobile trail. Timber in this area was almost completely burned in a 1967 fire.

The eastern slope

On U.S. 20, Santiam Pass marks the Cascade summit and the boundary between Willamette and Deschutes National Forests. Just west of the summit, hikers head north on the Pacific Crest Trail into Mount Jefferson Wilderness or south toward Mount Washington.

On the eastern flank of the Cascades, you drive high above Blue Lake, cradled in its deep volcanic basin below Mount Washington. The road descends through tall pines along the north shore of Suttle Lake. At its eastern end, a paved road provides lake access.

Popular Suttle Lake has three campgrounds; it also boasts a picnic area, swimming beach, and playground at its eastern end and a water-ski area at the western end. A 4-mile trail loops around the lake, and paths lead to other nearby lakes.

Another favorite destination is small Scout Lake, just south of Suttle Lake. To reach it, take the Suttle Lake-Blue Lake road for about 1½ miles, then watch for signs to Scout Lake. Firs and pines grow near its shore, and wide gravel beaches slope gently into the water. You can camp or picnic overlooking the lake and hike around its shoreline. In summer, Scout Lake warms enough for swimming.

Vacationing in the Metolius country

Many families and fishermen head for the famed Metolius country northeast of the Santiam Pass, a region renowned for superb—but challenging—fishing. Bubbling up from icy springs north of Black Butte, the Metolius races northward past the community of Camp Sherman, following a twisting course through tall ponderosa pines and parklike meadows. Fed by numerous springs and creeks, it passes several forest camps before entering a 1,500-foot-deep gorge on its way to Lake Billy Chinook—the reservoir behind Round Butte Dam—where it joins the Deschutes and Crooked rivers.

Resort accommodations and cabins are available, and in summer you can go horseback riding. Forest roads lead westward to campgrounds at Jack and Round lakes and to trailheads near the border of Mount Jefferson Wilderness.

The Metolius River Road. If you'd like to trace the course of a twisting mountain stream, take the river road north from Camp Sherman. It climbs high bluffs above the turbulent Metolius and dips into meadows near the river's edge.

The Metolius River and jumbled forest through which it passes seem to grow wilder as you go northward. The paved road ends at Lower Bridge Campground, but a dirt road—rutted and rocky—continues along the river as it begins to bend eastward toward the desert country. If you venture into the long-abandoned apple orchard, watch out for rattlesnakes.

To vary your return route, cross the river at Lower Bridge Campground and return over the west side forest road.

On foot. For intimate glimpses of the Metolius, take a walk along the river trail; you'll see springs spilling out of grassy banks and discover shady eddies where rainbow trout are seldom bothered by anglers. The trail begins at Lower Canyon Creek Campground and follows the river 2½ miles to the state fish hatchery at Wizard Falls. It continues downstream 3 miles to Bridge 99 and another 1½ miles to Candle Creek Forest Camp.

A marked side road forks east from the Camp Sherman road to a spring marking the head of the Metolius; a short paved path leads to the fenced-in spring. The river widens rapidly as it cuts through the meadow.

A 2-mile trail winds through the open timber to the lookout station atop 6,415-foot Black Butte. Hikers are rewarded with views of the Three Sisters and Broken Top on the way up; from the summit you can see Cascade peaks north to Mount Adams.

Sisters. Once Indian trails converged in this vicinity; now the Santiam Pass and McKenzie Pass highways join at Sisters, forming the town's main street before forking again toward Redmond and Bend. Campers, fishermen, hikers, and hunters use Sisters as a convenient supply point. Most stores are being remodeled to reflect an old western town, complete with false fronts, verandas, and hitching posts.

Southeast of town, Sisters State Park straddles Squaw Creek. Set in a shady grove of pines and junipers, the park offers picnic tables, fireplaces, and a place where travel-weary children can run and play.

From Sisters a paved road leads 17 miles south to Three Creek Lake, a peaceful alpine tarn just east of the Three Sisters Wilderness.

Up the McKenzie

From Springfield, State Highway 126 heads eastward, closely paralleling the McKenzie River for more than 40 miles.

Boating is a way of life on the river, and most of the people who live along the McKenzie are as much at home on the water as they are on the road running beside it. In riverside communities—Leaburg, Vida, Blue River, and McKenzie Bridge—professional river men spend much of their time in high-prowed, motorless McKenzie drift boats, guiding visiting fishermen through tricky rapids and strong currents to the deep holes where fighting trout hide.

Above the town of Blue River, dams harness the waters of the Blue River and the McKenzie's South Fork. You'll find campgrounds and boat ramps beside both Blue River and Cougar reservoirs, where

Hiking along the Cascade skyline

Winding for more than 400 miles among the forests and high peaks of Oregon's Cascade Range, the Pacific Crest National Scenic Trail provides a well-signed route through the state's high country.

First posted by the Forest Service in 1920, the skyline trail covers approximately 2,400 miles from the Canadian border to Mexico, linking the high mountain routes of Washington, Oregon, and California. It was designated a National Scenic Trail in 1968.

Oregon's 420-mile portion of the route begins at the Columbia River Highway east of Cascade Locks and winds south along paths first followed by animals and later by Indians, who gathered olallie (huckleberries) on the mountain slopes to dry for their winter food supply. Snowy peaks loom in spectacular panoramas along the route, which passes through five mountain wildernesses and skirts a sixth. Many short side trails lead to trout-filled mountain lakes. The trail crosses the California border east of Copco Lake.

Most back packers take about a month to complete the entire Oregon portion of the trail. However, trans-Cascade highways and forest back roads provide access, making it feasible for you to enjoy small portions of this primitive country even on weekend trips.

In most years, the best period to travel the trail is between mid-July and September, although some portions of the trail may be passable in early July and early October. Trail elevations range from 4,000 to 7,100 feet, and hikers often find snowy stretches on northern exposures until August. Forest Service personnel provide up-to-date information on trail conditions. Topographic maps are available from the U.S. Geological Survey office, Denver Federal Center, Denver, Colorado 80202.

In the mountains, you must be prepared for great variations in weather, for the temperature may drop suddenly from 80° or 90° to below freezing. Midsummer snowstorms occur occasionally. Mosquitoes can be a problem in some regions. All improved camps are outside the wilderness areas, usually at road crossings. Along the trail, running streams are plentiful, particularly on the western slope, and you'll find plenty of camping places from which to choose.

If a pack trip is more to your liking, horses and pack animals are available in some areas for trips into the mountains. Write to the forest supervisor of the appropriate national forest for information on packers and outfitters. Stock grazing areas are limited, so plan to carry feed for your animals. □

Log bridge *spans the sparkling waters of French Pete Creek in the lushly forested McKenzie River watershed.*

Harmonica-playing *wanderer takes a musical break beside the roaring creek.*

fishermen report catches of coho salmon, rainbow trout (often called "redsides"), kokanee, and native cutthroat. Water levels are lowered in summer to provide storage for the flood season; by late summer, it's often difficult to launch boats.

Near Belknap Springs, State 126 veers north toward Clear Lake and the Santiam Highway, while the old McKenzie Highway—State 242—climbs in winding curves toward the summit of McKenzie Pass (closed in winter).

Covered bridges. Below Vida you pass the Goodpasture Bridge (cover photo), long a landmark on this stretch of the river. Two other bridges can be found south of the highway. East of the Cougar Dam turnoff, take McKenzie River Drive to Rainbow, where the Belknap Bridge spans the river. Another covered bridge, no longer in use, is a mile south of the highway on Horse Creek Road, south of McKenzie Bridge.

Hiking and fishing. The wooded hillsides, fish-filled lakes, and rugged terrain of the Willamette National Forest offer endless recreation opportunities. Additional information on forest excursions, hiking trails, and lakes is available on request from ranger stations.

Up the South Fork

East of Blue River, a forest road branches off State 126 up the McKenzie's South Fork, skirting Cougar Reservoir and passing several small riverside campgrounds. Occasionally you see remnants of turn-of-the-century mining activity.

From the road along the South Fork, numerous trails lead into the mountains toward the western boundary of the Three Sisters Wilderness. You hike through tall forests of fir and hemlock, past alder groves and vine maple, and along rushing streams and high ridges.

The lower valleys are snow-free almost the year around, but spring is perhaps the most enjoyable time to explore, when wild rhododendrons, iris, and other forest wildflowers bloom extravagantly. Sunlight filters through the lofty conifers, dappling luxuriant undergrowth.

An easy day's hike departs from Echo Picnic Ground and follows the East Fork 5 miles along a river trail. Another pleasant hike that even novice back packers enjoy is the 5-mile trail through the quiet wilderness valley of French Pete Creek. In autumn, huckleberry pickers head for the trail across Indian Ridge, southwest of French Pete Campground. Check with the Blue River ranger station for information on trail conditions.

The Clear Lake cutoff

About 5 miles east of McKenzie Bridge, State 126 veers sharply northward along the upper McKenzie, intersecting U.S. 20 some 20 miles later. No towns disturb this forest route. Lovely in any season, it is especially enjoyable in early summer and fall—white dogwood blossoms and the fresh, pale green of vine maple herald spring; masses of pink rhododendrons bloom in late June; and hillsides of gold and scarlet vine maple add riotous touches to autumn color.

Lava beds. During the past 3,000 years, several lava flows from Cascade volcanoes blocked the ancient bed of the McKenzie, creating Clear Lake, Beaver Marsh, and several spectacular waterfalls. Portions of the highway cut through the black lava.

Waterfalls. From parking areas near the highway, short trails lead to Koosah and Sahalie falls on the upper McKenzie. A third waterfall, Tamolich, is below Koosah but accessible only by trail.

Located near Ice Cap Creek Campground, Koosah (the Chinook Indian word for *sky*) drops 73 feet over a ledge. Trails lead to a view point and to the top of the falls, where you can look down the McKenzie canyon. Watch out for poison oak.

About a half-mile north, Sahalie (meaning *high* in Chinook jargon), plunges 100 feet over a rim into a clear pool edged by lush ferns and moss-covered rocks.

Clear Lake. A geological curiosity, Clear Lake lies high in the Cascades 4 miles south of U.S. 20. One of the clearest and coldest of Oregon's mountain lakes, it preserves within its calm waters an old and unusual forest.

When lava dammed the McKenzie nearly 3,000 years ago, water gradually filled the valley behind the barrier, covering the forest and killing the trees. Due to the cold (about 43°) mineral-free waters and the absence of strong currents, the tree snags have been preserved beneath the surface of the lake and are visible to boaters.

In summer you can rent rowboats at the lake resort, or you can launch your own canoe or kayak. Motorboats are prohibited. You'll find picnic areas along the shore. Campers can stay in Coldwater Cove Campground; rustic cabins are also available. Trout fishing is usually good, especially at the south end of the lake. A big spring at the lake's north end is a source of the McKenzie River.

River trail along the McKenzie

Hikers can follow the sparkling waters of the upper McKenzie along a 13-mile riverside trail. Beginning about a mile east of McKenzie Bridge, the foot trail is accessible from several places along State 126. A trail map is available at the ranger station east of McKenzie Bridge. Several campgrounds are located near State 126 and the trail.

Beginning hikers will enjoy the first 10 miles of the trail, east and north to Deer Creek through old-growth Douglas fir. You can break the distance into several short hikes. From Deer Creek to Trail Bridge, the 3-mile hiking trail veers away from roads, and the route is accessible only at each end.

An additional 11 miles of trail, from Trail Bridge north to Clear Lake, are planned for construction. When completed the upper trail will traverse part

of the Cascade lava beds, pass through Beaver Marsh, and skirt the three waterfalls of the upper McKenzie—Tamolich, Koosah, and Sahalie.

The rugged Mount Washington Wilderness

Spanning the Cascade summit between the Santiam and McKenzie highways, the wilderness area surrounding Mount Washington offers strenuous challenges to hikers and mountain climbers.

Dominating the region is the austere peak, topped by a craggy pinnacle, its steep volcanic flanks deeply carved by glaciers. South of the mountain, great floods of black lava have spilled across the slopes, leaving huge jagged boulders. Cinder cones and islands of trees dot lava flows.

Travel in this formidable and desolate area is limited to hikers and pack animals. The Pacific Crest Trail provides the main access, entering the wilderness near Big Lake on the northern border and west of Dee Wright Observatory on the McKenzie Pass.

Mountain lakes. Big Lake Campground, south of U.S. 20, is the northern takeoff point for trips into the wilderness. Don't forget to bring mosquito repellent. From the trailhead at the end of the road, the Patjens Lakes are a 2-mile hike up Hidden Valley.

From State Highway 242, you can drive in to the

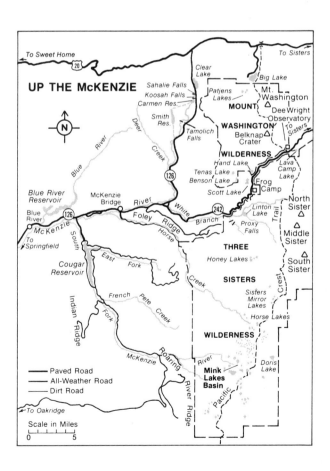

campground at Scott Lake, then set out on foot for Benson and Tenas lakes about 3 miles beyond. Major wilderness lakes are stocked with rainbow and brook trout.

If you want to get away from civilization but don't feel equal to a long pack trip, take the short trail to Hand Lake, a small jewel in an alpine setting only a half-mile off State 242. Watch for the trail sign about a mile above the Scott Lake turnoff.

Climbing the peak. One of the most popular rock climbs in Oregon, 7,802-foot Mount Washington has challenged many parties since it was first climbed in 1923. The ascent should be undertaken only under qualified leadership and with proper equipment. The final climb of the pinnacle is through rock chimneys and up sheer walls.

The old McKenzie Highway

For 37 miles State 242 weaves up and over Oregon's highest east-west pass. Not a road for hurrying, the scenic route across 5,324-foot McKenzie Pass winds through tall Douglas fir forests, traverses the state's largest lava beds, edges two wilderness areas, and offers superb views of some of the Cascades' mightiest giants.

From early September into October, fall color adds another reason for driving this mountain road. But don't wait too long, for at the first heavy snowfall—usually in late October or early November—the McKenzie Pass is closed for the winter.

State 242 begins to climb as it leaves its junction with State 126 near Belknap Springs, first passing through Douglas fir forests, then twisting in steep hairpin turns up Deadhorse Grade, named in pioneer days when this was a wagon road across the mountains. Short spur roads lead to forest camps, waterfalls, and high mountain lakes.

You drive through miles of lava country, so desolate it once served as a training ground for moon-bound astronauts. From the top of the pass, views of the Cascade peaks are stunning. Then it's a pleasant drive down the eastern slope through pine forests to the small community of Sisters.

Two short walks. About 10 miles east of the McKenzie junction, a half-mile trail goes south to Proxy Falls, a pair of misty, 200-foot cascades. You cross a narrow lava flow, then enter the forest. Rhododendrons and bear grass bloom along the trail in summer, and scarlet vine maple is prevalent in fall. At the fork, the left trail leads to the base of Upper Proxy Falls; the right fork leads to a view point opposite Lower Proxy Falls.

Just below Alder Springs Campground, a 1-mile trail leads southeast to Linton Lake. You walk through a forest and cross a lava flow on your way. In summer watch for penstemon and other trailside flowers. Trout fishing is usually good.

Stop at the summit. At the summit of McKenzie Pass, Dee Wright Observatory is built atop the lava. You can look through 11 windows in the stone tower and see 11 different mountain peaks.

Paved trail loops through the lava at McKenzie Pass summit. Astronauts trained near here for moon trips.

At the base of the observatory, a paved path leads you safely into the fields of jumbled lava. Along the half-mile Lava River loop trail, signs help you understand the geological features of the McKenzie Pass. Pick up a copy of the interpretive folder at the start of the trail; it traces the development of this volcanic wonderland and points out interesting features of the lava flows.

If you have several hours to spare, you can hike north from McKenzie Pass on the Pacific Crest Trail to Little Belknap Crater. Its summit is an intriguing maze of old lava tubes and vents.

Three Sisters Wilderness

Stretching south from the old McKenzie Highway, the vast Three Sisters Wilderness area rides the crest of the central Oregon Cascades. First recorded by Peter Skene Ogden in 1825, the Three Sisters form the most majestic alpine group in the range.

During the past few thousand years, more volcanic activity has occurred in this region than in any other part of the entire Cascade Range. Hikers will see volcanic mountains and cinder cones, lava flows, obsidian creeks, and lava-dammed lakes.

Winding for 45 miles along the skyline, the Pacific Crest Trail links hiking paths from the western and eastern slopes. Some 240 miles of trails lace this rugged yet inviting country, weaving through volcanic fields and grassy meadows to craggy peaks and tree-rimmed mountain lakes.

From the north the main entry points are Frog Camp and Lava Camp Lake, both near State 242. On the west, the forest road up the McKenzie's South Fork leads to trails through Olallie Meadows and along Roaring River Ridge. Hikers and horsemen climb the southeastern slopes on trails originating at lakes located along the Cascade Lakes Highway (State Highway 46); several packers lead trips up the eastern slope into the wilderness area. For more on this region, see page 123.

Hiking wilderness trails. When you see the mountains at close range, the distant look of awesome grandeur dissolves, and you see their gentle appearance. "A friendly wilderness," one hiker called it.

Trails within the area range from those easy enough for a family's day hike to routes challenging the most experienced hikers. Before beginning a trip, check current trail conditions and obtain a wilderness permit at the nearest ranger station— Blue River or McKenzie Bridge (for west side trails) or in Bend or Sisters (for east side routes).

From the west, forest roads follow Foley Ridge, Horse Creek, and the McKenzie's South Fork almost to the wilderness border. Hiking trails take you into cool green rain forests, by rushing trout-stocked streams, through rock gardens filled with vividly colored wildflowers.

On the drier eastern slope, trails start at four lakes—Sparks, Elk, Lava, and Cultus—outside the wilderness area near the Cascade Lakes Highway (see page 123). This is great vacation country. As you walk these trails, you'll see streams emerging from clear cold springs and meandering through meadows, trees skirting small lakes, and cinder cones rising above long streams of lava on the mountain slopes. The east side offers easier access —but you'll find more people, too.

Fishing lakes. The southern part of the wilderness is a fisherman's paradise with more than 300 lakes strewn across the mountains. Favorite destinations are the Mink Lake Basin, the Horse Lake group, and Doris Lake, all reached on trails from Elk Lake; Green Lakes, accessible from Sparks Lake; and the Sisters Mirror Lake group, reached from either Elk or Sparks lakes. Long trails up the western slope also lead to lakes along the crest.

On the northwestern border, trails lead in from the Foley Ridge Road to the Honey Lakes.

Mountain climbing. For mountaineers, the Three Sisters are among the most popular of Oregon's major peaks. All top 10,000 feet elevation. Most formidable of the three is North Sister; South Sister has become the favorite climb.

Access to North and Middle Sister is via Frog Camp on State 242. Climbers approach South Sister on a long but easy climb from Sparks Lake by way of the Green Lakes Basin.

Other varied climbs in the wilderness area include Broken Top, The Husband, The Wife, and Little Brother.

Riders water their horses and take a respite from the saddle on a Three Sisters Wilderness excursion.

Across the Willamette Pass

Angling southeast from Eugene, the Willamette Pass Highway (State Highway 58) parallels the Middle Fork of the Willamette to Oakridge, then follows Salt Creek toward the summit.

Dams now control the upper waters of the Willamette and its main tributaries, which until recent years flooded parts of the Willamette Valley with depressing regularity. Dexter and Lookout Point reservoirs, on the Middle Fork some 20 miles southeast of Eugene, are popular destinations for boaters, water-skiers, and fishermen.

Further upstream is Hills Creek Dam and Reservoir, 3 miles south of Oakridge. Forested hills provide a scenic backdrop for small parks where you can launch boats or have a picnic. Nearby Forest Service campgrounds provide overnight facilities.

A land of lakes and streams

The Willamette Pass Highway is a scenic corridor leading to superb recreation land. Near Oakridge the Middle Fork of the Willamette is enlarged by four additional streams—its own North Fork, and Salmon, Salt, and Hills creeks—draining a vast watershed. Along the Cascade crest, dozens of lakes and miles of trails attract hikers and fishermen to Willamette National Forest.

Salt Creek Falls offers a good excuse to stretch your legs when you're driving along U.S. 58. You can hike to the top or down to the bowl at its base.

In autumn, maple trees along the route paint hills and stream banks in brilliant gold.

Oakridge. Hub of Willamette highways and forest roads is Oakridge, 43 miles southeast of Eugene on State 58. In the wooded foothills of the Cascades, many residents rely on the forests for their livelihood. Each spring Oakridge hosts a community-wide Tree Planting Festival, reforesting the hills with Douglas fir seedlings.

In Green Waters City Park beside the river, you'll find picnic tables, sports facilities, and a nature trail. East of Oakridge, picnickers enjoy creekside sites at Blue Pool Forest Camp.

Salt Creek Falls. A few miles west of the summit you glimpse Salt Creek Falls, half screened by tall conifers, south of the highway. For the best views, follow easy trails from the parking area to the top of the waterfall or down into its misty bowl.

Willamette Pass Ski Area. From December to March, families from the Eugene area make the short drive to the Willamette Pass summit for a day of skiing. Instruction is available, and you'll find a snack bar and ski shop.

Exploring forest back roads

If you enjoy back-country exploration, explore some of the choices off the Willamette Highway. Check with Forest Service offices in Lowell or Oakridge for current road conditions and recreation suggestions.

In the low foothills, Fall Creek (see page 78) makes a pleasant destination for a Sunday picnic or a fishing weekend.

From Westfir, the North Fork Road follows the Willamette upstream toward the mountains. Nearing the Three Sisters Wilderness, the road veers north, ultimately linking up with the forest road along the McKenzie's South Fork (see page 106).

Salmon Creek Road heads northeast from Oakridge, past Salmon Creek Falls and up toward its Cascade headwaters. You can hike to the Salmon Lakes (brook and rainbow trout here) or take side roads along Black Creek or to Spirit Lake.

South of the highway, forest roads follow the Middle Fork of the Willamette and Hills Creek. Campgrounds are located along the Middle Fork road, which ends deep in the mountains south of Diamond Peak. Portions of this road follow the 1864 Oregon Central Military Wagon Road and the earlier emigrant route across the summit. A primitive road branches 3 miles south to Opal and Timpanogas lakes, and you can hike in to lovely Indigo Lake. From the Timpanogas junction, a narrow and winding dirt road follows the northwestern shore of Summit Lake and continues east to Crescent Lake.

Waldo Lake Recreation Area

Lying high on the slopes of the Cascades just west of the Willamette Pass, Waldo Lake was scooped out by glaciers eons ago. Snowy peaks are reflected in its clear blue waters, and evergreens border its shoreline.

Eighteen miles east of Oakridge on State 58, a 12-mile paved access road branches north to the lake. Three campgrounds are located along the eastern shore. The lake's north and west sides have been left in a primitive state, accessible only by boat or trail. To preserve the peaceful alpine atmosphere, motorboats are limited to a speed of 10 m.p.h. on the 6-mile-long lake. Motorbikes are prohibited on most trails, and no horses are allowed on the trail along the lake's east shore.

Anglers are most successful during early morning and late evening hours, and in June and October rather than in midsummer. Waldo is stocked annually with rainbow and brook trout.

A 20-mile loop trail circles the lake, and other trails give hikers access to the forest's quiet glades. Many small but good fishing lakes surrounding Waldo are reachable only by trail.

Gold Lake, south of Waldo, is also accessible by road, but you'll hear no noisy motorboats here—though you might see a canoe gliding silently through the still waters. From the Gold Lake Road you can hike in to the Marilyn Lakes.

Snow blocks these access roads in winter, and the forest route to Waldo Lake becomes a marked 9-mile snowmobile trail.

Diamond Peak Wilderness

South of State 58 another wilderness area straddles the Cascade crest around 8,744-foot Diamond Peak. Formed during the volcanic period and later deeply carved by glaciers, the peak is often climbed by mountaineers. In the northern part of the wilderness, the steep precipices of Mount Yoran also offer fine rock climbing practice.

The Pacific Crest Trail enters the wilderness west of Odell Lake, continuing southwest past Summit Lake. Access to the western slopes of the wilderness are from the Hemlock Butte Road and from forest roads west of Crescent and Summit lakes (part of an old pioneer route across the mountains).

Dozens of small lakes, gouged by moving glaciers, surround Diamond Peak. Many can be reached only by cross-country hiking. Lakes deep enough to support fish are stocked regularly, but you may have to share lakeside locations with hungry mosquitoes.

Current information on trails and wilderness recreation is available from the Rigdon ranger station in Oakridge (State 58) or the Crescent ranger station (U.S. Highway 97).

High Cascade lakes

On the eastern side of the mountains, State 58 skirts the northeast shore of Odell Lake and passes east of Crescent and smaller Summit lakes. All three have lakeside campgrounds and boat ramps. These popular spots are crowded in summer.

Odell and Crescent lakes have resorts where you can purchase supplies, arrange accommodations, and rent boats. Summit Lake lies west of Crescent Lake on a forest road. In these lakes you'll catch rainbows, kokanee, and Dolly Varden trout.

The Pacific Crest Trail touches the western ends of Odell and Crescent lakes, providing easy access into Diamond Peak Wilderness and other parts of the high country. Trails south from Crescent Lake lead through rolling countryside to many secluded lakes and pothole ponds. Mosquitoes can be pesky here.

North of State 58, forest roads lead to Davis Lake, where you'll find boat ramps and three campgrounds along the shore.

Lone motorboat breaks the broad surface of Odell Lake, one of several large lakes near U.S. 58. Behind the thick forests rises snowy Diamond Peak.

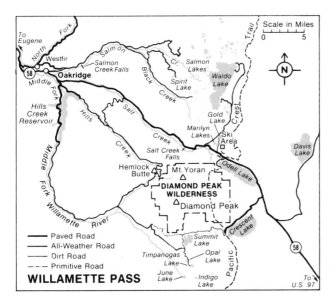

WILLAMETTE PASS

Along the Umpqua

Named for the Umpqua Indians, who once fished these streams and roamed these hills, Umpqua National Forest stretches from the summit of the Cascades down the timbered western slopes toward Roseburg. Twisting through the forest, tumbling over rocky ledges, and plunging in misty waterfalls are the North and South Umpqua rivers and their numerous tributaries. In autumn, the Umpqua country is ablaze with fall color.

Fishing on the Umpqua is superb—it's regarded as one of the state's best fishing streams. Here anglers catch rainbow, cutthroat (sea-run and resident), brown trout, Chinook and silver salmon. Steelhead runs occur both in summer (June to October) and winter (late November until March). Thirty miles of the river—from Rock Creek upstream to the Soda Springs power plant—are open to fly fishing only. Steamboat Creek and its tributaries are closed to all fishing.

Back in the wooded foothills you can still find Indian caves and the remnants of century-old gold mines (see page 112). Campsites and picnicking areas are located along main routes and near fishing lakes; elsewhere, rustic shelters are scattered through the hills.

North Umpqua Highway

Winding beside the North Umpqua and Clearwater rivers for more than 50 miles, State Highway 138 offers a water-level route from Interstate 5 to Diamond Lake, Crater Lake National Park, and U.S.

97. Numerous riverside campgrounds provide sites varying from thick forests with wild rhododendrons and ferns to open, sparsely wooded areas. Short trails lead to bubbling springs or secluded waterfalls. Scenic side roads follow the Little River and Steamboat Creek.

State 138 meets the North Umpqua River about 16 miles northeast of Roseburg at Glide, where an annual spring wildflower show is a local tradition.

Not far from the Glide Ranger Station, the North Umpqua and Little rivers collide head-on; near the view point, rangers have labeled many of the forest flowers, plants, and shrubs.

Trails. From the highway, you can take a 1-mile trail through rain forest vegetation to the site where Fall Creek tumbles through a rocky cleft.

Upstream from Bogus Creek Campground (between Wright Creek and Mott Bridge), a scenic 5-mile riverside path provides access for fishermen and a pleasant interlude for hikers.

For a longer trek, take the 9-mile trail up attractive Boulder Creek (near Boulder Flat Campground), past interesting rock formations.

Waterfalls. At Toketee Lake, forest roads branch off the highway, border the lake, and follow the North Umpqua River northeast. On this route you can take a half-mile trail along white water to a view point of graceful Toketee Falls; stop for a look at Umpqua Hot Springs and continue on the back road to Lemolo Lake.

State 138 now follows the Clearwater River upstream past a series of waterfalls, each with its campground and scenic trails: Watson Falls, at 272 feet, highest in southern Oregon; Whitehorse Falls, tumbling through the campground into a shady pool; and Clearwater Falls, sparkling as it cascades over a 30-foot drop. At Lemolo Junction, a paved road leads north, circling Lemolo Lake and providing access to Lemolo Falls and Cascade trails.

A trio of enjoyable detours

Paved side roads branch north and south off State 138, leading to a self-guided forest tour, more waterfalls, gold mines, a nature trail, and several small lakes.

Along the Little River. On the 27-mile road between Glide and Lake-in-the-Woods, you can see Wolf Creek Falls, follow a short nature trail up Wolf Creek, camp or picnic in the forest, fish for trout at several lakes, and take short hikes to Yakso Falls and Hemlock Falls.

Up Steamboat Creek. Northeast of Steamboat, a paved road follows Steamboat Creek into the Calapooya Mountains. A favorite destination is Steamboat Falls, 7 miles upstream, where you'll find a small camping and picnic area. An important salmon and steelhead spawning stream, Steamboat Creek is closed to all fishing. Often you'll see the migrating fish traveling up a fish ladder or trying to jump the falls.

To the Bohemia Mines. Another road, paved most of the way, heads north up Canton Creek to the old mining district on the slopes of Bohemia Mountain (see page 79).

Vacationing at Diamond Lake

Below Mount Thielsen's jagged pinnacle and somber green slopes spread the blue waters of Diamond Lake. Located 4 miles from the north entrance of Crater Lake National Park, Diamond Lake is a favorite family vacation spot. Campgrounds and picnic areas are scattered along its shore, and a resort on the lake's east side offers year-round accommodations.

You can rent a boat for lake fishing, and riding horses and pack animals are available from June to September.

Superb fishing draws anglers to the Umpqua in quest of steelhead, trout, and salmon.

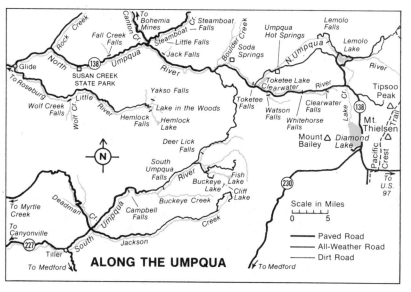

ALONG THE UMPQUA

Trails. In summer, the Diamond Lake Information Center can provide maps, brochures, and recreation suggestions. Short trails you might enjoy include the ½-mile lakeside nature trail and a 2-mile route along the north shore to the fish hatchery at Lake Creek.

West of the lake, a 7-mile path traverses the Rogue-Umpqua divide through old-growth timber and open meadows.

To the east, trails climb through alpine timber and pumice flats to 9,182-foot Mount Thielsen, Tipsoo Peak, and Maidu Lake, all along the Pacific Crest Trail.

Water sports. Sandy beaches attract swimmers and sunbathers, while fishermen cast their lines both from boat and shore, pulling in good catches of rainbow and Kamloops trout.

Snow trails in the southern Cascades

In the south Cascades, a number of marked snow trails provide fun for skiers, snowshoers, and snowmobilers. Access to most of the trails is from State 58 (in the Odell and Crescent lakes area) and from State 138 near Diamond Lake.

Trail information is available at Forest Service ranger stations at Oakridge on State 58, Crescent and Chemult on U.S. 97, and Toketee on State 138. Ask for the comprehensive *South Cascades Snow Trails* brochure containing information on marked snowmobile trail routes, accommodations, and winter services.

Snowmobile trails in the region range from the easy 1½-mile Odell Lake-Crescent Lake Airstrip route to the 80-mile-long South Cascades Trail, a challenging 3-day trip combining three of the area's marked routes.

Among many possible day excursions are a pair of loop trails, each 13 miles in length, circling Diamond Lake and Crescent Lake; both offer wintry views of nearby peaks. A 12-mile route goes south from Diamond Lake to a view point on Crater Lake's north rim; snowmobiles must stay on marked trails in the national park.

Skiers and snowshoers will have the trails to themselves on the 12-mile Diamond View trail south of Odell Lake and on the Howlock and Thielsen trails east of Diamond Lake.

Diamond Lake freezes over in winter; in some years anglers fish through the ice when trout season opens in spring.

River road up the South Umpqua

Less well-known is the South Umpqua, which joins the North Umpqua near Roseburg. From Canyonville, State Highway 227 follows the river upstream about 24 miles to Tiller. Inquire at the ranger station here for information on campgrounds, forest roads, and trails.

The highway continues south toward Medford, while a forest road branches northeast from Tiller, closely following the river.

Dusting of snow sets off Crater Lake's brilliant blue and the deep green of bordering conifers. Wizard Island's lava cone rises near the shore.

Waterfalls. The South Umpqua also has its waterfalls—Campbell Falls, about 12 miles above Tiller, and South Umpqua Falls, 9 miles further upstream, where a wide expanse of water cascades over interesting rock formations. Picnic grounds are located nearby.

Hike-in lakes. Horsemen and hikers will find trails leading south to Fish Lake and to neighboring Buckeye and Cliff lakes; best lake fishing is in spring and fall.

Crater Lake National Park

In a state filled with spectacular scenery, Crater Lake ranks in a class by itself. A sapphire jewel cradled by encircling cliffs, it is the deepest lake in the United States—1,932 feet—and sixth deepest in the world. Its surface is approximately 6,177 feet above sea level, and rugged rock walls tower as much as 2,000 feet above the water.

Figures mean little as you gaze at the lake; its moods change with the light, the weather, and the season. Whether you first see its deep blue waters reflecting a mirrorlike panorama of cliffs and clouds, shimmering like molten silver on a midsummer afternoon, or framed by a rocky rim powdered with snow, it's a sight you'll long remember.

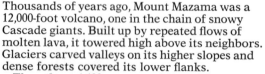

A mountain blew its top, and Crater Lake was formed

Thousands of years ago, Mount Mazama was a 12,000-foot volcano, one in the chain of snowy Cascade giants. Built up by repeated flows of molten lava, it towered high above its neighbors. Glaciers carved valleys on its higher slopes and dense forests covered its lower flanks.

Then about 6,600 years ago, Mount Mazama blew its top. In a series of climactic eruptions, earthquakes shook the mountain. Gases and steam burst upward, blocking out the sun. Frothy, red-hot pumice spewed forth, filling the valleys and covering the land for miles around. Fissures beneath the mountain drained away more of the molten rock.

Mazama's great cone became a huge shell covering an empty pit. Shaken by the volcanic forces and deprived of underground support, the peak collapsed with a thundering roar. When the skies finally cleared, the mountaintop was gone. In its place was a vast bowl, more than 5 miles across and 4,000 feet deep.

Later volcanic activity inside the caldera formed the cinder cone now known as Wizard Island.

Over the centuries, rain and melting snow accumulated in the caldera, forming a deep intense blue lake. Amazingly pure, the water supports little aquatic life. □

Oregon's only national park, Crater Lake lies high in the southern Cascades in the caldera of a collapsed volcano. Discovered in 1853 by a prospector searching for a rumored lost mine, the unique lake received national park status in 1902.

When to visit

Crater Lake National Park is open the year around, but full services and accommodations are available only in summer.

Entrances. The all-year entrance is State Highway 62, cutting across the park's southwestern corner.

Along the highway you'll see forests now growing where molten lava once poured down the mountainsides. Creeks have cut deep canyons through beige beds of pumice, ash, and cinders.

From State 138 the north entrance road crosses a pumice desert to the lake's north rim. This road is closed from the first heavy snowfall, usually in mid-October, until late June.

Accommodations. Perched on the rim overlooking the lake, Crater Lake Lodge is open from mid-June to mid-September. "Christmas" is celebrated August 25 with a decorated tree and carolers; often a late August snowfall adds a wintry touch. A dining room and cocktail lounge overlook the lake. Rustic cabins are also available. Transportation can be arranged between Klamath Falls and the park.

You'll find a cafeteria and gift shop at Rim Village, where picnic supplies, souvenirs, and other small items can be purchased. It is open daily in summer, weekends and holidays only the rest of the year.

Campgrounds. Within the park, campsites are located near the south entrance (Mazama Campground) and on the road to the Pinnacles (Lost Creek Campground). If weather permits, they remain open from mid-June until late September. No campsites can be reserved. Dogs and cats are permitted but must be kept on a leash or in your car at all times; animals are not permitted in buildings or on park trails. The Rim Village area, atop the crater rim, is a picnicking and day use area.

Summer programs. Park rangers conduct an extensive program for visitors; check posted schedules for the day's events.

Early in your visit, stop at the Sinnott Memorial overlooking the lake; plan your visit to coincide with the ranger's short talk on the geologic origin of the lake (usually scheduled hourly in summer from 9 A.M. to 6 P.M.).

In the nearby exhibit building, examples of the park's plants, rocks, and wildlife are on display, and you can purchase maps and booklets about Crater Lake and the park.

CRATER LAKE NATIONAL PARK

To Diamond Lake

Crest Trail

Pacific

Rim
Cleetwood Trail
Llao Rock
Cleetwood Cove
Hillman Peak
Wizard Island
Crater Lake
Drive
The Watchman
Bybee Creek
Discovery Point
Cloudcap
Sinnott Memorial
Phantom Ship
Mount Scott
RIM VILLAGE
Garfield Peak
Sun Notch
Kerr Notch
Castle Creek
Park Hqs.
Applegate Peak
Wildflower Garden
LOST CREEK CAMPGROUND
To Medford
Vidae Fall
Crest Trail
Munson Cr.
Wheeler Cr.
Sand Creek
Godfrey Glen
Grayback Ridge Motor Nature Trail
The Pinnacles
MAZAMA CAMPGROUND
Annie Creek
Sun Creek
Pacific
To Klamath Falls

Paved Road
Unpaved Road

Scale in Miles
0   1   2

Rangers conduct a variety of "discovery hikes," or you can explore on your own. Illustrated evening programs are presented in Crater Lake Lodge and Mazama Campground.

Winter at Crater Lake. Snow and ice cast a magic spell over the park, transforming it into a winter wonderland. As you drive through high snowbanks, firs and hemlocks appear quilted in dazzling white. Snowy cliffs rim the indigo lake. The coffee shop remains open to thaw skiers and other visitors.

Check at park headquarters for information on cross-country skiing and other winter activities. Since the park averages 50 feet of snow annually, be prepared; tire chains may be needed at any time.

Exploring the park

After viewing Crater Lake from the rim and learning how it was formed, you'll want to see more of the park.

A favorite excursion is the Rim Drive, a 33-mile route circling clockwise around the lake rim, high above the water. Snow closes the loop from mid-October until early July.

In summer a sightseeing bus makes the trip daily, leaving from the lodge and stopping at several view points. Or you can make the one-way drive in your own car.

To more fully enjoy the park's variety, take along a picnic and break your circuit with one or more side jaunts. You can take a self-guided nature trail through a wildflower garden, descend a zigzag trail to the lake for a boat trip, or hike to a high point for a panoramic view.

Nature trails. In July and early August, wildflowers are blooming throughout the park. In Castle Crest Wildflower Garden, near park headquarters, a trail traverses forest, swamp, meadow, and streamside terrain. Small labels identify many plants.

Near the park's south entrance, the 1½-mile Godfrey Glen nature trail parallels the steep canyon cut by Munson Creek. A booklet, available at the trail entrance, describes the terrain.

On the south side of the lake, motorists can drive the Grayback Ridge Motor Nature Trail, a scenic, low-speed road winding 5 miles from Lost Creek Campground to Vidae Falls on the Rim Drive. A guide booklet noting points of special interest is available at the beginning of the trip.

Early in the morning, you'll often see wildlife along the trails or near the rim. Bluejays and Clarks nutcrackers scold you in harsh tones from the trees, and chipmunks and golden-mantled ground squirrels scramble among the rocks searching for crumbs. Occasionally you'll glimpse a grazing deer, half hidden by trees, or a bear prowling the campground looking for the remains of a picnic lunch. Enjoy the wildlife from a distance.

Down to the lake. For a boat trip on the lake, you must hike down the Cleetwood Trail, a 1-mile switchback path descending from the north rim to the water's edge.

In summer sightseeing boats leave from Cleet-wood Cove for 2-hour trips around the lake. Often a naturalist goes along to point out geological features of the lake and rim (check the bulletin board at the top of the trail for current information). During the trip the boat makes a brief stop at Wizard Island and passes near Phantom Ship rock.

If you wish to stop over on Wizard Island, a trail leads through lava to the top of the cone, where you can look into the island's crater.

Fishing is legal on the lake, and no license is required. On Wizard Island fishing is best on the opposite shore from the boat landing.

Drive to the Pinnacles. From Kerr Notch on Rim Drive, a 6-mile road branches southeast to the Pinnacles. These needlelike pumice spires rise 200 feet out of Wheeler Creek Canyon.

Trails to view points. From Rim Village, the 1½-mile Discovery Point Trail heads north along the rim to the point where prospector John Wesley Hillman first saw the lake in 1853. The trail to Garfield Peak begins behind the lodge, climbing east along the rim wall to the peak some 1,900 feet above the blue water.

On the south rim, an easy, 10-minute walk from Rim Drive leads through hemlock forest and meadows to Sun Notch for a spectacular view of Phantom Ship. You'll enjoy the wildflowers in Sun Meadow in July.

Trails also lead to two mountaintop fire lookouts. Mount Scott dominates the eastern part of the park; a 2½-mile trail climbs steadily to the summit. On the western rim, an easy ¾-mile path leads from a trailhead parking lot along Rim Drive to the lookout atop The Watchman. A natural history museum and viewing platform are located beneath the lookout.

At Sinnott Memorial, *Crater Lake ranger talks on the area's geology and explains how the lake was formed. Check the park bulletin boards for special events.*

East of the Cascades

Discover this sunny land of broad vistas

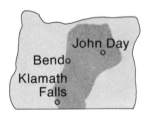

Cowboy gets ready to wrestle with steer in bulldogging event at Tygh Valley rodeo.

Juniper-strewn hills rise behind a cluster of Indian tepees at Kah-Nee-Ta vacation resort on the Warm Springs Indian Reservation.

The spacious, sun-drenched country of central Oregon is richly satisfying to persons who love the outdoors. From the pine-clad eastern slopes of the Cascades, a vast high plateau stretches halfway across the state to the Blue Mountains and the lonely southeastern corner.

Two main rivers—the Deschutes and the John Day—and their tributaries dominate the region, carving scenic canyons through the plateau as they wind north to meet the Columbia.

Intriguing geological features pervade central Oregon. Hundreds of volcanoes left their deep imprint on the landscape as they belched forth rivers of lava, cones of cinders, and fields of volcanic glass. Weathered buttes and mesas rise abruptly from the plateau. The massive stratified terraces of central Oregon are a legacy of the ancient landlocked lakes that once covered great inland areas of the west. Rockhounds can hunt for thundereggs, agates, petrified wood, and other semiprecious stones. Geologists have uncovered the fossilized remains of prehistoric plants and animals.

Central Oregon still kindles memories of the Old West. Indians roamed these lands, fur trappers and pioneer scouts explored its valleys and canyons, and sheepmen and cattlemen battled for grazing rights. Occasional ghost towns and tumble-down buildings testify to the hard life on the windswept prairie.

Crooked River *cuts a steep 300-foot canyon through colorful sedimentary rock at Smith Rock State Park. You view the winding river from a small picnic area.*

Hot lava *carved this underground tunnel at Lava River Caves State Park.*

Along the Deschutes

The Deschutes River dominates central Oregon; it is the region's principal life-giving artery. A complex and scenic waterway, it bubbles from underground springs in the southern Cascades and tumbles northward, cutting through ponderosa pine forests and lava flows.

In its central section, the Deschutes is joined by the Metolius and Crooked rivers, their waters expanding in a pair of deep reservoirs. It plunges another 100 miles northward through basalt-rimmed canyons to the Columbia. More than 150 years ago, French-Canadian trappers and traders named it *Rivière des Chutes* (River of the Falls).

The Deschutes has acquired an impressive reputation among fishermen for its redsides (native rainbow trout) and for runs of Chinook salmon in the spring and steelhead in the fall. When salmon and steelhead move upriver, every riffle and bar has its cluster of anglers.

The lower river

Fishermen know the lower Deschutes well; this splendid stretch of river offers some of the finest trout, steelhead, and salmon fishing to be found anywhere. In recent years, white-water boaters have taken up the challenge of the Deschutes rapids; river excursions start below Pelton Dam.

You can truly experience the canyon's grandeur and raw magnificence only from the river. At times the rugged, rocky gorge walls close in, and at other places they widen to border grass-fringed flatlands. Occasional trees and clumps of grass dot the shore. Rattlesnakes gravitate toward the water, so be alert. The valley can be quite hot in summer, though it is cooled in morning and evening by strong winds; mornings are fresh and sparkling.

Access to the lower river has improved since the Bureau of Land Management constructed a road downriver from Maupin and Sherars Bridge, a traditional Indian fishing site and location of a pioneer toll bridge. Stop at the BLM district office in Prineville for information about BLM campgrounds and boat ramps on the lower Deschutes.

Tygh Valley's All-Indian Rodeo

In cattle states like Oregon, many Indian cowboys are occupied with daily tasks of the corral and range; some are among the best rodeo performers.

On the 3rd weekend in May, Indian cowboys from all over the West gather in Tygh Valley, 32 miles south of The Dalles on U.S. Highway 197, to compete in traditional rodeo events. Other activities include Indian dance performances, a Saturday night dance, and a Sunday buckaroo breakfast.

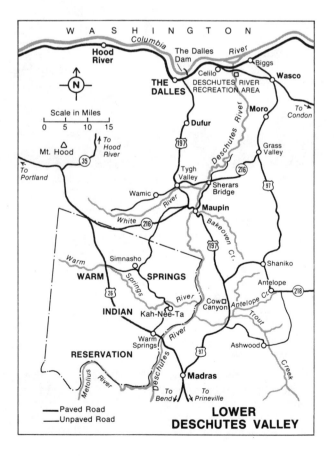

Shaniko, an echo of the Old West

From Biggs Junction on the Columbia, U.S. Highway 97 cuts southward east of the Deschutes.

The Old West lingers on in Shaniko—a scattering of weathered buildings in the middle of a grassland plateau. During the early 1900s, bitter range battles were fought nearby.

Seventy years ago Shaniko was in its prime—central Oregon's sole railroad terminus, center of a sheep raising and wool shipping industry, and headquarters for railroad construction workers building a new line up the Deschutes. By-passed by the new railroad, Shaniko's influence as a shipping and trading center rapidly waned.

Shaniko today. But Shaniko is no ghost town; it still has about 70 residents. Activity centers in the impressive two-story brick Shaniko Hotel, built in 1900; most of its rooms are occupied by pensioners who formerly worked on nearby ranches.

Shaniko's other buildings—and its sidewalks—are of wood. In recent years, efforts have been made to preserve historical remnants, including vehicles and household articles of bygone days.

Antelope and Ashwood. State Highway 218 cuts southeast from Shaniko to Antelope, another one-time stage station and rip-roaring frontier town. Poplar and locust trees shade the remaining buildings here and in Ashwood, 20 miles south by gravel road. Both towns thrived around the turn of the century but today are virtually deserted.

West of Ashwood, the gravel road back to U.S. 97 passes near the Priday agate beds.

Visit an Indian reservation

Visitors are welcome on the Warm Springs Indian Reservation. You can unroll your sleeping bag inside a tepee, ride horseback over sagebrush covered hills, enjoy Indian foods such as baked salmon and wild huckleberries, and attend tribal festivities.

The Confederated Tribes of the Warm Springs Indian Reservation have developed a multimillion dollar vacation resort — Kah-Nee-Ta — along the Warm Springs River. To reach it, drive northwest of Madras on U.S. Highway 26 to the community of Warm Springs, then continue 11 miles north.

Several dozen tepees cluster near the meandering river. *Nee-sha* (cottages with kitchens) and a hilltop lodge-convention center also provide accommodations; campgrounds and trailer hookups are available.

Natural hot springs warm the swimming pool, and a golf course extends along the river. Hiking, horseback riding, and tennis are other diversions; daily or seasonal reservation fishing permits are available. Activities may include Indian dance performances, storytelling, and arts and crafts.

Major events on the reservation include the Root Festival (early April), Pi-Ume-Sha Pow Wow and Treaty Days (June), Fun Day (July 4), and the Huckleberry Feast (August). For exact dates, check with the Madras Chamber of Commerce.

Madras, farming and recreation center

East of the Cascades, settlement proceeded slowly during the mid-19th century. But in 1855 treaties were drawn up with bands of the Wasco and Walla Walla Indians, and the first trans-Cascade road was completed in 1862. Homesteaders soon followed.

Madras, hub and county seat of sun-drenched Jefferson County, owes its agricultural prosperity to the railroad, which arrived in 1911, and the development of irrigation projects in the late 1930s. Peppermint, potatoes, and grass seed are cultivated on some 50,000 irrigated acres.

A town of about 2,000, Madras is a center for rockhounds, fishermen, boaters, and hunters. Water-skiers flock to the two reservoirs on the Deschutes. Anglers can fish the big lakes or nearby rivers, and hunters bring in deer and game birds.

Rockhounds gather in Madras during the Rockhound Pow Wow in June. If you're here in late October, you can watch working cowboys at the Oregon Horse Cutting Association annual show.

Cove Palisades State Park

West of Madras, the waters of the Deschutes are impounded behind a pair of dams. These reservoirs —Lake Simtustus behind Pelton Dam, and Lake Billy Chinook behind Round Butte Dam—offer splendid water-oriented recreation.

Central Oregon's most popular state park, Cove Palisades (sometimes called The Cove) borders the southeastern shore of Lake Billy Chinook near the confluence of the Crooked and Deschutes rivers. The Metolius River enters the lake from the west. Narrow watery fingers stretch back through the three river canyons.

For centuries prior to their impoundment, the rivers cut through many layers of lava, leaving the banded rim rocks exposed to view. These towering vertical cliffs provide a spectacular setting.

Cove Palisades State Park has a pair of shaded campgrounds, as well as picnicking and swimming areas, boat launching ramps and dock, and a marina (on the Crooked River arm) where you can rent boats and obtain supplies in summer. Lake fishing is outstanding from bank or boat. Water-skiers cut arcs in the center of the reservoir. In summer, evening programs are presented in an outdoor theater.

A road follows the canyon's east side down to the water (boaters can park and launch boats here) and to an observation building overlooking Round Butte Dam.

Ghost town explorers can follow a gravel road west of the park to now-deserted Grandview.

The Crooked River valley

Upriver from Lake Billy Chinook, the twisting course of the Crooked River carves its unique signature across the central Oregon landscape—cutting

Exposed layers of lava at Cove Palisades State Park are reflected in the waters of Lake Billy Chinook —named for a Wasco Indian who joined Fremont in 1843.

through narrow canyons, meandering across wide valleys, and swelling into reservoir lakes.

Fur trappers and frontier scouts passed through this country in the early 19th century. Ogden Scenic Wayside, overlooking an awesome stretch of the Crooked River canyon 8 miles north of Redmond, honors Peter Skene Ogden, a Hudson's Bay Company trader who explored this area in 1825-26.

Another splendid view point is Smith Rock State Park, where the Crooked River cuts a curving 300-foot-high canyon through colorful sedimentary rock. Thrusting high above the river, Smith Rock dominates the flat farm lands and lava plains for miles around.

East to Prineville

Prineville has a colorful past. As a young town in the Old West it saw Indian raids, range wars between cattlemen and sheepmen, and vigilante justice. Homesteaders struggled to exist on these windswept desert grasslands. Between Madras and Prineville you can still see a few windmills that pumped water for early 20th century farmers.

With a population of 5,300, Prineville is the largest and only incorporated town in sparsely settled Crook County. Livestock raising, lumbering, and mining are the county's principal industries.

Take a look at the splendid old Crook County Courthouse and its clock tower. The city is also proud of its City of Prineville Railroad, the only city-owned and operated railway in the United States. Built in 1918, the 18-mile-long railroad links Prineville to the main north-south line.

Rockhounding country. Rockhounds know this region as a rich source of semiprecious stones. You

Rockhounds search for prized agates and thundereggs

As a beachcomber you may have scanned the coastal sands in search of agates—but did you know these transluscent gems are found in the Willamette Valley, central Oregon, and Malheur County as well? Oregon is prime rockhounding country, where diggers also uncover treasured thundereggs, petrified wood, jaspers, fossils, and and obsidian.

Central Oregon probably offers the most concentrated beds of semiprecious gemstones for recreational rockhounds, but you can find minerals and fossils in all parts of the state. The state Travel Information office offers a folder on Oregon rockhounding areas; for more suggestions on digging sites, contact local chambers of commerce, rock shops, and Forest Service and Bureau of Land Management offices.

Rockhounding is usually a rugged and dirty pastime, so wear old clothing and sturdy boots. Tools should suit the digging conditions—shovels, picks, rock hammers, long handled chisels, or other pointed instruments are often used.

You can dig on federal lands, subject to certain limitations; check locally before you dig. Some private operators open their lands for digging; you usually pay by the pound for rock you haul away. In digging, avoid undermining trees or tunneling through unsupported soil or overhanging banks that might cave in. Fill in pits or trenches when you finish digging. Check before using power equipment.

Rattlesnakes are found in some areas during the warm months, so watch out for them in rock slides, around damp areas, and under old buildings and ledges.

Hobbyists enjoy sharing tips and exhibiting their prize finds; rockhounding clubs and commercial rock shops are local gathering spots. Gem and mineral shows—held annually in Sweet Home, Eugene, Medford, Roseburg, and Newport —attract good crowds. Thousands of hobbyists congregate at summer rockhound pow wows in Madras, Prineville, and Nyssa to buy, trade, and go on field trips to local digging sites. □

---

can dig for agate, limb casts, agatized jasper, and thundereggs on more than 1,000 acres of Prineville Chamber of Commerce mining claims on public lands; stop at the office for a map and information on digging areas. Rockhounds gather in Prineville for a Rockhound Pow Wow in early July.

Local events. In late May, the Central Oregon Timber Festival attracts contestants from all over the west. Regional artists display and sell their work at the Central Oregon Arts and Crafts Festival in Prineville's Pioneer Park each June. The outstanding Crooked River Roundup, part of the Rodeo Cowboys Association (RCA) rodeo circuit, comes in mid-July; pari-mutuel betting is an added attraction. Ranchers and farm families gather for the Crook County Fair in late August.

The tiny community of Powell Butte, southwest of Prineville on State Highway 126, attracts visitors from all over Oregon on the first Saturday of November. Local families stage the Lords Acre Auction, an old-fashioned fund raising social to benefit the community church.

Prineville Reservoir

The Crooked River winds through the city of Prineville; upriver is popular Prineville Reservoir and its state park and resort area. Several roads lead to various parts of the valley.

Located 18 miles southeast of Prineville, the reservoir offers boating, water-skiing, fishing, camping and picnicking, and nearby rockhounding.

A state park along the lake's north shore offers campsites and picnic areas spread over the juniper-dotted hillside. Facilities include a boat launching ramp, fishing piers, and a bathhouse and swimming area. Anglers fish for bass, rainbow trout, and catfish.

A small resort on the south shore offers boat rentals, tackle, and other supplies.

Into Ochoco National Forest

Pleasant day trips in this region offer a sampling of the upper river, the Ochoco Mountains, and local rockhounding sites.

One of the best side trips is the all-day excursion along upper Crooked River to Paulina and Big Summit Prairie. Four miles east of Paulina, turn north to Wolf Creek Campground. Forest Road 142 follows the creek, then veers west past the pastoral prairie, where cattle graze placidly. You continue to Ochoco Ranger Station and U.S. 26.

CROOKED RIVER VALLEY

Another away-from-it-all route continues east from Paulina to Suplee, Izee, and U.S. Highway 395; it is paved most of the way.

You can make a loop trip north of U.S. 26 past Stein's Pillar, a geological oddity northeast of Prineville. You head north of town on McKay Road, then return on Mill Creek Road to U.S. 26 near Ochoco Lake. Stein's Pillar protrudes like a solitary stone finger south of Mill Creek Road (about 8 miles north of U.S. 26). Some 30 million years ago, volcanic eruptions buried this area beneath ash and lava; the softer tufas gradually eroded, exposing the hardier crags, of which Stein's Pillar is the most prominent. Rockhounds find thundereggs on several digging sites north of U.S. 26.

Ochoco Lake State Park borders the reservoir 8 miles east of Prineville. Tent campsites, picnic tables, and a boat launching ramp are available.

The upper Deschutes

Upstream from Cove Palisades State Park, the Deschutes River parallels U.S. 97 past Redmond, flows through Bend and past Sunriver, then curves westward toward its Cascade headwaters.

This is central Oregon's prime vacation area, enhanced by a sunny dry climate, thick pine forests, scenic mountain lakes, fascinating geologic features, and opportunities for outdoor recreation the year around.

Redmond—reindeer and a rock garden

Redmond, a town of about 4,500 at the junction of U.S. 97 and U.S. 126, is a Deschutes vacation center in the heart of juniper country. Lumbering, cattle raising, dairying, and agriculture support the local economy. The Deschutes County Fair is staged here in early August, featuring rodeo events, horse racing, and a buckaroo breakfast.

Smokejumper base. Redmond Air Center at Roberts Field is the regional U.S. Forest Service base for training smokejumpers, the hardy firefighters who parachute to the scene of remote forest fires. In summer, you can observe training activities—including practice jumps from towers; phone 548-2177 to inquire about training times and arrange a visit to the facility.

Reindeer ranch. Two miles west of Redmond on U.S. 126, Ron Troutman raises reindeer for use during the Christmas season. The rest of the year, visitors are welcome to stop to see the animals.

Cline Falls State Park. This pleasant picnickers' oasis borders the Deschutes 4 miles west of Redmond on State 126. Picnic tables are scattered amid the juniper and willow trees along the river bank. Children can explore the grassy shore; anglers find fair to good fishing for rainbow trout.

Petersen Rock Gardens. When his collection of rocks and gemstones grew beyond manageable size, Rasmus Petersen began transforming his

Drooping willows and tall ponderosa pines line the Deschutes River as it passes Bend's Drake Park. Broad lawns slope to the water where waterfowl swim.

rocks into agate mansions, lava bridges, towers of petrified wood, obsidian castles, and traditional rock gardens. The attraction is open to the public southwest of Redmond.

Pause awhile at Bend

Bend has long been a place where travelers paused to rest and refresh themselves. Pioneers driving their wagons northeast toward the Ochoco Valley called this spot Farewell Bend; at a curve in the Deschutes River, they took a final look at their shady campsite, then headed northeast into sage and juniper country.

The town's name has been shortened, but its location at the crossroads of U.S. 97 and U.S. Highway 20 still makes it a logical stopping place. The Deschutes River flows through town.

Tall ponderosa pines and ancient gnarled junipers shade the sloping lawns at Drake Park, which curves along a wide and placid stretch of the Deschutes near the heart of town. Families lounge on the grass, young people paddle in canoes, and resident swans and geese share the stream with migrant waterfowl. Bend families celebrate the Fourth of July here with a full day of events.

Farther downstream is smaller Pioneer Park, landscaped with lawns and flower beds. East of U.S. 97, Juniper Park contains a swimming pool, sports facilities, and a children's playground.

Perched on a hill west of town, the buildings of Central Oregon Community College blend into a wooded setting on a hilltop site.

Deschutes County Pioneer Museum, at Greenwood and Harriman streets, has Indian artifacts and pioneer memorabilia; it is open afternoons from Tuesday through Saturday.

For a spectacular panorama of Cascade peaks, drive to the top of Pilot Butte, a 500-foot-high symmetrical cinder cone a few blocks east of town.

Waterside picnic sites. Fishermen and picnickers enjoy Robert W. Sawyer State Park beside the Deschutes just north of Bend. Another pleasant spot beside the river is Tumalo State Park, 5 miles northwest of Bend just off U.S. 20.

If you head west of Bend along sparkling Tumalo Creek, you can picnic at Shevlin Park, a large forest preserve 5 miles from town, or near 97-foot Tumalo Falls some 15 miles west of Bend, where creekside trails branch out from the picnic area.

Visit an observatory. From mid-June to mid-September, visitors are welcome at Pine Mountain Observatory, a University of Oregon research facility near the summit of 6,395-foot Pine Mountain. You can visit Thursday through Sunday from 2 to 5 P.M. and from 7 P.M. to dusk.

To reach the observatory, drive 26 miles southeast of Bend on U.S. 20; just east of Millican, turn south on Forest Road 2012 and proceed 8 miles to the site, keeping to the right.

In a casual atmosphere, astronomers answer questions and describe the observatory's research. On clear afternoons, the site affords a fine view of the Cascades and the Oregon desert. When schedules permit, visitors may gaze at the sky at dusk through the observatory's 24-inch telescope.

Outdoor fun at Sunriver

The resort development of Sunriver borders the winding Deschutes River 15 miles southwest of Bend. A lodge and residential areas face a pine-fringed meadow and a panorama of snowy Cascade peaks and dark green forests.

Sunriver's inviting bike paths lure this mother and child for a late afternoon ride. Paved trails wind through the resort's recreation and residential areas.

Since commercial development began in the mid-1960s, planning has emphasized retaining the area's natural beauty. Bicycles and electric carts are more popular than automobiles; a 17-mile network of paved trails links all parts of the complex. Sunriver also has its own airstrip.

Life at Sunriver is oriented toward the outdoors —fishing in nearby lakes or along the Deschutes, boating or canoeing on the river, horseback riding and bicycling on a web of pathways. You can play a round of golf or several sets of tennis, swim in an outdoor pool, or enjoy a nature trail—all without leaving Sunriver. The resort has its own nature center, and a resident naturalist conducts programs and field trips. Guest artists and craftsmen conduct summer classes. A miniature paddlewheeler makes trips on the Deschutes in summer.

Activity centers around the lodge, where visitors can obtain information on events and rental equipment; a small shopping mall is located nearby.

In winter, buses transport skiers up to Mount Bachelor. Snowshoe and ski touring enthusiasts follow winding trails across the countryside (rental equipment is available), and visitors enjoy horsedrawn sleigh rides across the snowy meadow.

The Cascade lakes

Stretching along the eastern slopes of the Cascade Range, Deschutes National Forest encompasses a 1½ million-acre preserve. In addition to the usual forest activities, you can explore a countryside shaped by volcanic activity. Recreation maps and information are available from the Deschutes National Forest office in Bend (211 East Revere) or at district ranger offices in Sisters and Crescent.

One of the loveliest parts of the Deschutes country is the Cascade Lakes region west of Bend. Numerous Forest Service campgrounds are sprinkled along the shores of lakes and streams, but you don't have to unroll your sleeping bag beside a campfire unless you want to. The Bend area has accommodations ranging from elegant resorts and condominiums (at Sunriver, Black Butte, and Inn of the Seventh Mountain) to comfortable motels—some with kitchen units—and rustic housekeeping cabins at lake resorts.

Bachelor's challenging slopes

Central Oregon's foremost ski resort—Mount Bachelor Ski Area—clusters along the northern slopes of Bachelor Butte (also called Mount Bachelor) about 22 miles west of Bend. Dry powder snow, sunshiny days, and challenging slopes attract skiers and racers from all over the West.

Skiing activity continues from November until June. Six double chairlifts and a triple chairlift transport skiers above timberline to the 7,700-foot level for superb downhill and slalom runs. Beginners have their own electric rope tow.

Three day lodges provide food service, warming

rooms, a ski shop, and equipment rentals, but no overnight accommodations are available at the ski area. Lessons and day care service are available. You can arrange for a guided cross-country ski tour to nearby lakes. Ski races are held several times each season, and in summer a racing camp attracts young skiers. During the winter season, bus service transports skiers to the area from Bend, Sunriver, and Inn of the Seventh Mountain.

The Cascade Lakes Highway

From Bend a paved road arcs west through fragrant ponderosa pines to some of the state's best fishing, boating, hiking, and camping. More than a dozen tree-rimmed mountain lakes lie near the main route.

The Cascade Lakes Highway (also known as Century Drive) climbs southwest from Bend over the 6,400-foot-high north shoulder of Bachelor, curves south around Crane Prairie Reservoir, and cuts east to return to U.S. 97 near La Pine. Some of the state's highest peaks are constantly in view.

Superb fishing draws many vacationers here, but families enjoy many other activities as well. More than two dozen Forest Service campgrounds offer picnic tables and campsites bordering the jewel-like lakes and clear cold streams. Rustic resorts are located at Elk, Cultus, and South Twin lakes.

The highway is generally free of snow by late June or early July and remains open until the first heavy snow in late fall. Mosquitoes can be pesky in summer. Many vacationers prefer late season vacations during the warm days and crisp nights of September and October.

Fishing. Brook and rainbow trout are found in most of the lakes, but anglers also pull in cutthroat, mackinaw (lake trout), kokanee (landlocked sockeye salmon), coho salmon, and whitefish. Hosmer Lake is famed for its landlocked Atlantic salmon. Trout, coho, kokanee, and whitefish are found in Crane Prairie and Wickiup reservoirs and Davis Lake.

Check local regulations, for they vary by lake and stream. Some waters have boat speed limits or restrictions on trolling or the use of boats or motors. Some lakes and streams are restricted to fly fishing only.

Water sports. You can sail, canoe, float a raft, or swim in chilly lake waters. Several lakes have marinas where you can rent boats and obtain tackle. Boat ramps are located near many campgrounds. Water-skiing is permitted on Cultus and Little Cultus lakes and Wickiup Reservoir.

Hiking and horse trails. From campgrounds and trailheads along the Cascade Lakes Highway, numerous trails cut across the forested slopes, many of them entering the lake-dotted alpine country of the Three Sisters Wilderness (see page 108).

Scores of small lakes are accessible to day hikers and weekend back packers. Pack and saddle animals are available. For information on trails, outfitters, or other recreation information, check

Sailboats and a canoe glide across tree-rimmed Elk Lake below the snowy South Sister. Cascade Lakes Highway heads west from Bend to a forest playground.

with the Deschutes National Forest office in Bend.

An easy day's trip begins ½ mile south of Elk Lake; the well-used trail goes west to Blow and Doris lakes, continuing into the Mink Lake Basin. Another good family trail cuts 3½ miles northwest from Elk Lake through wildflower meadows to Sisters Mirror Lake.

Trails to Big Green Lake begin north of Sparks and Todd lakes; climbers can veer off to ascend 9,165-foot Broken Top. Big Cultus Lake Campground is the trailhead for weekend hikers heading into the southern part of Three Sisters Wilderness.

Nesting ospreys. Perched atop the ghostly snags of Crane Prairie Reservoir, ospreys breed and raise their young. The fish-eating hawks nest here from April to September, protected from tree-climbing predators by the flooded reservoir. In July and August you can sometimes spot fledglings in nests.

The main osprey nesting area lies near the northwestern section of the lake; you can look at the birds (bring your binoculars) from an observation point north of Quinn River Campground. Often you'll see loons and herons as well. Another small nesting area is off the eastern shore.

Other activities. Flower lovers can enjoy the bright wildflowers blooming in alpine meadows and rocky crevices in July and August. Climbers and amateur geologists can explore the region's volcanic terrain; an accessible lava flow borders the northeastern shore of Davis Lake. Forest roads lace the area; check locally before you venture onto unimproved mountain roads.

Riverside forest camps

If you prefer riverside camping, you'll find several small picnic areas and campgrounds along the

Trail through the lava begins at the Lava Lands Visitor Center south of Bend. Molten lava once exploded through the volcano wall of Lava Butte.

Deschutes between Wickiup Reservoir and Bend.

At Pringle Falls, the river plunges through a narrow chute just downriver from the road. Big River Campground has a boat ramp, and La Pine Recreation Area, accessible from U.S. 97, is one of the larger state camping areas on the river.

Southwest of Bend, forest roads follow the west bank of the Deschutes and provide access to waterfalls where the river cuts through a lava flow.

Land of lava

Restless volcanoes have left dramatic imprints on central Oregon, making it possible for geologists to trace the story of major eruptions such as those of Mazama and Newberry. Some of the most interesting volcanic activity occurred during relatively recent geologic times—within the past few thousand years—and has been little altered by weathering or erosion.

Ancient Mount Newberry was the center of hundreds of small volcanoes scattered for some 70 miles over the Deschutes country east of the Three Sisters. Lava eruptions varied from frothy pumice and molten rivers to tiny cinders and glassy fields of obsidian.

Lava Lands Visitor Center provides an excellent introduction to this country. Afterwards you can take a more knowledgeable look at some of the lava flows, cinder cones, underground tubes, and buckled buttes and ridges identifying the violent eruptions that transformed this countryside.

Lava Lands Visitor Center

The fiery volcanoes that shaped this area provide the theme for Lava Lands Visitor Center 10 miles south of Bend on U.S. 97. Blending into the pines just south of Lava Butte, the Forest Service center interprets the fascinating story of volcanism and guides you to nearby examples where you see first-hand the effects of nature on the rampage.

Five dioramas recreate the Cascades' geologic history, and a relief map displays nearby points of interest. The center is open daily from May through October and weekends only in winter, weather permitting. Hours vary by season. Self-guided interpretive trails lead west from the center.

To the top of Lava Butte

North of the visitor center, a paved road spirals up Lava Butte, one of many miniature volcanoes in the Deschutes country. It hurled volcanic cinders into the air, gradually building up a cinder cone more than 500 feet high. About 2,000 years ago, the volcano disgorged a massive flow of magma which streamed northwest covering some 6,000 acres.

From the summit you look down on this black apron of lava, sprinkled with stunted conifers. Fingers of molten lava spilled into the Deschutes channel, blocking the river's flow and forming a big lake upriver. Eventually the river cut a new channel, forming several waterfalls.

From the summit observation tower, you have an outstanding view of the snowy Cascade peaks and the forested lava country. A paved trail allows visitors to stroll around the crater rim of Lava Butte.

Stay on the trail; off-trail hiking on the cinder slopes leaves long-lasting scars.

A spectacular underground lava tube

You can see another fascinating geologic feature at Lava River Caves State Park, about 1½ miles south of the visitor center. Thousands of years ago, a hot stream of lava broke out of the Mount Newberry foothills, leaving a long underground tunnel that extends nearly a mile through now-solid rock.

Located 12 miles south of Bend off U.S. 97, this unique state park is open daily from May through September; hours are 9 A.M. to 4 P.M. Visitors rent lanterns at a nominal charge, then descend into the cave to explore. The tunnel is open until 5 P.M.

Signs near the cave tell its dramatic geologic story. Then, lighted lantern in hand, you enter the tunnel opening—hardly more than a hole in the ground. Stairs bridge the abrupt drop over volcanic rocks to the floor of a large, cool chamber.

In the main tunnel, you make your way down the ancient course of a river of liquid rock. The tube averages about 35 feet in width, but in places it widens to 50 feet and reaches a height of 58 feet. The cave's walls and ceiling are marked by the lava stream, and in spots iciclelike projections of lava hang above your head.

The temperature inside the cave remains about 40° throughout the year. Pioneers used the cool cavern to preserve venison, and Indian artifacts were found near the entrance.

Trees cast by molten lava

Lava Cast Forest illustrates another intriguing aspect—"stone trees" formed some 6,000 years ago when molten lava from ancient Mount Newberry flowed into a living pine forest, forming lava casts around upright trees. Other trees were knocked over and encased in horizontal, pipelike casts. Eventually the charred trees inside the casts died and rotted away, leaving a stone forest of hollow lava tubes extending above the surface of the flow.

To reach Lava Cast Forest, drive about 15 miles south of Bend on U.S. 97 and turn east on Forest Road 195 opposite the entrance to Sunriver. The cinder road continues 10 miles, ending near a small picnic area among pine trees (no water).

A paved path meanders for nearly a mile through the jagged lava fields. Some casts extend 4 or 5 feet above the lava surface, their tubes penetrating up to 10 or 12 feet below. You can see the imprint of pine bark on the inner wall of some casts.

Newberry's massive volcanic crater

Ancient Mount Newberry was a massive fire mountain, around 12,000 feet high and some 25 miles in diameter at its base—the most imposing peak east of the Cascades. Lava drained from the restless volcano through faults and fissures, and the walls supporting its broad dome weakened. The giant shield volcano then collapsed within itself, leaving a large crater 4 to 5 miles in diameter.

Newberry Crater now cradles a pair of scenic lakes. To reach Paulina (pronounced Paul-EYE-nuh) and East lakes, drive about 24 miles south of Bend on U.S. 97 and turn east; the paved side road leads about 13 miles east to the lakes. Just west of Paulina Lake, the waters of Paulina Creek tumble from a semicircular rim into the canyon.

Forest camps along the lake shores are popular with vehicle campers. Tent campsites are available at McKay Crossing Campground beside Paulina Creek, and rustic resort accommodations are available at the lakes.

A short walk south of the main road near Paulina Lake, molten rock from within Mount Newberry created a large obsidian flow, believed to be the most extensive field of volcanic glass on the continent. An interpretive trail winds through the area. For generations, Indians chiseled arrowheads and spear points from the obsidian they found here.

In summer you can drive up an unpaved road to the summit of 7,985-foot Paulina Peak, named for the chief of a marauding outlaw band who for years terrorized the scattered settlers of the region. From the summit you enjoy a magnificent view.

Exploring lava caves

Many interesting lava tubes, some of them ice-choked, are found throughout the area. Inquire at the Deschutes National Forest office in Bend to see if any are currently open to visitors (summer only).

Arnold Ice Cave, one of the region's best known caverns, is located southeast of Bend near Forest Road 1821. Originally discovered by hunters, the cave served as a source of ice for the village of Bend; in 1910 ice from the cave sold for $40 a ton. The cave has been closed since the summer of 1975, when vandals dislodged boulders into its opening, shattering portions of the wooden staircase. Forest Service officials hope to reopen the cave in the summer of 1976.

One of the most interesting underground lava tunnels is ½-mile-long Lavacicle Cave located 52 miles southwest of Bend. Many stalactites and stalagmites decorate its interior. Entrance is limited to groups headed by a guide; you must make arrangements in advance through the Deschutes National Forest office in Bend. Visitors wear hard hats to guard against the jagged lava and enter the cave by crawling through a very small opening.

South to Klamath Falls

U.S. 97 cuts a direct swath south through scattered pine forests toward Klamath Falls and the California border. State highways head east across the plateau and west toward Crater Lake National Park and the southern Cascades.

As U.S. 97 nears Klamath Falls, it skims the eastern shore of Upper Klamath Lake, where you'll often see pelicans, western grebes, night herons,

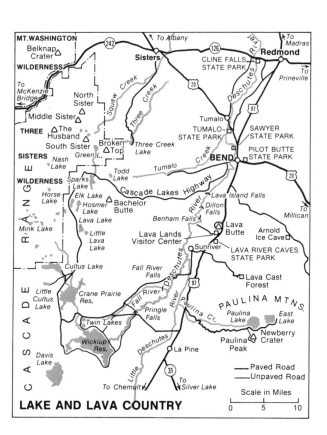

LAKE AND LAVA COUNTRY

and other waterfowl. Oregon's largest natural lake, Upper Klamath becomes a boating and sailing center in summer. Sportsmen fish for big rainbows in spring-fed tributary creeks and, in autumn, come here for duck and goose hunting.

A green oasis and logging museum

About 30 miles north of Klamath Falls, Collier State Park offers an inviting green lawn in the middle of pine and sagebrush countryside.

Families enjoy the velvety lawn and children's play area alongside the Williamson River. Fly fishermen head up Spring Creek to another picnic area; a path follows the creek downstream for about a mile.

Machinery and equipment used by early loggers are displayed under roofed sheds and in several log buildings west of the highway. Also exhibited are cross sections of enormous logs cut from Oregon forests. Behind the logging memorabilia, you can peer into various rustic cabins built by trappers, miners, loggers, and homesteaders and furnished with articles typically used by the owners.

Historic Klamath Falls

Settlement of the Klamath country was slowed by conflicts between local Indian tribes and homesteaders, culminating in the Modoc War in 1872-73.

In the late 1860s, settlers located near the spot where the mile-long Link River tumbled into Lake Ewauna; today you may see pelicans here. From this lake, the Klamath River flows across northern California to the Pacific.

The town grew rapidly after rail lines linked it to Weed (in 1909) and Eugene (in the mid-1920s). Klamath Falls became the marketing and distribu-

Indian baskets from Favell Museum collection in Klamath Falls represent the work of many tribes.

tion center for south-central Oregon's livestock, lumber, and agricultural products.

Klamath Indians represent a substantial portion of the local population. In late May, Klamath Falls hosts Pow Wow Days, featuring a parade, All-Indian rodeo, and dance presentations.

Geothermal "hot seat." Klamath Falls sits atop a subterranean reservoir of high pressure steam and hot water, used a century ago by Klamath Indians to cook their food and soothe sore limbs.

Fifty years later, residents dug the first crude wells to tap this hot subsurface water for home heating. Today several hundred businesses and families located in the "hot springs belt" utilize geothermal energy to provide clean and inexpensive heat and hot water for their houses, businesses, schools, and community hospital. A local dairy uses the heat in milk pasteurization, and hot-water coils beneath the pavement deice some city streets, sidewalks and driveways.

Geologists believe the Klamath Basin sits atop one of the earth's richest stores of geothermal energy, and private companies are now doing preliminary drilling on leased federal lands. Friction of shifting subsurface lava formations heats these underground streams.

City parks. Klamath Falls has a pair of fine parks overlooking its local lakes. Veterans Memorial Park, at the foot of Main Street near Lake Ewauna, has picnic tables and an old locomotive.

Moore Park borders Upper Klamath Lake at the northwestern city limits; drive north of town and take Nevada Avenue west across the river to Lakeshore Drive and the park. The large natural area includes picnic tables, sports and play areas, a nature trail, and a zoo and bird sanctuary. Often you can spot eagles and hawks resting in the trees.

Klamath County Museum. The history of the Klamath Basin—along with its geology, people, and wildlife—is detailed in this museum's exhibits. A fine display covers the Modoc Indian War. Located east of the business district at 1451 Main Street, the museum is open from 9 A.M. to 5 P.M. Tuesday through Saturday, 1 to 5 P.M. Sunday, with extended hours in summer.

Baldwin Hotel. During its heyday, this turn-of-the-century hotel hosted presidents Theodore Roosevelt, William Howard Taft, and Woodrow Wilson. The brick hotel backs against a rocky cliff at 31 Main Street in the old section of town overlooking the lake.

Victorian craftsmanship is evident in the panel of small, leaded stained-glass window panes above the front entrance and in hand-beveled doors and banisters. Though electric wiring has been updated, most plumbing fixtures and furnishings remain unchanged. Visitors may tour some historic downstairs rooms for a nominal charge.

Riverside nature trail. A ¾-mile nature trail along the Link River lets you combine bird watching with a bit of history. It follows an old roadbed along the river's south bank where Indians once camped,

Bird watching in the Klamath Basin

One of the greatest congregations of ducks and geese known on earth takes place each spring and autumn along the Oregon-California border. Millions of waterfowl move along the Pacific Flyway, funneling into the lakes and marshes of the Klamath Basin where they make a major stopover on their migration. Their flight range stretches from north of the Arctic Circle to south of the Mexican border.

Within a 50-mile radius of Klamath Falls, 5 national wildlife refuges host these varied migrant throngs—mostly ducks, geese, and swans, but also pelicans, cormorants, terns, phalaropes, stilts, avocets, curlews, cranes—a total of 250 species during the year. At times their numbers are almost beyond belief.

Where to go. North of Klamath Falls are two refuges—Upper Klamath, on the northwest shore of Upper Klamath Lake, and Klamath Forest, in a region known as the Klamath Marsh. To the south, Lower Klamath refuge spans the Oregon-California border, while Tule Lake and Clear Lake are wholly within California. Each refuge provides a slightly different habitat. At the refuge headquarters on Tule Lake, you can obtain leaflets describing all five refuges, along with maps and a bird list.

You'll see birds in any season, but spring and fall are the liveliest times. In May and June birds show off their beautiful mating plumage; many birds nest here and raise their young.

Autumn days are typically warm and bright, nights and mornings cool, stubble fields golden.

Skeins of ducks and geese approach in long wavering Vs as they prepare to land. Pheasants whir out from the high grass as you pass in your car.

To see the great congregations of birds, you must venture off the paved routes. Gravel roads and dike-top trails put you into close proximity with the birds. The leaflets are your guide; they not only keep you from getting lost, but also tell you where you must not trespass.

What to bring. Binoculars are almost a must. Borrow extra binoculars if you can, so that more than one party member can watch at a time. If you own a camera with a telephoto lens, you're in luck; a long lens makes extraordinary pictures possible.

Bring layers of warm clothing, a windbreaker, and light rain gear. To avoid alarming the birds, keep colors dull (khaki or straw colors) and avoid flapping belts or scarves.

Mosquitoes are a nuisance in some seasons, and only a good insect repellent seems to quell their enthusiasm. Dark glasses will add to your comfort. Bring a lunch and drinking water.

Some serious observers of wild birds favor setting up a simple blind from which to work. You can improvise a small tentlike structure from dark sheet plastic, burlap, or even boughs. Provide comfortable seating, for you may be in for a long vigil. Almost as good as a blind is your own car; birds may fly off at your approach, but they usually return soon and resume feeding if you stay quietly inside the auto. □

---

near the falls that cascaded into Lake Ewauna.

The trail begins just behind the Favell Museum parking lot near West Main Street; go through the turnstile and past the power plant. The thickets provide cover for small birds, pheasants, wild geese, and ducks.

Indian artifacts and western art

A splendid museum on the west side of the Link River combines regional Indian crafts and artifacts with art and sculpture by some 200 western artists.

The Favell Museum of Western Art and Indian Artifacts fills its own six-sided, stone building at 125 West Main Street near the bridge. Visitors can tour the private museum Monday through Saturday from 9:30 A.M. to 5:30 P.M. and Sunday from 1 to 5:30 P.M. (closed Mondays in winter).

Exhibit rooms display artifacts from tribes of the Columbia River valley and nomadic plains Indians, woodcarvings from Northwest coastal tribes, pottery and stonework crafted by Southwest Indians, and pre-Columbian artifacts from Mexico. Impressive arrowhead collections contain points made of various stones. Other displays include stone and bone tools, baskets, and beadwork.

Paintings, sculpture, and woodcarvings by contemporary artists from Oregon and the West are featured in the museum's gallery.

Agricultural valleys

Southeast of Klamath Falls, the Lost River meanders through some of the Klamath Basin's most productive agricultural valleys. Potatoes, barley, and oats are raised here, along with livestock.

Families can picnic and fish at Stevenson County Park on the Lost River, 11 miles east of Klamath Falls. From State Highway 140, roads branch southeast from Olene to the Poe Valley and from Dairy toward Bonanza and the Langell Valley. State Highway 39 follows the river southeast to Merrill, site of the Klamath Basin Potato Festival in October. Malin's showcase is Malin Park, with picnic tables and a swimming pool.

Across the plateau

Four main routes cross central Oregon's broad plateau, connecting U.S. 97 and U.S. 395. From

Madras, U.S. 26 cuts southeast to Prineville, across the forested slopes of the Ochoco Mountains (see page 120), and eastward along the John Day River (see page 134).

Lonelier routes are U.S. 20, connecting Bend and Burns; State Highway 31, a route traveled by John Charles Fremont and Kit Carson in 1843; and the Winnemucca to the Sea Highway, paralleling the state's southern border.

Eastward to Burns

U.S. 20 offers few diversions as it cuts southeast across the high plateau toward Burns. You drive through miles and miles of juniper and sage. Now and then a country road branches off into lonely grazing lands, and occasionally a vertical butte rises abruptly from the plateau.

For more on this region, see page 149.

The Fremont Highway

State 31 cuts diagonally across Lake County's semi-arid high plateau from La Pine on U.S. 97 to Valley Falls on U.S. 395. Probably the most interesting of the roads across the high desert, it was named in honor of John C. Fremont. As a 30-year-old Army lieutenant, he brought his party of explorers— including scout Kit Carson—over much of this route in the winter of 1843.

Scenery varies from corridors of yellow pine to high rocky passes offering sweeping views of distant valleys. Yellow daisies speckle the sagebrush hills in late spring, and the lakes—which recede in summer—are surrounded by green meadows. Rabbitbrush adds its golden autumn glory to the high desert in October.

Geological oddities offer interesting detours. Fossils and Indian artifacts have been uncovered in the area, but the collection of archeological materials (including fossils and arrowheads) on federal lands is prohibited unless authorized by permit.

State rest areas are located 33 miles southeast of La Pine and near the community of Summer Lake. You can also picnic at Fort Rock State Park, or detour south to camp in Fremont National Forest.

Lunarlike craters. Just east of the Klamath-Lake county line, a pair of explosion craters puncture the plateau. Though they resemble meteorite craters, they were blown out by volcanic forces.

Twenty miles southeast of La Pine, Forest Road 2523 branches south to make a 4-mile loop inside the forested lava crater called Big Hole. A few miles east, a marked side road leads from State 31 to a view point overlooking Hole-in-the-Ground.

Fort Rock State Park. A remnant of an ancient volcano, Fort Rock is a gigantic crescent of rock rimming a desert amphitheater. In isolated grandeur it towers some 325 feet above a desert lake bed east of State 31. A dirt road circles inside the rim, ending at a view point. Ancient artifacts found here indicate that prehistoric hunters inhabited one of the caves near the rock's base, which at that time bordered ancient Fort Rock Lake.

Forest campgrounds. Near the Silver Lake Ranger Station, forest roads climb south into the northern part of Fremont National Forest. You'll find campgrounds beside Silver Creek and Thompson Reservoir, a favorite trout fishing spot.

Desert side trip. A paved side road north of State 31 leads toward Table Rock, a 5,630-foot butte with a great view of the Fort Rock Valley and Christmas Valley, an isolated desert retirement development. Irrigated green fields now occupy once drab sagebrush flats. Nearby is Crack-in-the-Ground, a narrow but deep (up to 70 feet) split in the basalt that extends for 2 miles.

If you're prepared for desert travel, you can continue northeast from Christmas Valley on lonely unpaved roads to Fossil Lake, site of outstanding fossil discoveries (horses, camels, ancient birds and fish) by paleontologist Thomas Condon a century ago; farther on, drifting sand dunes are enveloping the ancient pines of Lost Forest. Carry water when you venture into the desert.

Shallow lakes and marshes. Southeast of the community of Silver Lake, several shallow lakes and marshy areas are all that remain of ancient landlocked lakes that filled the Fort Rock and Christmas Lake valleys in prehistoric times.

In fall and winter, hunters seek migratory waterfowl and upland game birds in marsh lands near the highway. The spring-fed Ana River empties into salty Summer Lake, and sand dunes rise behind its east shore.

Just south of Picture Rock Pass, Forest Road 290 serpentines along Winter Ridge. Fremont named Summer Lake and Winter Ridge on December 16, 1843, as he stood on the snow-crusted rim and looked down on the grass-rimmed lake glimmering in the sunshine more than 2,000 feet below.

Paisley. Largest community along this route, Paisley got its start in the 1870s as a stockman's town, and

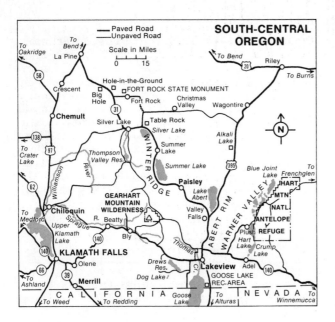

it still serves the ranchers of central Lake County. On a prominent corner is the unoccupied yet impressive Hotel Chewaucan. Broad green Chewaucan Marsh spreads for miles below town.

About 10 miles south, at the Narrows of the Chewaucan, look for ancient beach markings on the hills—former shorelines of Lake Chewaucan which covered this country in Pleistocene times.

Winnemucca to the Sea Highway

Paralleling Oregon's southern border is the Winnemucca to the Sea Highway, a 494-mile road linking major north-south routes and cutting across a rather empty piece of the west. From Crescent City, California, U.S. Highway 199 winds northeast to Grants Pass; you continue on Interstate Highway 5 to Medford, then take State 140 through Klamath Falls and Lakeview to Winnemucca, Nevada. More than 300 miles of the highway are in Oregon.

On the 96-mile stretch from Klamath Falls to Lakeview, you climb gradually as you move east; three passes are above 5,000 feet, and there are few trees. About 60 miles east of Klamath Falls, the Sprague River offers good sites to picnic, camp, swim, or fish. Hunters and fishermen can turn south at Bly toward the Gerber Reservoir area.

The wildest and loneliest part of the trip is the 207-mile stretch from Lakeview to Winnemucca. You cross high desert country, occasionally marked by unexpected streams and water holes. Deep Creek, about 20 miles east of Lakeview, offers good fishing in spring and fall. Check your gas gauge in Adel; no gasoline is available for more than 80 miles until you reach Denio, Nevada.

Southern Lake County

In this land of cloudless skies and expansive horizons, oceans of sage and rabbitbrush stretch toward upthrust rimrock buttes and colorful rolling mountains. Towering fault scarps jut high above the flat plateau.

During prehistoric times, great landlocked lakes covered much of this Great Basin region; their wind-whipped waters lapped at the mountain sides, creating still-visible terraces. Shallow alkaline lakes are the only remnants of these once-vast inland seas.

Some of Oregon's largest ranches snuggle into broad valleys in this range country, and it's far between towns. Often you'll see jackrabbits and coyotes. Occasionally, a fleet-footed antelope races across a dry lake bed. Mule deer abound in the pine forests, and upland birds rustle in the brush.

Beneath the Abert Rim

From Riley on U.S. 20, lonely U.S. 395 wanders south through alkali flats toward Lakeview and the California border. A state rest area is located south of dry Alkali Lake, 61 miles north of Lake-

Winnemucca to the Sea Highway winds through Deep Creek Canyon (rear) to Adel, where a roadside store offers provisions and gasoline for local ranchers and travelers.

view; in spring and summer, its green grass provides a refreshing contrast to the grey monotony of the sage desert. You'll find picnic tables and primitive campsites at Chandler State Wayside south of Valley Falls.

For nearly 20 miles, the route follows the base of the 30-mile-long Abert Rim, a massive fault scarp looming 2,000 feet above Lake Abert and the Crooked Creek Valley. Looking up, you can see layers of superimposed lava. Shallow Lake Abert is the brackish remnant of an ancient lake; its former shorelines are plainly visible high above the lake's current level.

South of Valley Falls, the country softens as sage and alkali flats give way to grazing cattle, pine trees, and prosperous ranches.

Lakeview's western hospitality

A pair of 40-foot-high wooden cowboys flanking a billboard map of the state welcome you to Lakeview, Oregon's "tallest town" at 4,800 feet elevation. Placed on U.S. 395 at the town's north and south entrances, the giant signs typify the friendly hospitality of this region. Hub and county seat of vast Lake County, Lakeview has a population of about 2,700 and serves as the marketing and shipping center for some of the state's largest cattle ranches. Pioneer days are recalled in the Schminck Museum.

The pine-covered ridges and wide-open spaces delight sportsmen, who come here to fish and hunt. Rockhounds search nearby for agates, petrified wood, jasper, thundereggs, and arrowheads.

If you enjoy the color and excitement of rodeos, you'll find good ones here. A junior rodeo is presented in June, and a major amateur rodeo draws outside contestants during the Labor Day weekend as part of the Lake County Fair.

Spouting geysers. Oregon's only continuously spouting geyser is a Lakeview landmark. North of town, "Old Perpetual" spurts a 60-foot column of 200° water into the air at 20-second intervals. Another hot geyser spouts every 2 hours at Crump Ranch north of Adel. Both geysers were triggered by well drillers seeking water in hot springs areas.

Goose Lake. Water sports enthusiasts head for this 30-mile-long lake on the Oregon-California border. You'll find campsites and picnic tables here, and a boat ramp offers lake access. Eight to 10 feet at its deepest point, the lake is slightly alkaline but supports lake trout. Wild Canadian honkers and other migrating waterfowl stop to rest and feed.

Ski area. From December through March, skiers can enjoy the powdery slopes at small Warner Canyon Ski Area, 10 miles northeast of Lakeview off State 140. The ski area operates Thursday afternoons, weekends, and during school holidays. Snacks are available at the day lodge.

Into Fremont National Forest

Logging roads provide access to the pine forests and inviting lakes and streams of Fremont National Forest. This country opens up in June. Except during hunting season, you'll probably have the mile-high campgrounds almost to yourself. For recreation information, stop at a Fremont National Forest office in Lakeview, Paisley, Silver Lake, or Bly.

If you'd like to sample this forest, take State 140 about 3 miles west of Lakeview and turn north on the Thomas Creek Road. About 26 miles northwest of Lakeview—beyond Dairy Creek—the road forks; Forest Road 2823 continues north to pine-rimmed Campbell and Deadhorse lakes (no motorboats), Forest Road 237 forks west toward Gearhart Mountain Wilderness and the town of Bly on State 140.

Dog Lake, Cottonwood Meadows, and Lofton and Drews reservoirs, all west of Lakeview, are other popular recreation areas.

Gearhart Mountain Wilderness

Rugged, rocky hiking is in store for persons who set out to climb 8,634-foot Gearhart Mountain. You can obtain trail information and a map at Fremont National Forest offices.

The main wilderness trailhead is about 16 miles northeast of Bly over the Bly-Dairy Creek forest road; a steep, rough but passable side road leads to the Lookout Rock fire observation tower—starting point of the 14-mile Gearhart Trail.

You hike steadily uphill for 6 or 7 miles northwest to the top of the rough, glaciated peak. A good overnight campsite is the large meadow at the head of Dairy Creek, about a mile south of the summit.

Canyons and ridges radiate in all directions from the mountaintop, and you'll see a large glacial cirque near the headwaters of Dairy and Gearhart creeks. From the top, the trail heads north along the ridge, then drops down to Gearhart Marsh and lovely Blue Lake, and continues to the northeastern wilderness entrance at Nottin Creek.

A chain of lakes in Warner Valley

Heading east from Lakeview, State 140 descends from the Warner Summit along Camas Creek. Sixteen miles east of U.S. 395, a paved side road heads north toward Plush and the Warner Valley, as State 140 continues east toward the Nevada border.

More than 40 miles long and about 12 miles wide, the prosperous and lush Warner Valley contains several large ranches and a long chain of lakes and marshes—a magnet for waterfowl hunters.

Surrounded by large ranches, the little hamlet of Plush serves local ranchers and sportsmen. Anglers head for Hart Lake or nearby Honey Creek. Rockhounds can hunt for "sunstones" (crystalline feldspar) north of Plush. Hunters come here not only for waterfowl, but also for deer, antelope, and game birds.

Hart Mountain's antelope and bighorn sheep

From the Warner Valley, Hart Mountain's massive volcanic ridge appears a barren monolith. Atop its plateau is Hart Mountain National Antelope Refuge, established in 1936 to protect a large herd of pronghorn antelope. Mule deer also browse on the upland plateau, bighorn sheep roam the rocky crags, and upland birds hide in the brush.

From Plush, a graded gravel road follows the base of the escarpment northeast. Then the road climbs steeply, winding to the top of the plateau (ascending more than 1,000 feet in 3 miles). From the plateau you can gaze over the valley's lakes, marshes, and hay fields—and to the desert beyond.

Stop at the Refuge Headquarters to check on road conditions and where to see wildlife.

Wheat country

The serpentine gash of the John Day River marks the beginning of central Oregon's wheat lands. East of the river, vast fields of ripening wheat cover the rolling hills of Gilliam, Morrow, and western Umatilla counties, stretching some 45 miles south from the Columbia.

State highways 19 and 207 are the main north-south routes connecting Interstate Highway 80N and U.S. Highway 26. Together with intersecting roads and highways, they cut across the ruts of the Oregon Trail, traverse the wheat plateau, and provide access to quiet farm communities and ghost towns. Farther south in Wheeler County, the scenery changes to the sagebrush-strewn hills and rocky gorges of the central plateau. Occasionally you'll pass an old homestead, usually shaded by tall poplars.

Vast golden fields of wheat stretch toward the horizon in sparsely-settled Gilliam County.

Steepled church in Lonerock, built in 1898, stands near boulder that gives the town its name.

The lower John Day River

For some 300 miles, the John Day River curves and twists across central Oregon's northern plateau—watering broad fields and pasture lands, carving through ancient rock formations, snaking between lonely hills toward the Columbia.

From Service Creek Bridge downstream to Tumwater Falls, a 147-mile-stretch of the lower river is a state-designated scenic waterway. For 31 miles—between Thirtymile Creek and East Ferry Canyon—the John Day is a wild river, essentially untouched by man. Trickling creeks and narrow side gulches lead into the steep-walled river canyon.

Few roads and fewer communities touch the lower river; outdoorsmen must explore it by boat. Day float trips can be arranged in Fossil.

Fishermen catch cutthroat, rainbow trout, steelhead, and salmon in season. In autumn hunters prowl this region in hopes of bagging game birds. Rockhounds discover thundereggs and agates.

Detours to the river

Gilliam County's main thoroughfare is State 19, cutting south from Arlington on Interstate 80N to Condon, the county seat. About 7 miles south of Arlington, a sign marks the highway crossing of the Oregon Trail.

Pioneers' river crossing. A few miles south of the Columbia, you can detour to the spot where covered wagons forded the John Day River. About 7 miles south of Arlington on State 19, turn west onto a paved road; you parallel the pioneer trail to Rock Creek, then continue 5 miles west by gravel road to the river. From the west, take country roads east from Wasco to reach the ford.

You see the river almost as the pioneers did—a rocky riffle about 100 feet wide. Crossing goes best if you have a 4-wheel-drive or other high clearance vehicle and ford in late summer when water is only hub deep. A bronze plaque on a boulder west of the ford gives historic details.

Wasco cutoff. From Condon, State 206 cuts 41 miles northwest to Wasco and 43 miles east to Heppner. You can picnic beside the John Day River at J. S. Burres State Park, 25 miles northwest of Condon.

Greenery amid the wheat fields

Capital of Gilliam County, Condon lies in the heart of the Columbia Basin wheat lands. Mature trees shade its pleasant city park—site of a big Fourth of July celebration which includes a patriotic program, parade, rodeo, fireworks, and other events.

Once the trading center for surrounding ranchers, Lonerock now is almost deserted. Only a few families live in this once-thriving community 20 miles southeast of Condon. Built around a huge, erratic lava boulder in a broad canyon, the town thrived in the 1890s. From above, it looks like a small New England village, its buildings clustering around a steepled church and imposing two-story school.

Along Willow Creek to Heppner

If you drive along State Highway 74 south from the Columbia, you get some insight into the character and gradual transition of wheat country towns. For almost 50 miles the road parallels Willow Creek from Interstate 80N to Heppner.

Homesteaders built the towns of Cecil, Morgan, Ione, and Lexington along Willow Creek; today these roadside settlements are only shadows of once vital farm communities. In the horse and buggy days, farmers and ranchers drove into town from miles around for social gatherings. But as their energy, money, and water gave out, many homesteaders departed. Today only a few small communities break the vast golden wheat fields.

Heppner. Sheltered by high domelike foothills, Heppner occupies a site on the valley floor of Willow Creek. A community of about 1,500, it is the largest town on the northern plateau and the hub of Morrow County.

Take a look at the sturdy Morrow County Courthouse, built of local stone. Items used by pioneer settlers are exhibited in the museum in Heppner's city library building. Ordinarily a slow-paced community, Heppner bursts with grassroots vitality in August during the Morrow County Rodeo.

Ghostly Hardman. Twenty miles southwest of Heppner on State 207, a sea of wheat fields isolates lonely Hardman. In its heyday, this farm town served the scattered families of the upper Rock Creek Valley; but when they could no longer make a living, the homesteaders drifted away.

A few families still live in Hardman, but the town's weathered buildings stand empty, drowsing in the sun, surrounded by weed gardens.

Through pine forests

South of Hardman, the wide plateau dips sharply as you enter Rock Creek Canyon; it separates the wheat growing region from range land to the south.

North of Spray, State 207 cuts across a forested spur of the Blue Mountains—part of Umatilla National Forest—noted for its fine stand of ponderosa pine. Hunters come here in autumn for deer and elk, chukar and pheasant.

You can camp, picnic, or fish at Bull Prairie Reservoir, a small but popular recreation area east of State 207. You'll find a boat ramp and a trail around the lake (no motors allowed).

Cattle country and fruit orchards

Ten miles south of Spray, a pleasant side road branches east of State 19 along the North Fork of the John Day River. On the 35-mile route to U.S. 395, scenery varies from orderly fields and fruit orchards to colorful red rock formations and brown hills spotted with juniper and pine. You drive through several small cattlemen's towns before meeting U.S. 395 at Long Creek.

Monument is a cozy little settlement beside the river; its interesting general store and buildings date back to stagecoach days. To the south, rugged buttes are sculptured into fantastic shapes and colored in a dozen different shades. You pass Sunken Mountain, where part of the mountain collapsed within itself; red cliffs rim the trees and grass in the depression. The small communities of Hamilton and Long Creek also serve nearby ranchers.

Where primeval animals roamed

Between the wheat lands and U.S. 26, you come upon a succession of startling contours—jagged peaks etched against blue sky, sharp pinnacles upthrust from solid rock, gashes carved through colorful volcanic formations, dome-shaped hills banded with colorful strata. A profound stillness hangs over the land.

Imbedded in these buckled hills are ancient fossils dating back as far as 50 million years to the time when alluvial plains covered this part of Oregon. Geologists and paleontologists have uncovered polished teeth and bones of now-extinct animals and perfect imprints of subtropical trees and plants. Ancient marine fossils have also been found. These remains have enabled scientists to trace evolution through millions of years. Parts of

JOHN DAY COUNTRY

Scale in Miles
0 5 10 15
—— Paved Road
—— Unpaved Road

this spectacular area have been set aside as John Day Fossil Beds National Monument.

Fossils and a ghost town

A few miles south of Condon you leave rolling wheat fields and enter ranch lands and sagebrush hills. Fossil lies about 20 miles south of Condon; it's another 22 miles through pine forests and scenic canyons to Service Creek and the river.

Fossil, Wheeler County seat, marks the intersection of State 19 and State 218. Giant cottonwood trees shade its square and belfried courthouse. For information on the region's history and geology, visit the free local museum (open Wednesday through Saturday in summer), housed in a former saloon and card room. You can dig for fossils in the sedimentary banks behind the high school; most fossils found here are prints of leaves, cones, and needle sprays from the Oligocene epoch.

Kinzua, a company-owned mill town and tree farm headquarters east of Fossil, has a 6-hole golf course open to the public.

Two shady roadside picnic areas invite you to stop. Dyer Wayside is 10 miles south of Condon; Shelton Wayside borders a creek 10 miles southeast of Fossil.

One of Oregon's more interesting ghost towns is Richmond, about 6 miles south of the Service Creek bridge on State 207 and ½ mile east down a country lane. Tall Lombardy poplars shade abandoned buildings—a school, church, store, and some houses—along the curving road. Once Richmond had its own literary and dramatic society; now sagebrush overruns the site.

Exploring the new national monument

John Day Fossil Beds National Monument, created in 1974, covers three separate areas. It is comprised primarily of three former state parks transferred by the State of Oregon to the U.S. government. Fossil collecting or digging is prohibited.

Early in your visit, stop at the monument headquarters in the town of John Day (420 West Main Street) for information on the area. Staff members are on duty from 8 A.M. to 4:30 P.M. daily in summer, weekdays only the rest of the year.

Sheep Rock section. Largest of the monument's three areas, this unit borders the river for some 7 miles. It begins 6 miles north of Dayville on U.S. 26 and continues north along State 19, encompassing the rich fossil deposits formerly included in Thomas Condon-John Day Fossil Beds State Park.

Near the junction of State 19, the John Day River and U.S. 26 wind through Picture Gorge, an awesome defile cut through high basalt cliffs. Several sets of ancient pictographs once were visible on the canyon walls, but most have been mutilated or obliterated by vandals.

Farther north on State 19, basalt-capped Sheep Rock provides a prominent landmark for travelers. A visitor center is planned at Cant Ranch, across

Sheep Rock, topped by a basalt cap, looms above the John Day River in the national monument. Eroded rocks have yielded fossilized remains of many animals.

the river from Sheep Rock, where you will be able to obtain an orientation map and learn about the natural history.

From Thomas Condon Viewpoint at the north end of the gorge, you gaze over the contorted hills rising above the valley and barren Sheep Rock striped by horizontal bands of pale green and buff. The colorful and spectacularly eroded rocks have yielded remains of numerous animals. Turtle Cove, named for turtle fossils found here, has yielded more than 100 different fossil species.

Painted Hills. Varying in hue with the changing light, these colorfully streaked, domelike hills and ridges exude an austere beauty. In early morning they present an awesome vista, as the first rays of light touch the banded buttes bringing out pastel shadings that gradually deepen to vivid shades of rust, green, gold, and charcoal.

Three miles west of Mitchell on U.S. 26, turn north on the paved, 6-mile road that follows Bridge Creek to the base of the hills. Streaks of various colors signal variations in the age and composition of the deposits.

Several old cottonwood trees shade a few picnic tables along Bridge Creek (pit toilets, no drinking water). The nearest Forest Service campground is at Ochoco Divide, 17 miles southwest of Mitchell on U.S. 26.

Clarno Unit. Northernmost of the three areas, this part of the monument is located along State 218 about 17 miles west of Fossil. A few picnic tables are scattered among small junipers at the base of a massive wall in the former Clarno State Park, 2 miles east of the river (pit toilets, no water).

In primeval days, animal life here included crocodiles, rhinoceroses, huge tapirs, peccaries, and several varieties of fox-sized horses, believed to be the ancestor of modern horses. Semitropical plant

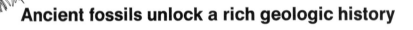

Ancient fossils unlock a rich geologic history

About 30 million years ago, camels, giant pigs, saber-toothed cats, and three-toed horses roamed the subtropical forests of eastern Oregon. Erupting volcanoes spit out clouds of ashes that smothered and trapped these prehistoric animals. Later eruptions locked in the plants and animals whose fossilized remains have become pieces to Oregon's paleontological puzzle.

These fossil beds are now part of the new John Day Fossil Beds National Monument, a 14,400-acre preserve in Grant and Wheeler counties. It encompasses one of the most outstanding natural depositories of prehistoric fossils on the North American continent.

The geologic unraveling of this country began more than a century ago when Thomas Condon, minister and paleontologist, saw fossils brought to The Dalles by a cavalry officer returning from an expedition. Condon soon explored the John Day country himself, uncovering plant and animal fossils dating back to eras when the dry hills were covered with lush subtropical forest.

Palms, redwood, magnolia, ginkgo, cinnamon, and fig trees flourished in the jungly forest. Rhinoceroses, tapirs, crocodiles, and four-toed horses inhabited the area covered by the Clarno Formation, created from eruptions during the

Eocene epoch 40 to 50 million years ago. In overlying layers of alluvium and volcanic ash—known as the John Day Formation—Condon found fossil remains of camels, giant pigs, saber-toothed cats, tapirs, and three-toed horses. Then followed the Picture Gorge Basalt flows, topped by the relatively recent fossil-bearing Mascall and Rattlesnake formations.

For millions of years, the John Day River and other streams cut through the accumulated layers, exposing the fossilized skeletons of Cenozoic animals and plants and carving out the steep cliffs.

The harvest of fossils in the John Day Valley is now history; most of the major discoveries were made in the late decades of the 19th century. Tons of fossils have been exhumed from the strata, and the fossil beds have been the training ground for America's top paleontologists. Examples of the fossils have found their way into museums all over the country.

In Oregon you can see major collections at the University of Oregon's Natural History Museum in Eugene and at the Oregon Museum of Science and Industry in Portland. Fossils are also displayed at the chamber of commerce office in John Day. ▢

---

fossils have been unearthed, and the famed "nut beds" yielded tropical fruits, nuts, and seeds from the Eocene period.

The John Day Valley

East of fossil country, the upper John Day River drains the western slopes of the Blue Mountains and irrigates a broad valley planted with alfalfa and rimmed by folded, barren hills. Cottonwood and willow trees mark the river's meandering course. Old farm houses and barns hide behind tall poplars near the base of the hills. To the southeast, the Strawberry Mountains form a rugged backdrop.

The discovery of gold on Whiskey Flat in 1862 triggered a rush of prospectors, and during the following decade some $30 million in gold was taken out of local streams.

Today's gold is in cattle ranching. Broad-brimmed hats and cowboy boots are everyday wear for suntanned ranchers. Memories of the Old West are revived when cowhands drive the cattle to greener pastures. Livestock have the right-of-way on roads in cattle country.

John Day, legendary cattle town

Located in the center of sprawling Grant County, the town of John Day is a stopping point at the intersection of two major highways—U.S. 26 and

U.S. 395. Appearing larger than its 1,800 population, John Day is also the supply center for the prosperous valley ranchers.

Each spring large livestock herds are driven along the town's main street during the annual cattle drive from winter pasture in Bear Valley to greener fields north of town.

A link with mining days is the Kam Wah Chung Building in Gleason Park, currently being restored as a museum. Built in 1866, the old stone landmark housed a trading post and general store catering to the needs of the Chinese miners during the boom days. It still contains relics including incense, joss sticks, and old records and letters written in Chinese.

Gold fever on Canyon Creek

After prospectors discovered gold on Whiskey Flat in June 1862, prospectors streamed into the region and a mining camp sprang up along Canyon Creek. At the peak of activity, some 10,000 miners and camp followers crowded into town. Pack trains loaded with supplies rumbled through Canyon City's dusty streets. Three times a week the Pony Express rider galloped into town from The Dalles, some 225 miles to the northwest. Later, freight wagons and stagecoaches lumbered to Canyon City over the old Military Road.

Millions of dollars in gold dust and nuggets were taken from the creek during the 1860s. Later miners scarred the canyon walls with hydraulic mining operations. You can still see tailings and mine tunnels along the canyon.

Many of the town's original buildings were destroyed during a fire in 1937, but several still stand on the banks above Canyon Creek. The St. Thomas Episcopal Church was built in 1876.

Days of '62. Life is quieter these days, but on the first weekend in June, Canyon City commemorates its golden era with the '62 Days Celebration, a lively festival featuring a parade, old-time dances, barbecues, and a medicine show.

Historical museum. One of the best local collections in Oregon is contained in Grant County's historical museum in Canyon City. Located beside U.S. 395, it contains rockhound and gold nugget displays, a gun collection, relics of the gold mining era and pioneer days, and Indian and Chinese artifacts. The museum is open from April through October; hours are 9 A.M. to 3 P.M. Tuesday through Saturday (also Sunday afternoons in July and August).

Near the museum is the old Greenhorn city jail, moved to this site in 1963, and the Joaquin Miller cabin, occupied in the 1860s by Cincinnatus (Joaquin) Miller, later to achieve fame as the "Poet of the Sierras."

Prairie City's mining museum

Another small town with a frontier atmosphere is Prairie City, 13 miles east of John Day. Nearby pastures support many prosperous cattle ranches.

DeWitt Museum has an interesting collection of mining relics of the 1860s including hydraulic hoses, tools, period clothing, and musical instruments. Some items revive memories of the Chinese coolies who worked local mines. The museum is open in summer from 9:30 A.M. to 3:30 P.M. on weekdays, and on Sunday afternoons.

Strawberry Mountain Wilderness

Rising in striking contrast to the irrigated John Day Valley and semi-arid plateau, the rocky peaks of the Strawberry Range dominate the country southeast of John Day. A narrow ridge of jagged peaks, the small but rugged range tops 9,000 feet at Strawberry Mountain, highest point between the Cascades and the Wallowas. The wilderness area encompasses several high peaks, tree-filled canyons, and five pristine mountain lakes.

You can obtain information, a wilderness permit, and a map at the Prairie City ranger station or at Malheur National Forest headquarters in John Day. Forest roads lead from Prairie City and Seneca to trailheads at the edge of the rugged wilderness.

More than 100 miles of trails lace the small wilderness; you can hike here from mid-July through October. An 18-mile loop trail links Strawberry Mountain and all of the lakes, or you can follow several shorter trails. In midsummer, masses of wildflowers bloom riotously across meadows and hillsides.

Horseback riding, hiking, fishing, and hunting are the main activities here. Lakes are open to year-round fishing (rainbow or eastern brook trout), though snow limits access much of the year. In addition to mule deer, elk, and bear, a small herd of bighorn sheep roams the western part of the wilderness.

Into Malheur National Forest

The pine-covered slopes of Malheur National Forest curve around the John Day Valley, covering the western slopes of the Blue Mountains and the flanks of the Strawberry Range. From U.S. 26 forest roads lead north to old mining sites along the Middle Fork of the John Day River (see page 141) and south to campsites near the river's southern headwaters. More forest camps are located near the North Fork of the Malheur River, which drains the slopes east of the Strawberry Mountain Wilderness.

South of Canyon City, U.S. 395 climbs through a stand of lofty ponderosa pines to the 5,158-foot highway summit dividing the watersheds of the John Day and Silvies rivers. North of the summit, a side road forks southeast along Canyon Creek to Canyon Meadows Lake, a pleasant site for boating and swimming. In winter families enjoy a snow play area near the summit of U.S. 395. The highway descends into the lush pastures of Bear Valley, and you'll see grazing cattle and occasional ranches as you follow the Silvies River south. A trio of creek-side camping areas are located east of Seneca.

Cattle ranching is big business in the John Day Valley. Buckled hills provide an interesting backdrop; willows and cottonwoods line the streams.

Northeastern mountains

Trace the pioneers' route along the Oregon Trail

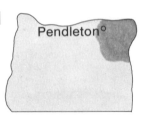

Pendleton°

Kicking bull attempts to dislodge rider during rodeo competition at Pendleton.

Abandoned store, its siding weathered and porch sagging, is one of a few buildings in ghost town of Bourne, an old mining camp in the Blue Mountains.

In Oregon's friendly northeast corner, the people live close to their land. Two splendid mountain ranges—the Blues and the Wallowas—tower above broad, prosperous valleys.

Interstate Highway 80N angles across this corner of the state, paralleling the Oregon Trail route from the Snake River to the Columbia. The region's major towns—Baker, La Grande, and Pendleton—are located along the highway. The awesome Grand Canyon of the Snake forms the state's northeastern boundary.

Prime recreation country, the mountains attract outdoorsmen who come to explore back-country trails on foot and horseback, fish in remote lakes and streams, ski on powder snow, and hunt for deer, elk, and game birds. You can enjoy exciting rodeos, stay on guest ranches, or visit ghost towns and pan for gold.

Along the Oregon Trail

The overland trek to the rich, green valleys of Oregon was a long journey, and a hard one. From the Missouri towns of Independence and St. Joe, pioneers headed toward the Oregon Territory. Beginning as a trickle in 1843, the westward migration

Horseback riders have a spectacular vantage point from moraine overlooking Wallowa Lake. You can rent horses for trips into the Eagle Cap Wilderness.

Lonely road borders rugged canyon cut by Snake River along northeast border.

swelled to a flood as more and more settlers made the arduous journey toward the fertile lands of the Willamette Valley.

Long trains of covered wagons, pulled by straining teams of oxen, lumbered across the great plains, through the Rocky Mountains, and along the Snake River. They crossed into present-day Oregon south of Nyssa, took a final look at the Snake at Farewell Bend, then made their way up the difficult Burnt River canyon.

Portions of the great trail, carved out by livestock hoofs and the narrow wheels of heavily loaded wagons, can still be found on the dry plateaus of eastern and central Oregon.

Baker—eastern Oregon's first "boom town"

After gold was discovered in California, tales spread of an Oregon stream literally pebbled with gold nuggets. According to legend, children of a pioneer party filled a blue bucket with the stones, then later tossed them aside.

In 1861 prospectors searching for the mythical Blue Bucket Mine discovered gold in Griffin Gulch, a few miles south of present-day Baker. The town became an important freight and stagecoach center, serving the miners probing the creeks and gullies of the Blue and Wallowa mountains. Prospectors, gamblers, and camp followers mingled with ranchers, cowboys, and sheepherders in the local dance halls and saloons or sauntered along the town's board sidewalks.

Business is still prospering in Baker, though today the economy is based on wheat and livestock. Hub of several highways, Baker is the gateway to forested recreation lands, ghost towns, and the Snake River country.

You can see samples of local gold—in dust, ore, and nuggets—displayed in the Baker branch of the U.S. National Bank, 2001 Main Street. A city park along the Powder River has a children's playground.

Haines—pioneer museums and hot springs

By-passed by Interstate 80N, Haines lies about 10 miles northwest of Baker on U.S. Highway 30. Though the town has only several hundred people, it boasts a good museum.

The Eastern Oregon Museum contains local family relics from the Oregon Trail era—grain cradles, fringe-top surreys, sod plows, candle molds, sleigh bells. You can even stand at an old saloon bar and put your feet on the rail. The museum is open daily in summer.

Hot springs near the town provide water for a naturally heated, warm-water swimming pool, open from mid-April to mid-September.

La Grande—hub of the Grande Ronde Valley

Surrounded by thriving farms and livestock ranches, La Grande spreads across the broad, rich valley of the Grande Ronde River.

Eastern Oregon State College is located here, the only 4-year institution of higher education east of

Oregon's Cascades. Each August outstanding student musicians study with professional musicians during the college's annual music camp.

In October the college community, local residents, and regional craftsmen join forces in a joyous Oktoberfest; traditional college homecoming activities are combined with the fun of a Bavarian beer fest.

From La Grande, highways branch north and west into the Blue Mountains and eastward to the Wallowas. A winding mountain road north of town climbs to the summit of 6,064-foot Mount Emily, where you have a splendid view of the wide Grande Ronde Valley and meandering river. Another pleasant side trip is the journey on State Highway 237, east from La Grande through farm lands and orchards to Cove.

Indian festival "at the cottonwoods"

For generations, native Americans representing varied tribes traditionally gathered in the land of Kop Koppa (a Nez Perce expression meaning "at the cottonwoods") in the Grande Ronde Valley, leaving their weapons behind in a gesture of peace and friendship.

Representatives of many tribes keep this heritage alive today in the annual Indian Festival of Arts held each June in La Grande. They gather to share their culture through displays of arts and crafts (both traditional and contemporary), Indian ceremonial dancing, and preparation of Indian food. A tepee village is erected. Highlight of the 3-day festival is a Saturday morning parade. For more information write Indian Festival of Arts, P.O. Box 193, La Grande, OR 97850.

Pendleton—a town with a western flavor

Backed by the Blue Mountains, Pendleton is the center of northeastern Oregon's wheat production area. Most roads leading to Pendleton cut through vast, rolling wheat fields, magnificently golden as they ripen under hot summer sun. The Umatilla River flows westward through the center of the city on its way to join the Columbia.

Pendleton is a town with a western flavor. You'll see plenty of Stetson hats and cowboy boots.

With advance notice, visitors can tour the Pendleton Woolen Mills plant on weekdays to see wool processed. Harris Pine Mills also welcomes visitors. Not far from Pendleton is the Umatilla Indian Reservation.

When it's Round-up time in Pendleton

For 4 days every September, Pendleton's usually quiet, elm-shaded streets resound with the beat of hoofs and the jingle of Indian trappings. One of the major western rodeos, the Pendleton Round-up got its start in 1910 when ranchers and farmers of the Umatilla Valley gathered to celebrate the end of the harvest.

Gunsight Mountain looms south of tree-rimmed Anthony Lake in the heart of the Blue Mountains, a favorite year-round vacation area.

Indians ride in tribal regalia during Pendleton's colorful Westward Ho parade.

Some of the nation's best rodeo riders compete in calf roping, saddle bronc riding, bulldogging, bareback riding, steer roping, and Brahma bull riding. Other special events include trick riding, wild horse races, branding, and stagecoach races.

Members of several Indian tribes set up a tepee village along the river, adjacent to the rodeo grounds; visitors are welcome to stroll through the encampment. The Indians compete in tribal ceremonial dancing and participate in the Happy Canyon pageant each evening.

Each day gets underway with a cowboy breakfast in Stillman Park—where you can eat your fill of pancakes, ham, eggs, and coffee—and ends with the historic pageant.

The lively Westward Ho parade is a colorful affair; you'll see costumed characters depicting pioneers, trappers, and prospectors; mounted Indians in full regalia; pack trains, stagecoaches, and Mormon carts; and ox teams pulling freight wagons. For more information write to the Round-up Association, P.O. Box 609, Pendleton, OR 97801.

The lower Umatilla Basin

Interstate 80N continues northwest from Pendleton toward the Columbia River. For a leisurely change of pace, take the road west from town which winds along the Umatilla River to Echo, a quiet community astride the Oregon Trail. Ruts left by

pioneer wagons are still visible west of town.

Hermiston, north of Interstate 80N at the junction of U.S. Highway 395 and State Highway 207, is the business hub of the lower Umatilla Basin and center of the region's potato harvest; a major part of the crop is converted into french fries and potato flakes at processing plants in Hermiston and Boardman.

Cold Springs National Wildlife Refuge, 6 miles east of Hermiston, offers a good place to watch migratory waterfowl in spring and fall.

The Blue Mountains

The cool pine woods and quiet, parklike meadows of the Blue Mountains provide a pleasant contrast to the warm, dry ranch land of northeastern Oregon. From Baker and La Grande the mountains are just a few miles west of Interstate 80N; the highway cuts through the range about 25 miles southeast of Pendleton.

Walk a short distance into the woods and you'll discover their delights: the fragrance of pine, the coolness of the forest when the valley is hot, the quiet peacefulness all around.

Pioneers migrating westward found the steep Blue Mountains a formidable barrier, difficult to surmount in their wagons. Now a modern divided freeway modifies the highway grade and provides spectacular views from Deadman Pass—cultivated fields patterned in abstract contours of green, yellow, and brown.

Ghosts of the golden past

The discovery of gold in Griffin Gulch in 1861 lured thousands of miners east from the Willamette Valley and north from California. Boom towns grew up around each new strike.

Another surge of activity came in the 1890s with the arrival of the railroads; spur lines penetrated the mountain valleys, and logging and mining camps dotted the hillsides. In the early years of the 20th century, gold dredges brought another mining revival; the giant machines chewed away at the river beds, leaving ugly mounds of waste gravel in their wake.

But the gold played out and the camps declined. Weather-beaten buildings, abandoned mine shafts, and crumbling foundations testify to the toll taken by heavy winter snows, fire, and the passage of time. Yet vestiges remain, enough to provide an intriguing glimpse of bygone days.

State highways 7 and 220 lead southwest from Baker into the historic Sumpter Valley mining district, now part of Wallowa-Whitman National Forest. You can travel paved roads to Sumpter and for a short stretch beyond; an all-weather road then continues west to Granite. Most roads leading to remote sites are graded gravel and dirt; inquire locally about road conditions. A Forest Service map (available for purchase in Baker) is helpful in identifying back roads.

If you want to try a bit of prospecting yourself, bring along a gold pan or build a sluice box and try some of the small creeks.

You'll find a Forest Service campground on the north shore of Phillips Reservoir, where a boat ramp, swimming area, and shoreline trail have been developed. Another small campground is located west of Sumpter.

Auburn. Seven miles south of Baker on State 7, a graded road leads 6 miles west to the site of Auburn. In 1862 it was the metropolis of the mining district and the first seat of Baker County. At its peak, Auburn had a population of 5,000 and was the second largest town in the state. But by 1868 the diggings had been worked out. Today few signs remain of the once-thriving town.

Sumpter. Once the crossroads of mining trails, Sumpter boomed when the Sumpter Valley Railroad arrived in 1896 and ore veins were opened in the Blue Mountains. The narrow-gauge network extended from Baker as far west as Prairie City. Nearly $16 million in gold was extracted here by placer and deep mining. Sumpter's business section—including numerous saloons—stretched seven blocks up the steep hill; the town even had an opera house where fancy-dress balls were held.

A generation later, giant dredges tore up the valley; one is there still, mired in gravel. A disastrous fire in 1915 wiped out most of the town, leaving only brick walls and foundations to indicate the size of the old settlement.

Granite. In contrast to most mining camps, Granite made its money on trade and its distributing and shipping business rather than on miners' vices. But when the mines were worked out, the town dwindled. Many weathered buildings remain.

Once virtual ghost towns, Granite and Sumpter have revived in recent years as the rising price of gold causes renewed interest in old mines.

Roads continue west up Congo Gulch to the Fremont Powerhouse and north to mines along Granite Creek.

Fremont Powerhouse. About 8 miles west of Granite, near the crest of the mountains, you can visit the Fremont Powerhouse, built in 1908 to provide electrical power for the mines and nearby towns.

Water was transported to the powerhouse through wood and steel pipelines from Olive Lake, about 8 miles to the west. Original items—used until the plant was closed down in 1967—include antique machinery and a blue Florentine marble instrument panel.

Bourne. From Sumpter an unimproved road heads about 7 miles north up Cracker Creek to the site of Bourne. Known in the 1870s as the boisterous mining camp of Cracker, in later years Bourne was notorious for many wildcat mining schemes hatched to fleece Eastern investors. In 1937 a cloud-

Huge dredges ravaged creek beds in search of gold-bearing gravel. This one is mired near the ghost town of Sumpter.

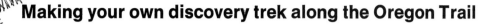

Making your own discovery trek along the Oregon Trail

Travelers who speed along Interstate Highway 80N through northeastern Oregon are never far from the route of the fabled Oregon Trail. Traveling in long wagon trains, thousands of pioneers pushed westward from Independence, Missouri, on a rugged 2,000-mile journey in search of a better life in the West.

The mass migration began in the spring of 1843, when a wagon train of 69 pioneers headed west, following the routes discovered by trappers and pathfinders. Each year the number of emigrants increased, peaking at 55,000 in 1850. Pioneers traveled by wagon train to Oregon through the 1870s, and travelers continued to arrive by wagon until the 1890s. Some 350,000 pioneers traveled the ruts of the Oregon Trail.

Leaving Independence at the first sign of spring, the travelers arrived at Old Fort Boise on the Snake River in late summer or early autumn. Another weary month and 400 difficult miles of travel still lay ahead.

Straining oxen pulled the creaking wagons across dusty plains and up steep slopes; today, a modern freeway reduces that month's journey to a few hours. Where pioneers camped or stopped to water their stock, state parks and rest areas now offer conveniences to motorists.

Yet time and the elements have not erased all signs of the old route. Wagon ruts still run for miles across parts of northeastern Oregon. South of Mount Hood on Laurel Hill, trees retain the deep gashes made by ropes used to slow the wagons' descent on the Barlow Road.

Oregon Trail interpretive displays in four state parks and seven rest areas along Interstate 80N recount the history of the trail, point out details of the local terrain, and discuss the route's influence on Oregon and its impact on the nation. Markers along the route relate historic details.

Write to the state's Travel Information Office (address on page 11) for a copy of a brochure on the Oregon Trail. It maps the route in relation to today's towns and highways, notes the location of interpretive displays, and describes the hazardous trip of the pioneers toward the fertile Willamette Valley. You can see pioneer relics in local museums along the route and at the Oregon Historical Society in Portland. □

---

burst diverted the creek, and a wall of water swept down the town's main street. Foundations and a few buildings are all that remain.

Whitney. Though surrounded by mining camps, Whitney was a logging town. Located about 9 miles south of Sumpter, Whitney was built in a large meadow near the North Fork of the Burnt River. A narrow-gauge railroad provided transportation and communication.

Weathered residences are scattered along the main street, and the deserted sawmill stands beside a log pond. Occasionally you'll see remnants of the old railroad, which transported lumber to northeastern Oregon towns.

Bonanza. From Whitney the 7-mile route to Bonanza heads northwest through meadows, along the river, and up Geiser Creek through pine forests. The mining camp grew up around the rich Bonanza mine. An aerial tram transported gold ore in buckets from the mine to stamp mills nearer town. Once one of the richest mines in the district, Bonanza today contains tumble-down buildings, the ruins of a stamp ore mill, and remnants of the old mine.

Greenhorn. Seven miles west of Bonanza (climbing some steep stretches on the dirt road) is Greenhorn, christened after two young men newly arrived from the East struck a rich vein of gold. Scattered ruins and isolated cabins mark abandoned mine sites. Greenhorn's population remains stable at three.

Along the Burnt River

State 7 leads southwest from Baker up the Burnt River to a junction with U.S. Highway 26 two miles north of Unity. East of Hereford on State 7, the Burnt River cutoff follows the river canyon through Bridgeport to Durkee and Interstate 80N.

You'll find camping and picnicking areas at Unity Lake State Park, near the U.S. 26-State 7 junction. You can go boating, swimming, and fishing in the lake.

The western slope

If you follow U.S. 26 northwest across the summit, you can detour to more old gold camps near the Middle Fork of the John Day River. Austin, 3 miles north of the highway, was a supply depot for many mining camps and a terminus of the narrow-gauge railroad from Sumpter. A few old buildings remain.

From Bates an enjoyable forest road follows the river to Galena and Susanville, where mines were worked in the early 1860s. The scenic riverside route also cuts through a large cattle ranch before intersecting State 395 north of Long Creek.

Anthony Lakes—a cool retreat

Twenty miles west of Interstate 80N by way of North Powder, the Anthony Lakes present a cool retreat on warm summer days. You climb by good road to the two larger lakes—Anthony and Grande Ronde—located above the 7,000-foot level. Several

Golden autumn foliage lines a quiet stretch of the Grande Ronde River in Red Bridge State Park near La Grande.

Skiers carve trails through powder snow at Anthony Lakes below the rugged peaks of the Blue Mountains.

smaller ones lie beyond the road and are reached by trails.

At Anthony Lake you can pitch your tent in shady Forest Service campgrounds (trailer sites also available) or picnic along the shore. Campsites are also located at Grande Ronde and Mud lakes.

Fishermen toss their lines in the quiet lake waters. Families find the lakes warm enough for summer swimming, or they can go berry picking. Hikers and horseback riders enjoy a network of maintained trails. The camps usually remain open through hunting season.

Two ski resorts with powder snow

The Blue Mountains are a long way from most of the state's population centers, but the area's dependable powder snow, rugged scenery, uncrowded slopes, and informal hospitality provide enjoyable skiing. Both resorts offer ski rentals and instruction.

Anthony Lakes. Lifts begin at 7,100 feet and top out near 8,000 feet, making this one of the highest ski areas in the Northwest. The high elevation and dry climate provide good skiing from November to May. A double chair and Poma lifts take skiers to packed slopes and untracked powder snow.

Located west of Interstate 80N in the heart of the Blue Mountains, about an hour's drive from Baker or La Grande, Anthony offers nearly 10 miles of good skiing terrain on nine runs. The ski area operates daily during the season. A day lodge and snack bar are located at the ski area. Snowmobile trails and race courses are nearby.

Spout Springs. Skiing lasts from November to April at Spout Springs, located about midway between Pendleton and Elgin off State Highway 204.

The ski area is about 2,000 feet lower than Anthony, but it offers more lifts and other facilities, including limited overnight accommodations. Two double chairlifts, T-bars, and rope tows can move 7,000 persons per hour to nine runs.

Spout Springs operates daily except Monday, plus holidays and daily during Christmas vacation. There's night skiing on Wednesdays, Fridays, and Saturdays.

The northern Blues

State 204 cuts through the northern stretch of the Blue Mountains, following an old short cut from the Oregon Trail to the Walla Walla Valley. Stagecoaches and other travelers stopped at the small settlement of Tollgate, 3 miles west of Spout Springs, to pay a toll as they passed through a large, wooden gate.

A lakeside campground is located at Langdon Lake, along the highway. Forest roads branch off the highway into Umatilla National Forest. Several campgrounds are located along the Umatilla River, east of the Umatilla Indian Reservation. At Umatilla Forks campground, a ¼-mile nature trail offers a glimpse of the forest wildlife community.

Boat trips. Two-day float trips on the Grande Ronde River usually start at Rondowa, at the mouth of the Wallowa River, and continue downstream to Troy. Good overnight camping spots are located at the mouths of Bear Creek and Elbow Creek. High water in spring and early summer makes the trip easier; later, rubber rafts must be pulled part of the way.

Wenaha Backcountry Area. Rugged ridges and steep canyons typify the Wenaha Backcountry Area, spanning the Oregon-Washington border in the northern reaches of Umatilla National Forest. Remote and roadless, the area attracts hikers, fishermen, and hunters. Scattered stands of evergreens —primarily Douglas fir and white fir—offer cover for wildlife.

From Tollgate, a scenic forest road (No. N50) follows the ridge of the Blue Mountains northeast to Troy. Forest Service campgrounds are located at Jubilee Lake, 12 miles northeast of the Tollgate junction, and at springs along the route. From Timothy Springs campground, a trail follows the South Fork of the Wenaha River for nearly 30 miles. Other trails also provide access from the forest road into the Oregon portion of the area.

The Walla Walla Valley

High on a northwestern flank of the Blue Mountains, just below the Washington state line, the waters of the Walla Walla River begin their journey toward the Columbia.

North and South forks curve southwest, converging just east of Milton-Freewater; hiking trails follow both waterways upstream into the forest.

Located about 5 miles south of the Oregon border, Milton-Freewater is the agricultural center of the upper Walla Walla Valley. Peas are a major crop, and the town hosts a Pea Festival annually in May. Fruit orchards—primarily apples, prunes, and cherries—and grain fields cover many acres as well. Marie Dorion Historical Park, south of town along the river, honors an Indian pioneer woman who with her family journeyed overland in 1811 with the Astor Overland Expedition, bound for Fort Astoria. She was the first woman to cross the plains and settle in Oregon.

Pioneer household goods from Oregon Trail and homesteading days have been collected in the Weston Museum, located in an old brick building in the community of Weston.

A lot of roads lead to Troy, too

Grand names embellish small communities throughout the West; in eastern Oregon, for example, you'll find Rome, Sparta, and Troy.

Near the Washington border, a number of local roads converge at Troy, a village at the confluence of the Wenaha and Grande Ronde rivers. Several families live here permanently. Horses are available for pack trips into the back country for hunting or up any of several roadless fishing rivers.

Float trips can also be arranged. A riverside campground is located just outside town.

The multispoked wheel of gravel roads radiating from Troy predates the modern paved highway (State Highway 3) about 16 miles to the east. Still important to the scattered ranchers of the region, these roads switchback up the dry sides of canyons to the wetter benches or breaks, where heavy timber begins.

Powwatka Ridge Road. This two-lane gravel road from Wallowa to Troy is kept open all year for the mail carrier's regular trips. It meanders through grassy hills and past scattered ranches, then ascends abruptly into the heavily timbered highlands of Wallowa-Whitman National Forest. From here you can take a last sweeping look back at the Wallowa basin and the snowy peaks of the Wallowa Mountains.

Dense timber thins to sparse ponderosa pine as you descend the north slope of Powwatka Ridge. Mountain vistas ahead are framed by pines and rail fences; a few ranches are still occupied.

Troy residents maintain that someone once took a road grader up the Powwatka switchback climb. If so, he deserves his place in history. For about a mile, the road is narrow, doubling back on itself six times and losing over 1,000 feet of elevation. If you are descending and spot approaching cars, wait at the wide places for them to pass.

State 3, though better paved, also has its share of switchbacks and steep slopes with deep valleys and gullies below.

Flora. Once a prosperous farming community, Oregon's northeasternmost settlement is now almost a ghost town. Many of its weather-beaten buildings stand empty and deserted on the open meadow, scoured to a silvery sheen by silt-laden winds. Grassy fields are carpeted with wildflowers in spring. Flora lies 2 miles west of State 3, about 35 miles north of Enterprise.

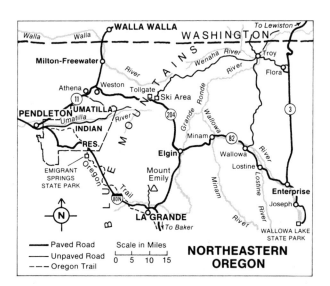

Forest road *snakes through trees along the ridge top on the route from Imnaha to the Hat Point view point.*

The last great Indian war

At the time white settlers moved into the Wallowa Valley, Old Chief Joseph was leader of a band of Nez Perce Indians who, for generations, had lived in the "valley of the winding water." In 1855 a U.S. government treaty made the valley part of the Nez Perce reservation, but over the next 20 years treaty changes and new government decisions reclaimed the land for the white settlers.

The old chief died in 1871 and his son, Young Chief Joseph, assumed leadership of the tribe. Living well on the abundant game of the mountains and annual runs of salmon, the Nez Perce band was understandably unwilling to leave the valley and retire to a reservation.

In 1877 U.S. troops were dispatched to forcibly evict the Indians from the Wallowa Valley. Led by the young chief, the Wallowa band retreated over 1,000 miles, repeatedly battling and defeating numerically superior federal troops. The Nez Perce warriors were finally subdued just a few miles from sanctuary in Canada.

The town of Joseph and Chief Joseph Mountain, rising west of Wallowa Lake, honor the young leader. Old Chief Joseph is buried in the Indian cemetery at the north end of Wallowa Lake, where a monument has been erected in his memory.

Relaxing at Wallowa Lake

Nestled at the northern base of the mountains is Wallowa Lake, the region's most popular recreation site. Scooped out by an ancient glacier during the Ice Age, the lake basin is still rimmed on east and west by lateral moraines; the glacier's terminal moraine, at the north end of the lake, became a natural dam backing up the lake waters.

Nearly 4 miles long, Wallowa Lake attracts many water sports enthusiasts. A resort and state park are located at the south end of the lake. Each September an Alpenfest is held at Wallowa Lake.

Wallowa Lake State Park. A popular destination for family recreation, the park has a large campground and two picnic areas. A boat launching ramp, bathhouse, dock, and swimming beach are located along the southwestern shore. Slide programs and nature talks are presented in the campground on summer evenings.

Many visitors spend their days on the water— boating, water-skiing, or fishing. Boats, canoes, water bikes, and other water sports equipment may be rented in summer. A park nature trail attracts strollers. Hikers and horseback riders ascend steep trails into the Wallowa Mountains; horses are available for day rides or longer trips.

Gondola ride up Mount Howard. From a terminal near the lake's southeast corner, the blue and white gondolas of the Wallowa Lake Gondola Lift climb silently to the summit of 8,250-foot Mount Howard. On the 15-minute ride, passengers survey the rugged peaks and green canyons of the Wallowas, the fields of the Wallowa Valley, the Imnaha Canyon,

Into the Wallowas

From La Grande, State Highway 82 makes a 70-mile eastward curve to Joseph, gateway to the Wallowa (first two syllables rhyme with *allow*) Mountains. Exciting canyon vistas and the drive beside stretches of the Wallowa and Lostine rivers make this a beautiful route. Renowned for the grandeur of its alpine scenery, the compact and rugged Wallowa range offers superlative wilderness recreation for hikers, horseback riders, fishermen, hunters, and rock climbers.

Campers and boaters headquarter around Wallowa Lake, lying at the head of the river below steep, forested peaks. Back packers and horsemen travel up steep valleys into Eagle Cap Wilderness. On the southern slopes of the range you will find the ghosts of once-roaring mining towns.

You drive northeast through the wheat fields of the broad Grande Ronde Valley to Elgin, a farming and lumbering center. The Elgin Stampede draws visitors each July for the Northwest Champion Horse Pulling Contest. The Eastern Oregon Timber Carnival attracts contestants from as far away as New Zealand.

Towns in this remote corner of the state retain a frontier flavor. Joseph, just north of Wallowa Lake, celebrates Chief Joseph Days the last weekend in July. Wallowa County's Bicentennial Museum is housed in the bank in Joseph.

The Wallowa Valley is the starting point for hunting and fishing excursions and pack trips into the Eagle Cap Wilderness. This is horse country, and several operators have pack and riding stock available; the Forest Service can provide a list.

and to the east, Idaho's Seven Devils Mountains.

At the upper terminal, check the bulletin board for special events. Two miles of nature trails meander through flowery meadows, past lingering patches of snow, and into groves of alpine fir, juniper, and whitebark pine to benches where you can spread a picnic lunch. Often you'll see elk and deer browsing in the alpine meadows.

The gondola lift operates daily from late May through Labor Day and on weekends until early October.

To Hat Point and Imnaha Canyon

Travelers willing to tackle steep, narrow, gravel roads can make two rewarding excursions from Joseph. Though it is a hard day's drive, you can combine both on a day's circuit. One road leads to an overlook on the rim of the mile-deep Snake River Canyon at Hat Point. The other climbs the scenic valley of the Imnaha River. Take along drinking water and a picnic lunch. Current road information is available in Joseph at the Forest Service office.

The road is paved for the first 30 miles, from Joseph northeast up Little Sheep Creek to the community of Imnaha. Check your gas gauge, for this is the last place to get supplies. Primitive campsites are available at Hat Point, and several small campgrounds are located along the upper Imnaha.

Hat Point. From Imnaha a single-lane unimproved forest road climbs steadily, with occasional turnouts, up the steep and dusty flank of Grizzly Ridge. At Five Mile Viewpoint, you have a splendid view of the rugged Imnaha Canyon, backed by the snow-tipped Wallowas. In 1973 a forest fire burned thousands of acres of timber southwest of Hat Point.

About 24 miles southeast of Imnaha you arrive at Hat Point, a lookout on the canyon rim. You gaze down on the Snake River, winding ribbonlike through the canyon more than a mile below.

Gondola glides smoothly to the summit of Mount Howard for a spectacular view of mountains and the Wallowa Valley.

The Snake's gorge is both the narrowest and deepest gash on the continent, averaging 5,500 feet in depth for some 40 miles. The Seven Devils Mountains loom on the Idaho side of the river; west and south you see the Imnaha River basin and the Wallowas.

Imnaha Canyon. From Imnaha a gravel road heads south up the scenic Imnaha River Canyon. By this route, Joseph is some 70 miles away. Cattle ranches are scattered along the route.

The road to Joseph forks west along Gumboot Creek. Fishermen and campers can continue along the Imnaha River Road to forest camps. From the trailhead at Indian Crossing Campground, a trail follows the river into Eagle Cap Wilderness.

Eagle Cap Wilderness

Some of Oregon's finest mountain country lies in the heart of the Wallowas within the boundaries of Eagle Cap Wilderness. Rugged granite peaks rise to nearly 10,000 feet above delightful alpine meadows and thick forests. Swift-flowing rivers—among them the Minam, Lostine, Wallowa, and Imnaha—radiate from Eagle Cap peak, cutting deep canyons through the mountain range and nearby plateaus. About 60 jewel-like lakes nestle at the base of steep slopes or hide in rocky basins.

You can drive up several scenic canyons to forest campgrounds on the edge of the wilderness, but no road penetrates to the high lakes. This paradise is reserved for hikers and horseback riders. Though many rugged hikers back pack into the wilderness, riding is more popular; trails are dusty and the terrain is hilly. Check with the District

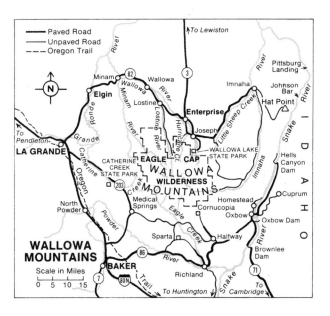

Ranger in Joseph before starting out. A free wilderness permit is required.

You can rent horses for short rides, day excursions, or long pack trips. If you like, a guide will pack you in and out, leaving you free to fish and explore the country within range of your camp.

High trails are usually blocked until late June, and patches of snow often remain the year around on the high peaks. Though most visitors come in July and August, the pleasant sunny days of Indian summer are especially enjoyable, often lingering well into October. Bring along some warm clothing, for evenings are crisp in the high country and you might encounter a brief storm in any season.

From Wallowa Lake. Favorite day trip destinations are Aneroid Lake, up the East Fork of the Wallowa River, and Ice Lake, up the West Fork Trail. Both lie in basins surrounded by high peaks.

Lake Basin, a 6-square-mile area of some 30 small alpine lakes in the heart of the wilderness, is a 9-mile trip from Wallowa Lake up the river's western fork.

Up free-flowing streams. Scenic routes lead up the rivers radiating from this alpine wilderness. Saddle and pack animals are available.

Vistas of high waterfalls, glacial canyons, mountain meadows, and immense marble peaks await riders and hikers on trails up Hurricane Creek and the Lostine and Minam rivers. The Minam is untouched by any road almost to its end and has been designated a state scenic waterway for its entire 45-mile length. Main eastern access to the wilderness is up the Imnaha River.

On the drier south side of the mountains, Eagle Creek provides an interesting route from Boulder Park into the high country.

The southwestern slope

From Baker and La Grande, roads lead into the southern foothills of the Wallowas where a century ago, miners found rich diggings.

State 203 makes a deep eastward curve through Union along Catherine Creek to Medical Springs. Union has some fine old brick buildings, and Catherine Creek State Park offers pleasant campsites and picnic tables. An unpaved forest road east of Medical Springs provides access to campgrounds along Eagle Creek. Abandoned logging roads make fine hiking trails.

One of the best ghost towns in the state is Cornucopia, about 11 miles north of Halfway off State 86. For over 50 years—until 1941—mines produced gold totaling $16 million, about half of Oregon's output. A 6,300-foot mine shaft provided access to 30 miles of underground tunnels. Heavy winter snows have taken their toll, but many sagging, dilapidated buildings remain.

Only a few remnants mark the once-flourishing gold camp of Sparta, southwest of Cornucopia, but hillsides show the scars of abandoned diggings. Starting life as a roaring boom town in the 1860s, Sparta produced more than $2 million in gold.

Eastward to the Snake

More than 200 miles of Oregon's northeastern border is rimmed by the Snake River, swelling into large reservoirs and narrowing as it tumbles and surges through Hells Canyon.

State 86 leads east from Baker to a series of hydroelectric dams—Brownlee, Oxbow, and Hells Canyon; guided tours through the generating plants are available on request. In late 1975, federal legislation created Hells Canyon National Recreation Area, ending 25 years of controversy over the area's future. Some 600,000 acres in Oregon and Idaho will be managed as wilderness by the Forest Service, and no new dams will be constructed in the scenic canyon of the middle Snake.

Roads parallel sections of the river, providing access to boaters and fishermen. Communities are scattered and small; you'll see a number of abandoned houses. Several riverside parks offer camping and picnic sites.

From the reservoir lakes, fishermen pull in bass, trout, crappies, and catfish. Below Hells Canyon Dam, fishing is good for trout and steelhead. The continent's biggest fresh-water fish—the white sturgeon—migrates up and down the Columbia and Snake rivers.

Riverside campgrounds

Fishermen and hunters can make their headquarters in Farewell Bend State Park, south of Huntington off Interstate 80N, or in any of four reservoir parks (three of them on the Idaho shore of the Snake River) maintained by Idaho Power Company.

Campsites, picnic tables, and a swimming area are available at Farewell Bend State Park. Boats can be launched and docked here, too.

Access to the reservoir parks is by paved roads off State 86. All four campgrounds have trailer spaces with electric hookups, picnic tables, boat ramps, and drinking water. Tent campsites are available at Woodhead Park, behind Brownlee Dam. Boat docks are located on the east shore of reservoirs behind Oxbow and Brownlee dams.

Boat trips on the Snake

Several companies operate 5 and 6-day float trips downstream from Hells Canyon Dam through the heart of the spectacular canyon. You can also arrange 1-day jet-boat trips downstream from the dam or upstream from Lewiston, Idaho.

Float trips. Oar-powered rubber rafts and wooden dories enter the Snake downstream from Hells Canyon Dam and float north past the Imnaha and Salmon rivers to the Grande Ronde, a distance of about 85 miles. Some operators float the entire 110 miles to Lewiston.

The steep, mile-high cliffs of Hells Canyon line the river for nearly 40 miles, from Homestead downstream to Johnson Bar. Farther north the valley opens into rolling hills occasionally marked

Riders pause in a high meadow north of Boulder Park on the southern slope of the Wallowa Mountains.

Challenging white water of the Snake River attracts boaters to the rugged canyon.

by ranches and abandoned homesteads.

An insurmountable barrier to fur traders and the wagon train pioneers who by-passed it, Hells Canyon yields many surprises. You float through challenging, fast-moving rapids and into placid waters that invite swimming. Vegetation varies from cool, green ferns to bright cactus blossoms. In side canyons and on ridges you can discover ancient petroglyphs, Indian caves, and old mines.

Water is highest and fastest on spring trips, when the canyon is at its greenest and the weather is pleasantly cool. Temperatures soar in summer, but the water is warm enough for swimming, and you can float alongside the boat in calm water. In fall the weather is cooler and fishing is excellent.

Jet-boat trips. You can also arrange jet-boat trips downriver from the dam to Wild Sheep Rapids and upstream from Lewiston to Johnson Bar. The mail boat makes regular trips upstream from Lewiston, and back packers can arrange travel to Pittsburg Landing or Johnson Bar. Fierce rapids block motor navigation between Sheep Creek and Johnson Bar.

A tortuous hiking trail

Rugged back packers can get a different perspective of the river on a tortuous hiking trail winding high above the churning waters. Access into and out of the canyon is limited. The trail follows the Idaho side downstream from Hells Canyon Dam, or you can arrange for a boat to drop you at a landing site and pick you up later. Check with a Forest Service ranger in Baker or Halfway (or in Idaho towns) before starting out.

Sources of drinking water are few and far between, and wood is scarce; bring a collapsible plastic water container and carry a small fuel stove. A topographic map is a necessity.

You'll look down on the swirling cascades and rapids, observe birds and animals at close range, see petroglyphs on canyon walls, and—below Hells Canyon—meet occasional ranchers and sheepherders who make this lonely area their home. Mailboxes are stuck on posts along the riverbank.

For back road explorers

Brownlee Dam makes a 50-mile lake of a wild, treeless section of the Snake; it is a fine place for crowd dodgers and—in season—chukar partridge hunters. From Huntington on Interstate 80N, an all-weather road closely follows the Oregon bank north for some 30 miles, climbing out of the canyon to the small town of Richland on State 86.

Along this sparsely settled, 38-mile route you'll see a few ranches and occasional private fishing cabins, but seldom even a fence—only the road, the hills, and the river. Sunflowers grow along the river bank in summer, and this is good bird-watching country from spring to fall.

Southeastern corner

Search for surprises in this spacious land

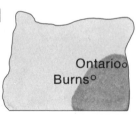

Great flocks of migratory birds pause at Malheur National Wildlife Refuge.

Sheepherders and dogs guide a flock of sheep along a desert road to new grazing lands. Look for sheep from April to July north of State 78.

The sprawling, sparsely settled southeastern corner of Oregon remains the state's least-known region, yet it holds plenty of surprises and challenges for the adventurous explorer.

On side trips you can explore green mountain meadows and vividly colored gulches, challenge the white water of the Owyhee River, fish in rock-rimmed reservoirs, go rockhounding or search for Indian artifacts, or stalk the wild birds and game that inhabit this rugged country. Large ranches still sprawl across range lands where, a century ago, cattle barons grazed immense herds.

Because relatively few highways penetrate this vast, silent country, you must sometimes venture off the paved roads to discover its special attractions. Passenger cars can safely navigate most of the improved roads, but the primitive routes are best probed by sturdy, four-wheel-drive vehicles. Inquire locally before setting out on unpaved roads, and heed the general rules for back country travel (see page 9).

The lonely plateau

Few roads intersect U.S. Highway 20 between central Oregon and the Idaho border. You travel

---

Awesome pinnacles tower over boaters floating the lonely Owyhee River. Most white-water trips begin at Rome and end near Lake Owyhee.

Succor Creek wends through rugged and colorful canyon north of Jordan Valley.

almost without interruption across grazing lands and sagebrush plateau dotted with buttes rising vertically from the plain. You may even glimpse a coyote or an antelope poised atop a rocky ridge.

In summer it's a long, hot trip. Temperatures may reach 100° in the shade — and there's almost no shade. You can plan ahead, though, to take advantage of the route's three desert roadside rest areas: at Brothers Oasis, 43 miles east of Bend; at Sage Hen, 16 miles west of Burns; and at Buchanan Springs, 24 miles east of Burns. At these areas you'll find water fountains and rest rooms, as well as picnic tables shaded by sun shelters.

At the community of Riley, U.S. Highway 395 veers southwest across range land toward Lakeview, more than 100 miles away. On this lonely road across the Oregon plateau, you parallel the route of an old Wells Fargo roadway. The small oasis of Wagontire offers a place for travel-weary families to stretch cramped legs. Another state rest area is located south of Alkali Lake.

Cattle country

The paved highways of southeastern Oregon cut through the heart of range land where the cattle frontier made its last stand. In the mid-19th century, tales of the region's well-watered valleys and grass-covered hills attracted hardy pioneer stockmen. John Devine came to the Steens Mountain country in 1869, and his Alvord Ranch became one of the finest in the region.

Most powerful of the cattle barons was Henry Miller who, with his partner Charles Lux, amassed a million acres and more than a million head of cattle. Miller also supervised the building of hundreds of miles of irrigation canals that brought water to the dry land.

Pete French settled in the Blitzen Valley in the early 1870s, weathered storms and droughts, and prospered on his vast "P" Ranch near Frenchglen. His daring and dominant personality made him a legendary figure. He died, as did many others in the lusty days of the Old West, "in the saddle"—by a bullet from a disgruntled sodbuster's gun.

Today cowboys still herd white-faced cows and calves on the lonely ranges of Harney and Malheur counties. Isolated private ranches remain on the scene, but large corporations hold most of the land. Ranching is big business in southeastern Oregon.

Oregon's largest county

Harney County's population is centered around Burns, the county seat, and neighboring Hines, where a lumber sawmill dominates the community.

Each September Burns hosts the Harney County Fair and Rodeo. A county historical museum, located north of town on U.S. 395, features Indian and pioneer artifacts. You can visit the museum Tuesday through Saturday (10 A.M. to noon, 1 to 5 P.M.) from June through September.

Burns stands in the center of good fishing and

hunting country. Nearby mountain streams yield rainbow trout, and in late summer and fall the county abounds with hunters. Forested campgrounds lie north of Burns on the southern slopes of the Blue Mountains. To the south is the Blitzen Valley, watered by streams from the western hillsides of Steens Mountain.

South from Burns

You can sample several of the region's surprises on a side trip south from Burns on State Highway 205. Here you can watch for wild birds and small mammals on a wildlife refuge, explore isolated settlements reminiscent of the Old West, and climb above the sagebrush plateau to picnic in green mountain meadows.

A unique local landmark is Pete French's Round Barn, constructed in 1880 and used by French and his "P" Ranch riders for breaking and exercising horses in winter. You'll find the barn, still in good condition, west of Diamond near the refuge.

Birdwatching at Malheur Refuge

Millions of migratory ducks and geese stop annually at the lakes and marsh lands making up the Malheur National Wildlife Refuge, located along State 205 about 30 miles south of Burns.

Though primarily a summer breeding and nesting area for migratory birds, the refuge also provides an important spring and autumn stop for waterfowl on the Pacific Flyway. Peak activity occurs from mid-March through May and in October and November. You'll want your binoculars.

In addition to migratory birds, you may also see upland game birds and small mammals such as muskrats, raccoons, coyotes, deer, and antelope.

Begin your visit with a stop at refuge headquarters on the marshy southern shore of Malheur Lake. Here you can get a map of the area, leaflets describing local birds and mammals, and information on current road conditions both in the refuge and elsewhere in Harney County. Mounted specimens of many birds inhabiting the refuge are displayed in the museum to aid identification.

A 42-mile, self-guided interpretive auto route leads visitors to points of interest in the Blitzen Valley. Roadside signs point out areas of varied wildlife habitat, Indian rock writings, and historic sites including the "P" Ranch.

A dirt causeway, used only by visitors and an occasional warden, parallels the main road through the center of the refuge and offers excellent wildlife watching. Southbound, you enter the causeway at the refuge headquarters; northbound, you pick it up about 2 miles east of Frenchglen, near the tall tower of the old "P" Ranch.

In summer, field classes in ornithology and other subjects are taught in the refuge. For information, write to the Director, Malheur Environmental Field Station (MEFS), Box 989, Burns, OR 97720.

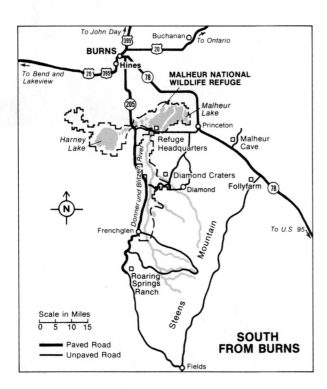

Round Barn about 13 miles west of Diamond was used by French and his men for breaking and exercising horses.

U-shaped Kiger Gorge is one of several glacial valleys on Steens Mountain. View point is near Steens Mountain Road.

From State 205 a side road leads east to the Diamond Craters, a small, isolated volcanic field. Its craters and domes are of special interest to geologists and rockhounds.

Frenchglen, a bit of the Old West

If this wide-open country becomes too lonely and you crave companionship, continue south on State 205 along the Donner und Blitzen River to Frenchglen, a hamlet near the southern tip of the refuge. The settlement is named for Pete French, perhaps the most loved—and most hated—of the region's cattle kings. Frenchglen's handful of buildings, reminiscent of a western stage set, includes a general store and the small Frenchglen Hotel.

State 205 continues south from Frenchglen toward the Nevada border. Paved as far as Roaring Springs Ranch, the all-weather road is usually in good condition. It follows the Catlow Valley southeast, intersecting with the Steens Mountain Road just north of Fields.

Dramatic Steens Mountain

Dominating the Harney plain is Steens Mountain, a giant geologic fault block. Rising high above the sagebrush and sandy grasslands, it stretches some 30 miles north and south and resembles a massive bulge in the earth's crust. At its highest point (9,670

feet at the head of Wild Horse Creek), the rugged eastern rim looms more than a mile above the flat alkaline sink of Alvord Desert. The western slope rises more gradually from a warm valley to cool mountain meadows. Two roads allow you to explore the different faces of Steens Mountain. Often this region is called simply "the Steens."

Steens Mountain Summit Road. From Frenchglen a loop road climbs gradually above the valley into aspen-bordered meadows watered by a network of trout-filled streams. As you climb, you leave the desert plants behind. Near the summit, dwarf alpine varieties flourish, nourished by moisture from the winter snows. Cattle graze in the high valleys; hawks and an occasional falcon soar above the canyons; game birds rustle in the underbrush; antelope and mule deer roam the west-facing slopes; and bighorn sheep seek the upper ridges.

A few lonely buildings, remnants of old homesteads, stand within sight of the road. Scenic view points, some reached by short trails, overlook deep glacial canyons, stream-fed lakes, sheer rock walls, and a broad, dry alkali lake.

Four Bureau of Land Management (BLM) campgrounds provide unimproved sites for camping and picnicking; for information and a map, stop at the BLM district office in Burns. Usually the road is free of snow from mid-July through October, but inquire before you make the trip. Sudden summer storms may make travel temporarily hazardous.

The Basques settled in Jordan Valley

The Basques first came to the West in Gold Rush days, but it was not until 1889 that they settled in Oregon's Jordan Valley. Within a few years the settlement had become a thriving Basque colony. Some of the newcomers became sheepmen, while others worked as stonemasons, miners, merchants, or hotel keepers. Other groups of Basques settled in northern Nevada, in communities on both sides of the Oregon-Idaho border, and in California's central valley.

From their homes in the Spanish and French Pyrenees, the Basques brought their own cultural traditions—a unique language, lively music and folk dances, regional foods, even the sport of *pelota*, a game similar to handball.

Numerous second and third-generation Basques still live in Jordan Valley and other Oregon and Idaho border towns. They congregate occasionally for folk dancing during the winter, at the Jordan Valley rodeo in mid-May, and for the Basque picnic in Boise the last Sunday of July. Many are members of the Basque Center in Boise, which carries on Basque dancing, language, and traditions.

In Jordan Valley, stop and look at the pelota *frontone* (ball court), a stone structure hand hewn by Basque masons. Here for many years local Basques played pelota. The property has been deeded to the Oregon Historical Society, and local Basques plan to restore the frontone to its original condition.

Bottle collectors and nostalgia fans will enjoy a stop at the drug store here; unusual old items are displayed amid modern merchandise. □

Along the eastern face. Another gravel road, broad and well maintained (but hot and dusty in summer), provides access to a handful of remote ranches lying against the sheer eastern side of Steens Mountain. The road follows the escarpment north for 65 miles from Fields to State Highway 78 at Follyfarm, an agricultural ghost town.

Today Fields is a small community clustered around its general store and one-room schoolhouse, but at the turn of the century it was a prospering stage and freight station. Mule-drawn wagon trains loaded with borax from the nearby Alvord Valley departed from Fields for the railroad shipping point at Winnemucca, Nevada. Until a few years ago, large herds of sheep—guided by Basque herders and their dogs—used the road as a thoroughfare, and motorists occasionally encountered a dusty mule train transporting sheepherders' gear to summer camps in the high pastures.

Mann and Juniper lakes offer excellent rainbow and cutthroat trout fishing. Mule deer, antelope, and bighorn sheep roam the eastern face of the Steens, and chukar and quail are common in the canyons. The road parallels Alvord Desert and Alvord Lake, both unique geologic features. Another road continues north from State 78, with some dirt stretches, to connect with U.S. 20 near Harper.

A desert hiking trail

Recreation hikers are discovering the desert. A 150-mile route has been mapped through Harney County, part of a proposed national desert trail now under consideration by Congress. Though not yet a marked, well-traveled path, the trail offers relatively easy sections as well as challenging wilderness routes.

Spearheading establishment of this national trail is the Desert Trail Association, P.O. Box 589, Burns, OR 97720. In Oregon, organization members conduct introductory group hikes with experienced guides as well as more strenuous back packing trips into mountainous terrain.

The mapped portion of the trail cuts north from Denio, Nevada, through the Pueblos to the crest of Steens Mountain, down the Little Blitzen River and the Blitzen Valley to Page Springs, north past Diamond Craters, then east to Riddle Mountain. It follows game trails and sheepherders' paths, crosses alpine meadows, skirts shallow lakes and marshes, traverses sage-covered desert plateau, and passes old volcanic craters and caves.

Before setting out, hikers should get detailed trail information from the Association or from federal agencies. On some stretches of trail, water and fuel supplies are sparse. Hikers should carry at least 2 quarts of water per person and a small cooking stove. Most sections of the trail can be hiked all year long, but be prepared for extremes of weather and temperature.

To cool Malheur Cave

Fifty-two miles southeast of Burns, where Indian Creek Road wanders off from State 78, no shade trees ease the heat of a hot summer day. But at this arid intersection you're only a few minutes away from the 50° coolness of Malheur Cave.

After driving 3 miles north up Indian Creek Road, turn left at a small reservoir and drive the dirt track to a depression in the valley floor. Nothing else is in sight except the sagebrush flat and surrounding hills; but if you walk over and look into the dip, you'll see deep shadows beneath a low arch of rock—this is the 8 by 20-foot cave entrance.

You can enter the cave—really a large lava tube—without stooping, and you can easily walk down its gently sloping floor. Its dimensions get higher and broader as you walk deeper into the cave. Daylight penetrates about 400 feet to a large chamber; you can walk another half-mile (you'll need a flashlight) to where the cave ends at a fresh-water pool.

Obsidian chips on the ground outside date back to the days of Indian occupancy; with its fresh-water supply and small entrance (once barricaded with large boulders), the cave made a natural fort. It is now owned by the Masonic Order but left open for the public.

Eastward toward Idaho

Once a tedious 2-day journey by stagecoach over parched hills, the 114 miles between Burns and Vale can be covered today in about 2 hours.

Diversions along this stretch of U.S. 20 are few, and the change from sagebrush-covered hillsides to irrigated farm lands near Vale comes as a surprise. Water, impounded in reservoirs on the Malheur and Owyhee rivers, is diverted by canals to irrigate vast fields of potatoes, onions, and sugar beets. Lakes formed behind the region's dams are popular for fishing, boating, and water-skiing. The Malheur River and its tributaries challenge a fisherman's skills. Rockhounds search for gemstones on BLM land in the Stinkingwater Mountains, and canoeists paddle on the Malheur's Middle Fork. Hunting for upland game birds—especially partridge, chukar, and quail—begins in mid-October.

As you cross into Malheur County, adjust your watch ahead an hour to Mountain Standard Time.

Side roads off U.S. 20

Only a few intersecting roads—and still fewer settlements—interrupt the highway as it winds across the plateau. Oregon's desert has supported few communities, most of them prospering briefly as stage or railroad stops and declining when transportation routes changed.

Small communities such as Drewsey and Diamond are often Saturday night gathering spots for local cowboys. If they are a little dustier and pack less hardware than their television counterparts, don't be disappointed—you're seeing the real thing.

Drewsey. Eighteen miles east of Buchanan Springs, a paved road branches north to Drewsey, a stage-coach stop (called Gouge Eye) in the 1880s when cattlemen, gamblers, renegades, miners, and adventurers kept things lively in this region. Today many buildings stand empty, and only a few dozen people remain. The community church and old-fashioned general store mirror another era. Some of the settlement's old buildings were damaged by a fire in November 1975.

On U.S. 20, pull off the road at the summit turn-out atop Drinkingwater Pass for a memorable view.

Juntura. With fewer than 100 people, this attractive little valley town is the largest community on the route. Take a look at its quaint railroad depot.

Here the north and south forks of the Malheur River merge, and U.S. 20 parallels the winding river eastward. Tall Lombardy poplars mark the ranches in small valleys along tributary creeks.

Reservoirs. From Juntura, a wide gravel road follows the river's north fork to Beulah Reservoir, stocked with rainbow trout. You'll find a campground on the access road and picnic sites and a boat ramp at the reservoir.

You can also fish for trout and warm-water fish at Warm Springs Reservoir, south of Juntura.

Westfall. At Harper another paved road marks the lonely route to the ghost town of Westfall. Buildings stand deserted, and grazing cattle roam freely through the town, yet a post office (open only 2 hours a day) serves ranchers who drive from miles around to deposit and pick up mail.

Green farm lands

Emigrant wagon trains journeying westward along the Oregon Trail left Fort Boise at the confluence of the Boise and Snake rivers, forded the Snake south of Nyssa, and proceeded west to the Malheur River, which they crossed near Vale. The weary pioneer families paused briefly to bathe in the near-by hot springs and launder travel-soiled clothing. Then the wagon trains pushed on toward the greener pastures of the Willamette Valley.

Today the huge Vale and Owyhee river projects provide water so that previously unusable land is now abundantly productive. Vale, the county seat, and its larger neighbors, Ontario and Nyssa, are the regional trading and population centers, with roads converging from several directions.

The irrigated fields of eastern Malheur County support a diversified agriculture of potatoes, onions, sugar beets, and corn—all processed locally —as well as seed crops, grains, hops, and peppermint. The county leads Oregon's beef production

When cut, knobby round thundereggs reveal crystals and agate. Look for them in central and eastern Oregon.

Red and buff-colored rock walls and basaltic canyons rim Lake Owyhee south of Ontario.
Fishermen cast for bass and crappies. You can camp and picnic at Lake Owyhee State Park.

and supports a major dairy industry as well. Ranchers sell their cattle, sheep, and hogs at weekly livestock auctions in Ontario and Vale.

Tree-shaded community parks in both towns provide recreation centers for residents and rest stops for visitors. Treasure Valley Community College in Ontario arranges cultural activities and stimulates local service projects, in addition to providing an impressive variety of special-interest and vocational programs; students on the campus range from junior high pupils taking special programs to persons of retirement age.

Vale hosts several rodeos, including special festivities on the Fourth of July. Ontario's Japanese-American community celebrates with an Obon Festival in July, and in mid-August the county's residents gather in Ontario for Malheur County Fair activities.

During the first week of August, Nyssa sponsors its annual Thunderegg Days celebration. Thousands of rockhounds from all over the United States and Canada congregate in the small town to trade stock and secrets about their favorite hunting spots. Local guides conduct free tours to nearby rockhounding areas where visitors can search for thundereggs, petrified wood, and agates. For more on rockhounding, see page 120.

Oregon's desert corner

From the irrigated vegetable fields in northern Malheur County, paved roads lead south toward the rugged desert. Outdoorsmen savor this land of solitude where herds of wild horses still roam free.

Lake Owyhee

Keystone of the massive Owyhee irrigation project is Owyhee Dam, southwest of Nyssa. A paved access road follows the Owyhee River; spectacular rock formations and seasonal wildflowers make this an enjoyable trip.

Bordered by rugged cliffs in rainbow colors, Lake Owyhee is an oasis in the desert wilderness. Accommodations and boat rentals are available at the lakeside resort. Lake Owyhee State Park, on the eastern shore, provides camping and picnicking sites and a boat ramp.

The lake has more than enough crappies (pronounced "croppies") for every fisherman, along with the more aloof bass, trout, and coho salmon. Rockhounds search for thundereggs, agate, and jasper in nearby canyons. You can arrange a boat excursion to explore some of the lake's rugged side canyons, at their most spectacular in spring. Hunters find deer, antelope, and upland game birds such as chukar, Chinese pheasant, and quail.

White water trip down the Owyhee

One of the least-known river runs in the West is the trip down the Owyhee through an awesome gorge in Oregon's remote southeastern corner. The river is navigable only in the spring, after enough snow has melted to provide water deep enough to cushion the rapids.

Scenery along the river is spectacular. The Owyhee flows—sometimes gliding quietly, sometimes tumbling in white water rapids—through a 1,000-foot chasm. Sheer walls tower on either side of the canyon; rock spires, balanced rocks, and multicolored geological formations attest to eons of wind and water erosion.

Occasional slopes along the river are verdant with grass and bright with wildflowers. En route, you may glimpse deer, coyotes, a band of wild horses, beavers, or otters. Wild ducks and geese nest along the river; a golden eagle may soar overhead. Petroglyphs in the rock walls of the canyon mark ancient Indian camps.

Most trips put boats in the water near Rome, on U.S. 95, and end near Lake Owyhee. The 5-day excursion covers more than 50 miles.

Prize specimens await rockhounds

Rockhounds know this country as a source of prime rock specimens—thundereggs, petrified wood, jasper, and agates. Inquire in Ontario or Nyssa for directions to the best hunting grounds on public lands. The BLM district office in Vale and the Ontario Chamber of Commerce issue maps marking the region's popular rockhounding areas. Be aware, though, that unimproved roads can be difficult to negotiate after heavy rains.

Succor Creek Canyon (still spelled "Sucker Creek" by some old-timers) is the main hunting ground for thundereggs, one of the most distinctive and most sought-after stones in the state. Knobby and round, these agate-filled nodules reveal beautiful and colorful designs when cut and polished. The best specimens are dug from bedrock several feet below the surface.

Other good rockhounding areas are Leslie Gulch Canyon, Painted Canyon, and Dry Creek. Agates and petrified wood have been found north of Jordan Valley. More information on Oregon rock hounding appears on page 120.

Canyon country

Only a handful of Oregonians have explored the stark yet colorful canyon country a few miles west of the Idaho border. About 8 miles south of Adrian, an improved gravel road branches off State Highway 201; this is the route into Succor Creek Canyon.

From rolling hills and sagebrush plains you enter a canyon whose rocky walls rise steeply toward brilliant blue sky. Eagles nest in the overhanging rocks and soar overhead.

The road you're on was once an old stage route. One station was located on the canyon floor near the present site of Succor Creek State Recreation Area; the only lingering signs of the old stage stop are several yellow rose bushes flourishing near a western cottonwood tree and a Lombardy poplar. Another station was at Rockville, 16 miles farther up the canyon. The stage road continued south of Jordan Valley to San Francisco.

Exploring Succor Creek Canyon. On warm summer days, the canyon's cool beauty is reason enough for a detour. On its way north to join the Snake River, Succor Creek has cut deeply into the multicolored canyon walls. Though the scenic all-weather road is only lightly traveled, you will usually find someone poking about—hunting for thundereggs, taking photographs, painting, or even fishing—though fishing is generally wasted effort. Campsites, picnic tables, and drinking water are available in the canyon.

Leslie Gulch. Approximately 7 miles south of Succor Creek Canyon, another improved gravel road branches westward, winding about 14 miles through rugged mountains—known as the Owyhee Breaks—down to the southeastern shore of Lake Owyhee.

Visitors have described this virgin country as resembling the awesome, colorful canyons of the Southwest. The final 10 miles of the road are the most spectacular: in subdued light or bright sunshine the sandstone cliffs become a palette of changing colors—soft lavenders, beiges, grays, vivid reds, umber, and gold. Some formations gleam as if polished. Though the canyon has not been extensively explored, Indian writings and artifacts have been found.

Until a few decades ago, Leslie Gulch and other nearby canyons served as corrals for the wild horses roaming the Owyhee Breaks. Cowboys and settlers drove the mustangs into box canyons, bar-

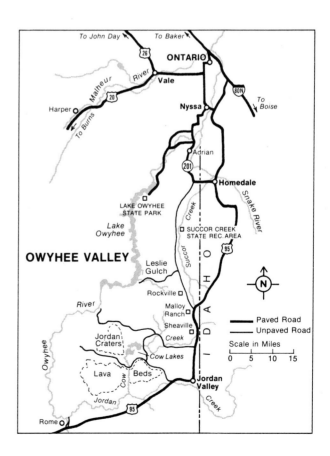

ricaded them, and sold most of the horses to the army for its mounted troops. You may still see wild horses or bighorn sheep in the area.

Down at the lake's edge, you can fish or launch small boats.

Wildflowers. During May, except in especially dry years, the hillsides and valleys of this canyon region are bright with wildflowers—yellow arrowleaf balsamroot, pink phlox, bright red Indian paintbrush, white serviceberry. Their delicate fragrance adds a delightful bonus to a spring trip.

Masses of purplish blue camas give marshy meadows the appearance of shallow blue lakes in late May and June. The edible roots of the blue camas were an Indian diet staple. Look for a good camas display at the southern end of the Succor Creek Canyon road, along U.S. 95 between the creek and the Idaho border.

Back road to Jordan Craters

The lonely dry wastes surrounding the Owyhee River contain a wealth of lava formations from relatively recent (probably within the past 2,000 years) volcanic events. The latest of these created the lava flows northwest of Jordan Valley.

Dark and barren, this lava field covers 60 square miles, culminating at the Jordan Craters where several small volcanic cones surround a larger one.

The unpaved road into the craters leaves U.S. 95 at Cow Creek, just south of Sheaville. Seven miles

Eroded cliffs of sedimentary rock capped by lava form the Walls of Rome, rising above a dry side canyon of the Owyhee.

west you cross the creek. At the 10-mile point, turn right at the back road intersection and continue 3 miles, fording a small creek. Fifteen miles from the highway, lava beds appear on your left; a mile farther you reach another intersection, where you should turn left. Seven miles beyond (23 miles altogether from U.S. 95), another left turn puts you onto the final 2-mile stretch to the craters.

Direction signs have been erected along the route, but cattle often knock them down. Inquire in Jordan Valley before setting out in this area; often you can arrange to tour the region with a local driver-guide. BLM maps of the area may be purchased on weekdays at the BLM office in Vale.

Jordan Craters is a colorful place. Lava clinkers in and around the craters are burnished with blue, gray, green, brown, and purple. Lichens add touches of yellow, apple green, and red.

Most of these lava fields are pahoehoe, a lava flow that is fairly smooth and easy to walk on. A well defined path leads up the slope.

Five miles beyond the craters on the same road, a pasture gate crosses the county road on the brink of the Owyhee Canyon. You look down on a memorable view—a chaos of buttes and canyons stretching to the northern and western horizons.

Cow Lakes. Lava that blocked the flow of Cow Creek gets the credit for forming Cow Lakes. Hunters and back-country explorers occasionally use the small BLM trailer campground on the southeastern shore of Lower Cow Lake.

The Three Forks area

West of Jordan Valley, unpaved roads lead south from U.S. 95 to the confluence of the South, Middle, and North forks of the Owyhee River. This lonely area is not for the timid driver; though the roads are fairly good, you may not meet anyone for hours. Wild and primitive, the 25-mile stretch of the river between the Idaho border and Three Forks is part of Oregon's scenic waterways system. Some Owyhee white water trips begin at Three Forks.

This rugged countryside was the site of the last big Indian uprising in the Pacific Northwest. Angered by the loss of their lands to white settlers, the Bannock Indians joined parties from the Paiute and Snake tribes in 1878 and went on the warpath, ravaging the region before being defeated and dispersed by federal troops.

The massive, weathered Walls of Rome

As you speed along U.S. 95 past Rome, you have no hint of the geological marvel just 3 miles to the north—the Walls (or Pillars) of Rome. An unpaved road leads to the site.

Mile-long walls of eroded lake sediments form the vertical sides of a dry tributary canyon of the Owyhee River. From almost every angle the scene resembles a forgotten city of antiquity. A lava cap atop the walls provides shapes easily taken for battlements and towers. From the road you walk about 100 yards to the base of the cliffs.

Some Books About Oregon

The lore of Oregon—past and present—is extensive. Below is a sampling of the many books that amplify various topics or explore particular regions of the state in depth. You'll find many other excellent books about Oregon—many of them by small Northwest publishers—in local bookstores.

Applegate Trail and **Barlow Road** by Walter Meacham. Portland, OR: Oregon Historical Society, 1947. These two booklets chronicle the hardships and adventures on these historic pioneer routes.

East of the Cascades by Phil F. Brogan. Portland, OR: Binfords & Mort, 1971 (3rd ed.). A history of the early days in eastern Oregon.

Exploring Crater Lake Country by Ruth Kirk. Seattle, WA: University of Washington Press, 1975. Colorfully illustrated, the small book provides background on the area's geology, plants, wildlife, and history with suggestions for enjoying the park.

55 Oregon Bicycle Trips by Nick and Elske Jankowski. Beaverton, OR: Touchstone Press, 1973. Cyclists will find ideas for trips near Portland, in the Willamette Valley, and along the coast. The illustrated guide contains maps and information on distance, riding time, and road conditions.

The Geologic Setting of the John Day Country by the U.S. Department of the Interior/Geological Survey. Washington DC: U.S. Government Printing Office. This booklet provides geologic background on the fossil country and outlines geologic points of interest on a loop trip.

Indian Relics of the Pacific Northwest by N. G. Seaman. Portland, OR: Binfords & Mort, 1967 (2nd ed.). An illustrated layman's guide to Indian artifacts of the region.

Mt. Hood: Portrait of a Magnificent Mountain by Don and Roberta Lowe. Caldwell, ID: Caxton Printers Ltd., 1974. A fine tribute to Oregon's majestic peak.

The Oregon Desert by E. R. Jackman and R. A. Long. Caldwell, ID: Caxton Printers Ltd., 1964. Factual and entertaining, this anecdote-filled book describes the history and development of eastern Oregon.

Oregon for the Curious by Ralph Friedman. Caldwell, ID: Caxton Printers Ltd., 1972. This paperback guides motorists to historic sites and backcountry exploration in all parts of the state.

Oregon Geographic Names by Lewis A. and Lewis L. McArthur. Portland, OR: Oregon Historical Society, 1973 (4th ed.). This definitive text traces the derivation of almost 5,000 Oregon place names.

Oregon Ghost Towns by Lambert Florin. Seattle, WA: Superior Publishing Co., 1971. Historical anecdotes on now-deserted mining camps and farm towns with information on remaining structures.

Oregon Ski Tours by Doug Newman and Sally Sharrard. Beaverton, OR: Touchstone Press, 1973. This guide describes 65 trails for cross-country skiers.

Oregon II and **The Oregon Coast** by Ray Atkeson, text by Archie Satterfield. Portland, OR: Graphic Arts Center, 1974 and 1972. These handsome books depict Oregon's spectacular scenery in color.

Oregon Under Foot by D. E. McMullen. Beaverton, OR: Touchstone Press, 1975. This OMSI Press guide offers a pocket-size visual reference to Oregon gemstones, well-illustrated with color photographs.

Portland, A Historical Sketch and Guide by Terence O'Donnell and Thomas Vaughan. Portland, OR: Oregon Historical Society, 1976. Filled with anecdotes, this factual and informative guide traces Portland's history and outlines various tours.

A Portrait of Oregon, edited by Robert B. Pamplin, Jr., text by Thomas K. Worcester, photography by Robert Reynolds, illustrations by Howard Snapp. Portland, OR: Oregon Historical Society, 1974. An affectionate look at various facets of Oregon.

70 Hiking Trails: Northern Oregon Cascades by Don and Roberta Lowe. Beaverton, OR: Touchstone Press, 1974. Hikes of varying lengths and over different types of terrain are described.

Space, Style and Structure: Building in Northwest America, edited by Thomas Vaughan with Virginia Guest Ferriday. Portland, OR: Oregon Historical Society, 1974. This impressive and well-illustrated 2-volume work examines community life styles and representative buildings of the Pacific Northwest from prehistoric times to the present.

Steamboat Days on the Rivers by Fred W. Wilson and Earle K. Stewart. Portland, OR: Oregon Historical Society, 1969. Handsomely illustrated with photographs, this paperback book recalls the era of steamboats on the Columbia and Willamette.

Steen's Mountain in Oregon's High Desert Country by E. R. Jackman and John Scharff. Caldwell, ID: Caxton Printers Ltd., 1967. A splendidly illustrated book focusing on this unusual mountain.

Index

Photographers